MW01097015

Principles of
BIBLICAL HERMENEUTICS

Principles of
BIBLICAL HERMENEUTICS

by
J. EDWIN HARTILL, D.D.
PROFESSOR OF BIBLE
Northwestern College, Minneapolis, Minnesota

ZondervanPublishingHouse
Grand Rapids, Michigan

A Division of HarperCollins*Publishers*

PRINCIPLES OF BIBLICAL HERMENEUTICS
Copyright 1947 by
J. Edwin Hartill

Requests for information should be addressed to:
Zondervan Publishing House
Grand Rapids, Michigan 49530

All rights reserved. No part of this publication may be reproduced, stored in a retrieval system, or transmitted in any form or by any means—electronic, mechanical, photocopy, recording, or any other—except for brief quotations in printed reviews, without the prior permission of the publisher.

ISBN 0-310-25900-2

Printed in the United States of America

00 01 02 /DC/ 55 54 53 52 51 50

This edition is printed on acid-free paper and meets the American National Standards Institute Z39.48 standard.

FOREWORD

Every man's learning is dependent upon the knowledge of others. I am thoroughly aware of this as I have compiled these notes. It is impossible to present, with them, a correct bibliography, or honest credit to all from whom I have gathered facts and inspiration for study.

However, I wish to acknowledge in particular the large part the late Dr. R. L. Moyer played in giving me my basic training and a desire to search the Scriptures. Much of the outline of this book is in the original form which Dr. Moyer used in his Hermeneutics class at Northwestern.

I trust that as you study these principles, your understanding of the Word and your love for its truth may deepen, so that you may more ably pass it on to others.

September, 1947   DR. J. EDWIN HARTILL

Table of Contents

The Bible and the Bible Student

Hermeneutics is a science of interpretation and termination. The word is derived from a Greek god, Hermes, who was the messenger and herald of the gods, and the interpreter of Jupiter. Biblically, Hermeneutics is a science of interpreting the Bible.

Aim—to make known the different principles of Bible study which must be followed if one is to be a student of the Word of God, and desires to know the Word of God and how to handle it aright.

The Bible

A. Designation

I. The Bible.

Our English word "Bible" comes from the Greek words "Biblos" and "Biblion" which mean "the Book." It is not called "Biblos" because there are sixty-six books, but because of its preeminence over all books. It is named *The Book* in Ps. 40:7, and Heb. 10:7.

There are apparent discrepancies in the Bible but that doesn't mean the Word is untrue. The mistakes were man's errors in translating the Bible. There is one Book and One Person, the Christ.

This title was given us by John Christianson of Constantinople. (398-404 A.D.)

II. The Word of God.

Heb. 4:12, "For the Word of God is quick, and powerful, and sharper than any two-edged sword, piercing even to the dividing asunder of soul and spirit, and of the joints and marrow, and is a discerner of the thoughts and intents of the heart." II Cor. 2:17; Mk. 7:13; Rom. 10:17; I Thess. 2:13.

Of all the names given to the Bible this title is perhaps the most significant and impressive. It signifies divine authority and is used frequently in the O.T., and about forty times in the N.T.

III. The Scripture or Scriptures.

The Bible is called "the Scripture" in Mk. 12:10, 15:28; Lk. 4:21; Jn. 2:22, 7:38, 10:35; Rom. 4:3; Gal. 4:30; II Pet. 1:20. It is called "the Scriptures" in Matt. 22:29; Mk. 12:24; Lk. 24:27; Jn. 5:39; Acts 17:11; Rom. 1:2; II Tim. 3:15, and II Pet. 3:16.

This designation is found once in the O.T. in Dan. 10:21. It was used more frequently in the early church than it is at present. Some fifty-two times the title is found in the N.T. It comes from a Latin word meaning "writing."

IV. The Old and New Testament.

The word "testament" means covenant, and by this term God designated the relation that existed between Himself and His people. "Testament" is used thirteen times in the Authorized version, but is translated "covenant" in the Revised version.

The O.T. or Covenant was given at Mt. Sinai and concerns the Jewish race. The N.T. or Covenant was made in the upper room and concerns believers. This was sealed by the blood of the Lord Jesus Christ.

Heb. 9:15 "And for this cause he is the mediator of the New Testament, that by means of death, for the redemption of the transgressions that were under the first testament, they which are called might receive the promise of eternal inheritance." II Cor. 3:6, 14; Lk. 22:20; I Cor. 11:25; Heb. 12:24.

V. The Oracles.

Oracles originally meant the place where the Word of God was kept and from which it was communicated. It also has the thought of a person proclaiming the Word. This designation is found approximately fourteen times in the O.T. and 4 in the N.T. II Sam. 16:23; Ps. 28:2, Acts 7:38; Rom. 3:2, Heb. 5:12; and I Pet. 4:11.

VI. The Way.

This designation is seldom used. It is found in the N.T. as a title of Jesus Christ. It reveals the way in which obedient followers must walk.

VII. Precepts.

Prescribed truths. It means "placed in trust" and has to do with the conduct and conscience of man. Fulfilling of precepts brings enjoyment of the promises.

VIII. Statutes.

This means fixed obligations and comes from the root meaning "to engrave." These statutes are fixed and engraved by the hand of God.

IX. Commandments.

God's word is given with authority and lodged with us as a trust. Not to obey the word of God is an act of rebellion.

X. Judgments.

His judgments were made in infinite wisdom. By them we must judge, and by them we must be judged. The Bible is a guide which is just and right.

B. Declaration.

II Tim. 3:16 "All scripture is given by inspiration of God, and is profitable for doctrine, for reproof, for correction, for instruction in righteousness."

If every scripture is inspired by God obviously there can be no scripture which isn't inspired by God.

I. The meaning of Inspiration.
   a. It is more than human genius. We sometimes read of the inspiration of Shakespeare. This is false for his was human genius not inspiration. Divine inspiration appears only in the Bible. Shakespeare quoted from the Word of God over 500 times. The Bible is more than human genius; there is no degree in inspiration.
   b. More than Illumination.
   Illumination refers to the influence of the Holy Spirit; this is common to all Christians, which enables them to understand spiritual truths. Spiritual illumination is conditioned by yielding to the Holy Spirit.
   c. More than Revelation.
   There are two kinds of records in Scripture:
   1. Record of truth directly revealed by God.
   2. Record of events that occurred in the writer's experience. Inspiration superintends the communication of all truths.
   d. Inspiration means literally "God-breathed;" it is the breath of God expressing itself through a chosen instrument—a human personality.
   We cannot explain the manner in which the Holy Spirit enabled the writers to accomplish the task, but we believe it.
   II Pet. 1:21—"For the prophecy came not in old time by the will of man; but holy men of God spake as they were moved by the Holy Ghost."

II. The extent of Inspiration.
   We believe in full inspiration; we reject partial inspiration. There are those who say that the Bible *contains* the Word of God. We believe that the Bible IS the Word of God.
   All scripture is God-breathed, and this means that no scripture is inspired more than any other scripture.
   Daniel wrote words given him by divine inspiration that he could not understand. Notice Dan. 12:8, 9. In II Sam. 23:2 we read, "the Spirit of the Lord spake by me, and his word was in my tongue."
   Other scriptures are: I Pet. 1:10, 11; Exod. 20:1; Exod. 24:4; Exod. 35:1; Isa. 1:2; Jer. 1:4; Dan. 9:21; Dan. 7:1; Amos 1:1; Rev. 1:1.

III. Proofs of Inspiration.
   a. Proof of Scripture itself.
   1. Its preeminence in literature.
   2. Its preservation.
   3. Its transforming power.
   4. Its unity throughout.
   5. Its scientific accuracy.
   b. Proof of the spade of Archaeology.
   Over 5,000 places, spoken of in Scripture, have been found by the archaeologists.
   c. Proof of fulfilled prophecy.
   Example: Ps. 22.

C. Divisions.

I. Into testaments.
   Old and New Testaments.
II. Into books.
   a. English division of the Old Testament (39).
   1. Pentateuch 5
   2. History   12
   3. Poetry   5
   4. Prophecy 17
      (1) Major 5
      (2) Minor 12
   b. Hebrew division of the O.T. (24 books).
   The Hebrews never spoke of I and II Samuel or I and II Kings until the translation of the Septuagint Bible in 285 B. C. When seventy Jews began to translate into the Greek, they found that it took so much space, that they divided some books into two books. Poetical books were not divided. Luke 24:44 tells of the O.T. division.

c. English division of the N. T. (27).
   1. Historical 5
   2. Epistles   21
   3. Prophecy   1

III. Into Chapters.
There are 1189 chapters in the Bible, and they are man-made. Credit for this is given to Stephen Langdon who died in 1227. Originally chapter division was thought to have been done by Cardinal Sancto who died in 1263, but Stephen Langdon is still given credit for the work.

IV. Into Verses.
There are 31,163 verses in the Bible. This division is also man-made, and was done in 1550 A.D. by Sir Robert Stevens. The Geneva Bible, printed in 1560, was the first Bible to be printed in verse form. The Revised Version of 1881 has not the verse division. There are 3,566,480 letters in the Bible.

D. Digest.

A birds'eye view of the Bible will be a great help in the understanding of the Word.
 I. History—God's history of the past.
  1. Heavens and earths were created.
   2. Satan's first rebellion.
    3. Earth prepared for man.
     4. The headship of the first man.
      5. Man's subjection to Satan.
       6. Mankind dealt with as a whole.
        7. Construction of Babylon.
         8. Israel called and blessed.
          9. Times of the Gentiles.
           10. The first advent of Christ.
            11. The ministry of Christ covers life and death.
             12. Church called out.

 II. Prophecy—God's Revelation of the future
             12. Church called up.
            11. The ministry of the AntiChrist.
           10. The Second advent of Christ.
          9. The times of the Gentiles—close of Tribulation.
         8. Israel recalled and given blessing.
        7. Destruction of Babylon.
       6. Mankind dealt with as a whole.
      5. God's subjection of Satan.
     4. The headship of the Second Man (Christ).
    3. Earth perfected for man.
   2. Satan's final rebellion.
  1. The new heavens and new earth.

  1. Heaven and Earth were created.
     Gen. 1:1 "In the beginning God created the heaven and the earth."
     This was the world that then was.
     II Pet. 3:6 "Whereby the world that then was, being overflowed with water, perished."
     There is no date, information, nor calendar for original creation. We must distinguish between create and make. Out of nothing by the word of His power, the heavens and earth were created. This is an appeal to faith, not reason. Reason can never discover who God is. God reaches our reason through our faith, and not our faith through our reason.
    2. Satan's first rebellion.
       Gen. 1:2 "And the earth was without form, and void; and darkness was upon the face of the deep. And the Spirit of God moved upon the face of THE WATERS."
       "Was" is translated "became" in verse 2.
       Isa. 45:18 "For thus saith the Lord that created the heavens; God Himself that formed the earth and made it; he hath established it, he created it not in vain, he formed it to be inhabited; I am the Lord, and there is none else."
      3. Earth prepared for man—Gen. 1:2—2:3.
         In verse 2 we begin with the Spirit brooding over the face of the water.
        4. The headship of the first man.
           Adam was first as man but second in person, for Satan was a headship also. The blessing of God rests upon the renewed creation.

5. Man's subjection to Satan—Gen. 3.
   The one who marred the first creation, mars the new creation. Adam identifies himself with Eve's sin and sin enters into the human race. Jesus identified Himself with our sin, and brought salvation into the world. Written in the close of the chapter is the provision of a covering for sin in the skins of animals slain. Blood was shed. The entire race was brought into subjection to Satan.

6. Mankind dealt with as a whole.
   Gen. Chs. 4-11:
   4—Result of sin in world.
   5—Death reigning.
   6—Corruption reigning on the earth.
   7—Beginning of the flood.
   8—Flood at its height.
   9—Flood at its end.
   10—Man's dominion and responsibility—9:25,26.

7. Construction of Babylon Ch. 11.
   Idolatry instituted.

8. Israel called and blessed.
   You must properly place Israel if you want to understand the Word.
   a. From call of Abraham to the Exodus.
      (1) Abraham
      (2) Isaac
      (3) Jacob
      (4) Joseph
   b. From Exodus to death of Joshua.
      Joshua fully established in the land.
   c. The Judges.
   d. The Kings.
   The Captivities.
      Jer., Ezek., Obadiah, Esther, Ezra, Nehemiah.

9. Times of the Gentiles.
   The period of time during which Jerusalem is politically under Gentile supremacy. Lk. 21:24.

10. The first advent of Christ.
    Gal. 4:4,5 "But when the fullness of the time was come, God sent forth his Son, made of a woman, made under the law, to redeem them that were under the law, that we might receive the adoption of sons."

11. The ministry of Christ covers life and death.

12. Church called out.
    Church is a company composed of both Jews and Gentiles.

Romans—Justification.
Corinthians—Church.
Galatians—Liberty from the law.
Ephesians—Heavenly character.
Philippians—Walk of church.
Thessalonians—Hope.
Jude—Church earnestly contends.
Timothy, Titus, Philemon—Danger from what might be called Gentile idolatry.
Hebrews, James, Peter—Danger from what might be called Jewish apostasy.
I John—Nature of fellowship.
II John—Limits of fellowship—excludes.
III John—Extent of fellowship—includes.

II. Prophecy—God's revelation of the future.

12. Church called up. I Thess. 4:16,17 (rapture).
    This has to do with every believer in Christ.

11. The ministry of the Anti-Christ. Christ was the truth; he (anti) is the lie.

10. The second advent of Christ.
    a. He came to the manger.
    b. Now He comes to the throne.

9. The times of the Gentiles—close of Tribulation.

8. Israel recalled and given blessing. Isa. 11.
Jer. 32:33 "And they have turned unto me the back, and not the face: though I taught them, rising up early and teaching them, yet they have not hearkened to receive instruction."
Ezek. 36:37 "Thus saith the Lord God, I will yet for this be inquired of by the house of Israel, to do it for them; I will increase them with men like a flock."
Rom. 11.

7. Destruction of Babylon (city razed).

6. Mankind dealt with as a whole.
Matt. 25:31,32 "When the Son of man shall come in his glory, and all the holy angels with him, then shall he sit upon the throne of his glory: and before him shall be gathered all nations: and he shall separate them one from another, as a shepherd divideth his sheep from the goats."
Joel 3:12 "Let the heathen be wakened, and come up to the valley of Jehoshaphat, for there will I sit to judge all the heathen round about."

5. God's subjection of Satan.
Rev. 20:1-3.

4. The headship of the second man (Christ).
Isa. 2:11; Micah 4; The Millennium (1,000).

3. Earth perfected for man.

2. Satan's final rebellion. Satan is loosed from his prison and deceives the people.

1. The new heavens and new earth.
In Peter—"The heavens and earth shall pass away."
In John—"A new heaven and a new earth."

The Bible Student

A. Preparation (What is necessary).

I. Personal Preparation.
a. Personal relationship to Christ—a regenerated person. I Cor. 2:11 "For what man knoweth the things of a man, save the spirit of man which is in him? even so the things of God knoweth no man, but the Spirit of God."
b. Positive persuasion concerning inspiration.
It is *The* Book, not *a* Book. We must approach with bare head and bended knee. The Bible student should never put a question mark where God puts a period.
c. A passion and desire to know the Book.
d. Prayer for discernment.
Martin Luther said, "To pray well is to study well."
e. A predisposition to obedience.
A great teacher will not teach those who refuse to obey. If we are to know the Word, we must do the will of God.
f. Persistence in study.
It is well to remember that our idle days are the devil's busy days.

II. Practical Preparation.
a. Own a good Bible—American or Revised edition.
b. Own a good Concordance, such as "Strong's" or "Young's."
c. Possess a good notebook.

B. Promotion (What is gained).

I. Profound knowledge.
If you study the Scripture you will become a possessor of a profound knowledge. Rom. 15:4 "For whatsoever things were written aforetime were written for our learning, that we through patience and comfort of the Scriptures might have hope." II Pet. 3:15-17; I Pet. 2:2; Lk. 24:25-27; John 1:45; John 5:46; John 5:39; I Cor. 15:1-4.

II. Personal Faith.
Rom. 10:17 "So faith cometh by hearing and hearing by the 'Word of God'." As we study, faith increases. Faith rests upon the Word of God.

III. Purification of Life.

John 15:3 "Now ye are clean through the word which I have spoken unto you."

John 17:17 "Sanctify them through thy truth: thy word is truth."

There is cleansing power in the Word of God.

Moody once said. "The Bible will keep you from sin or sin will keep you from this Book."

Ps. 119:69; Gal. 3:16, 17.

IV. Preparation for Service.

II Tim. 3:16, 17; Eph. 6:17 "And take the helmet of salvation, and the sword of the spirit, which is the word of God."

Our duty is to continually preach the Word. God honors the Word, not the person.

V. Power in Ministry.

If you use the Word of God you will be prepared for service and will have power in your ministry. The Word is profitable for doctrine, for reproof, for correction, and for instruction in righteousness.

C. Proposition (What shall be done).

I. Practice its truth.

Col. 3:16 "Let the word of Christ dwell in you richly in all wisdom; teaching and admonishing one another in psalms and hymns and spiritual songs, singing with grace in your hearts to the Lord."

If you proclaim its truth, practice what you preach.

Heb. 4:2; I Thess. 1:9, 10; I Thess. 2:1-12.

II. Proclaim its truth.

If you don't practice, don't proclaim it. Walk in its light, bow to its authority, cling to its integrity, obey every precept, feed on its treasure, and hide it in your heart.

CHAPTER TWO

The Dispensational Principle

I. DISPENSATIONAL PRINCIPLE.

Unless one understands the dispensations, one cannot understand God's Book, and it becomes a Book of confusion and contradictions.

a. Definition—A dispensation is a period of time during which God deals in a particular way with man in respect to sin and man's responsibility. The word "dispensation" means "administration" and is first found in I Cor. 9:17.

b. Divisions.

Someone has truly said, "time is an island in the sea of eternity, which is divided into different dispensations or periods of time."

1. The Dispensation of Innocence.

(a) From the creation of man to the fall of man. Gen. 1:26-2:23.
Period of years not known.
  (1) This is the innocent or unfallen state when the subjects knew neither good nor evil, being neither holy nor sinful, but being free to choose when good and evil were placed before them.
Adam wasn't righteous because he hadn't chosen good.
Adam wasn't sinful because he hadn't chosen sin.
  (2) Man was on probation.

(b) Man's responsibility—Gen. 2:8, 9, 16, 17. Man must choose whether he will believe God's Word or the statements of Satan.

(c) Failure of man—Gen. 3:6.
  (1) Man chose to believe Satan rather than God. Satan said, "ye shall be as gods—ye shall not surely die." His purpose was to people the earth with fallen creation.
These same lies of Satan are the foundation of present-day apostasy.
Many of the "isms" of the present day can be traced back to the verse which we just quoted, Gen. 3:4. Examples are Eddyism—"ye shall be as God"; Russellism—"ye shall not surely die"; Modernism—"yea hath God said."

(d) Consequences of man's failure—Gen. 3:14-19.
  (1) Judgment on Satan.
  (2) Judgment of the woman.
  (3) Judgment on the earth.
  (4) Judgment on man.
  (5) Promise of the seed to deliver—Gen. 3:15.
After viewing all of these judgments the necessity of the Savior is seen. Notice in this verse that prophecy had its birth in failure.

(e) Moral condition—one of perfection until sin came in.

(f) Divine mercy—Gen. 3:15—a promise of victory.

2. The Dispensation of Conscience—"with knowledge."

(a) From fall of man to flood—1656 years—Gen. 3-7.
  (1) Begins with man in a fallen condition—having knowledge and guided by his conscience.
  (2) Man is now outside the garden. A flaming sword is placed at the east of the garden to keep him away.
  (3) This dispensation shows what happens when man is guided only by his conscience.

(b) Man's responsibility—Gen. 4:7.
He is to choose between doing good and doing evil. He insists on evil.
Gen. 4:7 "If thou doest well, shalt thou not be accepted? and if thou doest not well, sin lieth at the door. And unto thee shall be his desire, and thou shalt rule over him."
If man had not done good, the sin offering was at the door. (This seems to be the first promise of Christ as a sin offering.)
Cain and Abel were both sinners, but Abel recognized the necessity of blood-shedding.

(c) Failure of man—Gen. 6:5, 11, 12.
Man is exceedingly wicked, for we read, "God saw that the wickedness of man was great."

(d) Consequences of man's failure—Gen. 7.
Judgment through the flood.

(e) Moral condition—became worse and worse.
  (1) Begins with birth of Cain, made in Adam's likeness, and fallen.
All men at the beginning of the dispensation are fallen.

13

(2) Refusal of Cain to make his sacrifice as God commanded (that is, through the shedding of blood) marks the beginning of rebellion toward God.

(3) This is followed by refusal of man to accept the will of God.

(4) The decline of the race follows.

(5) The moral condition becomes pitiful.

(6) Destruction of man seems the only way to remedy the condition.

(f) Divine mercy— Gen. 7:1.

Eight people are saved out of the flood to begin the new dispensation.

3. The Dispensation of Human Government.

(a) From the flood to the confusion of tongues—Gen. 8:1-11:9, 427 yrs.

Noah was a righteous man, the only man God could find who believed Him—Gen. 8:20; Heb. 11:7. Noah was saved with 7 others.

(b) Man's responsibility—Gen. 9:1.

Noah was given the same position which Adam occupied in the first dispensation; he was to govern for God. As a responsibility, it has never ended, and it will not end until Christ takes over the government.

Noah was given the power of capital punishment—Gen. 9:6, "Whoso sheddeth man's blood, by man shall his blood be shed, for in the image of God made he man."

The reason—raising the hand against one created in God's image indicates hatred of God Himself.

(c) Failure of man. Gen. 11:1-4.

(1) Unless man can govern himself, he cannot govern others.
Noah's downfall—Gen. 9:20-23 (intoxicated).

(2) Building of Tower of Babel.

((a)) An organized political and religious rebellion against God.

((1)) Idolatry and apostasy.

((2)) Failure comes always from disobeying God.

((3)) Unification here, is shown to become blasphemous. Unity may be all right but God was left out of the picture completely. The only worthwhile unity looks to God.

((4)) Man exalts himself. We read the words, "make *us* a tower."

(d) Consequences of man's failure—Gen. 11:5-9.

Confusion of tongues and the dispersion of the people.

(e) Moral condition.

Could not have been worse. It so angered God that He destroyed their plan, through the confusion of tongues.

(f) Divine mercy.

God was merciful to them in their idolatry and sought another man who would follow Him.

4. Dispensation of Promise.

(a) From the call of Abraham to the Exodus—430 years.
Gen. 11:10-15:21.

(1) Abram's condition—probably was in idolatry, but he listened to God. His faith began when he left Ur. He became righteous when he believed God's promise concerning his son.

(2) God's promises and covenants—Gen. 12:1-3; 13:14-17; 15:6.

(b) Man's responsibility—Gen. 26:2, 3.

(1) To stay in the land which God gave to him, and not to go down into Egypt which is a type of the world.

(2) Abram doubts God's word, and when famine comes, he goes to Egypt for food. Abram could not have died in spite of the famine, because the promises of God had not been fulfilled.

(c) Man's failure—Gen. 47:1.

All of Jacob's house went down into the land of Egypt.

(d) Consequences of man's failure—Ex. 1:8-14.

Slavery in Egypt—sin and idolatry.

(e) Moral Condition.

They turned to the gods of the Egyptians and became idolatrous—Ezek. 20:7-9.

(f) Divine mercy.

Deliverance and preservation of Israel.

5. Dispensation of Law.

(a) From Sinai to Calvary—the exodus to the cross—1491 years. Man's condition at the beginning of this dispensation—Ex. 19:1-8. Trusting in his own strength instead of depending on God— "All that the Lord hath spoken we will do."

(b) Man's responsibility—Exod. 19:5.
   To keep the law; includes 10 commandments and all laws, social and civil.
   These were given to the people of Israel only—Rom. 2:12; 9:4.
(c) Man's failure—II Kings 17:7-17, 19; Acts 2:22-23.
   They failed to keep the law, and the only One who did keep the law was crucified by them.
(d) Consequences of man's failure—II Kings 17:1-6, 20:25:1-11.
(e) Moral condition—Fallen.
(f) Divine mercy.
   Shown in the fact that judgment upon Jerusalem and on the nation of Israel was withheld for 40 years after the crucifixion.

6. The Dispensation of Grace.

(a) From the descent of the Holy Spirit to the descent of Christ—(Acts and Epistles).
   (1) Man's state at the beginning—a lost condition—Rom. 3:9-20; Eph. 2:2. There are two classes of people in the world—saved sinners and lost sinners.
(b) Man's responsibility.
   (1) To believe in the Lord Jesus Christ. John 3:36; Acts 16:31; John 1:11-13; Rom. 4:5; 5:1, 2; Eph. 2:8, 9; Gal. 5:6; Tit. 3:5. Man is not saved by works, but by faith alone.
(c) Man's failure.
   (1) Become lovers of themselves, of money, and of pleasure more than lovers of God—II Tim. 3:1-7.
   (2) Having a form of godliness but without power.
   (3) Would make God a liar through unbelief, which is the most colossal failure of the dispensations—I Jn. 5:10.
(d) Consequences of man's failure.
   God will give them up to their unbelief—I Tim. 4:1-3; II Tim. 4:3, 4.
(e) Moral condition.
   Fallen and sinful.
(f) Divine mercy.
   God has provided salvation for the whole human race.

7. The Dispensation of Judgment or Tribulation.

(a) From the rapture of the church to the millenium—Rev. 6-19; Dan. 12:1; Jer. 30:7.
   (1) State of man at the beginning—I Thess. 4:16-18.
      ((a)) The church is taken away, which means there is a race on earth that does not have in it the "salt" to prevent corruption—II Thess. 2:10-12.
      ((b)) The Holy Spirit, omnipresent, will still be here to deal with sinners; but since the church is gone, He will no longer be active in connection with the church.
(b) Man's responsibility.
   To recognize God and to worship God—Rev. 14:6.
(c) Man's failure.
   The men who are evil will not repent—Rev. 9:20, 21; Rev. 18:21-24.
(d) Consequences of man's failure.
   Utter destruction—Ps. 2:1-6; Rev. 14:20; Zech. 14:4; Rev. 19:17-21.
(e) Moral condition.
   A godless group of people from whom all restraint has been taken by the removal of the church.
(f) Divine mercy.
   Shown by the saved Gentiles and sealed Israelites.

8. The Kingdom dispensation.

(a) From the descent of Christ to the Great White Throne Judgment—1000 years—Psalms 2 and 11.
   (1) Man's state at the beginning.
      ((a)) Under the personal reign and rule of Christ—Acts 15:14-17; Ps. 2:6; Matt. 24:29, 30; Isa. 24:23.
(b) Man's responsibility.
   Obedience and submission to the King, and also to worship Him—Ps. 2:12; Isa. 65:20; Ps. 67:4; 86:9; Zech. 14:17.
(c) Man's failure.
   Feigned obedience. Man will follow Satan—Ps. 66:3; Rev. 20:7-9.
(d) Consequences of man's failure.
   Destruction caused by fire coming down from God out of heaven—Rev. 20:9.

(e) Moral condition.
    Fallen and unrepentant.
(f) Divine mercy.
    God provides a new heaven and a new earth.

9. Summary of Dispensations.

In each dispensation the trend of man is away from God. The responsibility of man in each dispensation is to believe the Word of God and to obey Him. At the end of each dispensation, God gives man up to his own way.

Each dispensation shows that evil is headed up in a person or persons.

1st Dispensation—Satan and the fallen woman.
2nd Dispensation—Sinful angels.
3rd Dispensation—Nimrod.
4th Dispensation—Pharaoh.
5th Dispensation—Judas, Scribes and Pharisees.
6th Dispensation—Modernists.
7th Dispensation—Anti-Christ.
8th Dispensation—Satan.

Each dispensation ends in a world crisis.

1st Dispensation—Expulsion of man from the garden.
2nd Dispensation—The flood.
3rd Dispensation—Confusion of tongues.
4th Dispensation—Bondage of the chosen race.
5th Dispensation—The cross of Christ.
6th Dispensation—The rapture of the church.
7th Dispensation—The wrath of God and the binding of Satan.
8th Dispensation—Fire from heaven.

In each dispensation God comes down.

1st Dispensation—God came down to the garden.
2nd Dispensation—God talked with Noah.
3rd Dispensation—God said, "Let us go down."
4th Dispensation—"I am come down" (burning bush).
5th Dispensation—Incarnation of Christ.
6th Dispensation—The Lord shall descend.
7th Dispensation—Coming to earth.
8th Dispensation—Still upon the earth.

10. Rightly dividing the Word of Truth.

(a) There are statements in the Bible which apparently are contradictory, and to avoid confusion one must follow the rules given below in dividing the Truth.
    (1) Not only must Truth be divided into dispensations, but it must be divided *in* the same dispensation.
        Examples—Compare Matt. 10:5, 6 with Mark 16:15.
        The first command was given by Christ before it became evident that the Jews would reject Him. The second command was given after His crucifixion and resurrection.
        Example—Compare Luke 9:3 and Matt. 10:9, 10 with Luke 22.36.
        Above rule applies to this. *"But now"* makes the difference.
        Example—Compare Isa. 2:4 and Joel 3:10 and II Tim. 3:1.
        Applies to dispensation of Judgment and Kingdom and Grace.
        Example—Compare Psa. 58:10 with Rom. 12:17, 21 Law and Grace.
        Example—Compare Rev. 20:12 with II Cor. 5:10. One is judgment as to whether or not men are saved, and the other is judgment as to the works done after salvation.
    (2) One must never take truth that belongs to a past dispensation and bring it up to the present.
        ((a)) Roman Catholicism (mixture of Paganism, Christianity, and Judaism) brings the earthly priesthood of the Law up to the present dispensation.
        ((b)) Seventh Day Adventism brings the Law which was given to the Jewish people down to this dispensation—Rom. 7:4-6.
    (3) Never take truth from a future dispensation and try to apply it to the present.
        ((a)) Russellism—The 144,000 mentioned in Rev. 7 taken from the judgment dispensation.
        ((b)) The Church belongs to this dispensation; and Abel, Noah, Abraham, etc. do not belong to the Church.

(4) Do not take statements applying to any other dispensation and try to make them fit the present.

> Example: Gen. 6:3—belongs to Conscience.
> Luke 11:13—belongs to Law.
> Rom. 8:9—belongs to Grace.
> Jn. 7:27-39—belongs to Doctrine of Holy Spirit.

(5) Do not put the present into the future.
The church is not going into the tribulation.
This period is connected with the Jews, and is "The time of Jacobs trouble"—Jer. 30:3; Dan. 12:1.

Chart of the Eight Dispensations

DESIGNA-TION	INNO-CENCE	CON-SCIENCE	HUMAN GOV'T.	PROMISE	LAW	GRACE	TRIBU-LATION	KINGDOM
CITATION	Gen. 1:26-28; 2:23	Gen. 3:8 & 23	Gen. 8:1	Gen. 12:1; Ex. 19:8.	Ex. 19:8	Jn. 1:17	Dan. 12:1 Jer. 30:7	Eph. 1:1
LIMITA-TION	Creation to fall	Fall of man to Flood	Flood to Tower of Babel.	Call of Abraham to Exodus.	Ex. to Cross. Sinai to Calvary.	Descent of H.S. to descent of Christ.	Ascent of Church to descent of Christ.	Descent of Christ to Great W. Throne.
DURATION	Unknown	1656 yrs.	427 yrs.	430 yrs.	1491 yrs.	1900 yrs.	7 yrs.	1000 yrs.
CONDI-TION	Man in innocence. Not ignorant.	In sin— Gen. 6:5, 6.	Noah now righteous leader. Man governing.	Idolatry and nation scattered.	Bondage to Obedience and disobedience.	All the world guilty before God.	Intense suffering.	Living in Kingdom of Glory.
OBLIGA-TION	Not to eat of the tree of knowledge of good and evil.	Do good and choose right— Gen. 4: 6, 7.	Govern for God— Gen. 9:5, 6.	To stay in land of promise— Gen. 12:5.	To keep the law.	To accept Christ, believing.	Worship God & refuse to worship Beast.	To submit to the Son.
TRANS-GRESSION	Disobeyed and ate. Lust of flesh, eyes, pride of life.	Did evil— Matt. 24:37, 38, 39.	Building Tower of Babel— Gen. 11:4.	Went into Egypt.	Failed to keep the law.	Failed to accept Christ.	Repented not. Worshipped Beast.	Feigned obedience.
CONDEM-NATION	Curse on man—Gen. 3:14-19.	God destroyed flesh— Gen. 6:13.	Tongues confused— Gen. 11:7.	Slavery.	Division of No. & So. Kingdoms. I King. 11:29-40.	Judgment & eternal damnation.	Battle of Armageddon. Destruction.	Fire devours them— Rev. 20:9.
CULMINA-TION	Expulsion from garden— Gen. 3:24.	Flood— 8 saved.	People scattered— Gen. 11:8.	In Egypt under Pharoah.	Calvary. Christ fulfilled law.	Rapture of church from world.	Armageddon.	Cast into Lake of Fire.
PREDIC-TION	Promise of the Redeemer. Gen. 3:15.	Ark—salvation— Gen. 6:18. New Covenant with Noah.	Confusion in Government.	Promise of seed thru Abraham. More definite now— Gen. 22:18.	Isa. 9:6, 7. "For unto us a child is born."	I Thess. 4:16, 17.	Matt. 24:29-31.	New heavens and new earth.
CORRECTION OR INSTRUCTION	They would not be as God (as Satan said).	Conscience not sufficient to bring man to God.	No hope in human government.	God did not abandon world when He chose Abraham.	The law will not save.	Eph. 2: 8-9.		

CHAPTER THREE

The Covenantal Principle

II. THE COVENANTAL PRINCIPLE.

a. Definition of a covenant.

1. An agreement or a contract between men or between men and God.
   (a) God, in grace, undertakes to do things for men.
   (b) A compact or fetter—that which binds together.

2. Kinds of covenants in the Bible.
   (a) Conditional—depends upon man.
   Exod. 19:5—"*If* ye will obey"—Formula.
   (b) Unconditional—depends upon God.
   Gen. 9:11—"I will"—Formula.

3. Not every covenant has its sign—only four.
   Noahic—the rainbow
   Mosaic—the Sabbath
   Abrahamic—circumcision (unconditional)
   Davidic—The Son

b. Divisions.

1. Edenic Covenant.

(a) Constitution of the covenant—Gen. 1:28-30; 2:15-17.
Orders life of man in Eden—his relationship to God.

(b) Contents of the covenant.
   (1) Man is responsible—to replenish the earth.
   (2) To subdue the earth to the needs of the human race.
   Possibly this means the forces of the earth as well as the beasts.
   (3) To have dominion over the animals of the creation—Psa. 8:3-9.
   (4) To restrict himself to a vegetable diet. This command has been changed.
   (5) To dress the garden. Before the fall, this would be an easy task.
   (6) To keep the garden. "Keep" means to guard or protect, and implies a warning against an enemy who might appear.

(c) Conditions of the covenant (IF).
   (1) To abstain from eating of the tree of the knowledge of good and evil.
   (2) Failure to do this resulted in physical death.

(d) Conclusion of the covenant.
Expulsion from the garden.

2. Adamic Covenant.

(a) The Constitution of the covenant.
Made with Adam in Eden, before the expulsion. It is unconditional and consists of a curse and a promise—Gen. 3:14-19. To order life of man outside Eden.
   Cherubim—Holiness of God.
   Seraphim—Uncleanness of people of God.

(b) The Contents of the covenant.
   (1) The curse of Satan—3:14.
   (2) The judgment on the woman—3:16.
      ((a)) Multiplied conception.
      ((b)) Maternal sorrow.
      ((c)) Subordination to man, the headship being invested in man.
   (3) The judgment on the man—3:17.
   The ground is cursed for his sake, and he must labor for his living.
   (4) The curse on creation—3:18.
   Caused to bring forth thorns, thistles, etc., and all things which tend to make cultivation difficult.
   See Gen. 3:17, Sorrow—toil.
   (5) The promise—3:15.

(c) The Conclusion of the covenant.
Runs on to the renovation of the earth by fire.

3. Noahic Covenant.

(a) The constitution of the covenant—Gen. 8:20-9:17.
  (1) Made with Noah after coming out of the ark. It is *unconditional*, and the rainbow is **the sign.**
  (2) Noah is wiser than Adam, because he had seen that God could destroy as well as create. He and his family were not ignorant and superstitious, for they did not worship the ark, but worshipped God.
  (3) Noah's sacrifice was a sweet-smelling odor to God, and formed the basis of the Noahic covenant—Gen. 8:20.

(b) Contents of the Covenant.
  (1) God promises that He will not again curse the ground—8:21,22. He recognizes the fact that man is in sin and cannot do anything but sinful deeds, and promises that He will not curse the ground because of this.
  (2) He will not again destroy all the living by the water of a flood—8:21,22.
  (3) The natural order of the seasons shall prevail.
  (4) Men (Noah and his family) are commanded to be fruitful and replenish the earth—9:1.
  (5) Man again has dominion over the animal creation.
      The animals will fear man—Gen. 9:2,3.
  (6) Their diet is changed to include meat, but as far as possible, it must be bloodless. (For physical good of man; blood is carrier of disease)—9:4.
      God is trying to impress on them the sanctity and holiness of blood; points forward to Christ. The Jews are very careful in this respect.
  (7) The law of capital punishment is established—9:6.
      Lifting up the hand against man, made in the image of God, shows rebellion in the heart against God.
      This law has never been abolished.
      Before this time the murderer was dealt with by God, but now is dealt with by man. In the days of the cities of refuge, a man found guilty was given over for punishment.
  (8) This covenant included animal creation.
      Beasts shall learn to prey upon each other.

(c) Conclusion of the covenant.
    The renovation of the earth by fire.

(d) Sign of the covenant, or the token of the covenant—bow in the cloud—Gen. 9:13-17.

4. Abrahamic Covenant.

(a) Constitution of the covenant. Gen. 12:1-3.
  (1) A seven-fold promise, to which added information is given from time to time. Gen. 13:14-17; 15:1-18; 17:1-8.
  (2) Condition of the world when Abram was called—Idolatry. Isa. 51:1,2; Josh. 24:3.
  (3) Abram's home at the time when God called.
      Ur of the Chaldees was a large, prosperous seaport, in one of the most productive regions of the world.
  (4) The act of laying on the altar the five beasts and birds represents the Oriental method of making a covenant, whereas the present day method is to sign a paper—Gen. 15:8-15.
      Each party to the agreement walked between the pieces of the animals. Abraham went to sleep, and God was the only One Who walked through.
  (5) The slain beasts may typify the death of Christ, and the birds of prey the powers of evil trying to take away the efficacy of Christ's death.

(b) Contents of the covenant.
    (First given in Gen. 12:2,3, but additions and explanations were given from time to time.)
  (1) "I will make of thee a great nation."
      ((a)) "Thy seed shall be as the dust of the earth, and as the stars of heaven . . . I will make thee exceeding fruitful, and I will make nations of thee, and kings shall come out of thee."
      ((b)) This covenant made with a man, childless and aged.
      ((c)) This nation was the Jewish race, and came through Isaac, the promised seed. In the days of David and Solomon, this was the great nation of the world and it is the miracle nation of all time.
          ((1)) Today they number over 20 million, and have been preserved as a race for 4,000 years.
          ((2)) They are the only nation which can trace its ancestry to one man, Abraham.
      (Additions)
          ((1)) Descendants of Ishmael—a wild man; "his hand will be against every man, and every man's hand will be against him; and he shall dwell in the presence of his brethren."

[a] Ishmael was not the promised seed, but he was part of the promised multiplication of Abraham—Gen. 17:15-22.

[b] The descendants of Ishmael through his twelve sons are the Arabian race or nation—I Chron. 1:29; Gen. 25:16.

The history of this nation is remarkable, and is another testimony of the truth of God's Word.

[c] They have dwelt in the presence of the other nations, and have retained their freedom until this day.

[d] Their hand is against every man and every man's hand is against them.

In 622 after the rise of Mohammed, they left their desert home, and under the name of the Saracens, they conquered a large part of the civilized world, and as conquerors, every man's hand was against them, and their hand was against every man.

[e] Their customs of living and dress have remained unchanged, and they are just like Ishmael. They are a wild people, living in tents in the desert.

[f] They can be accounted for only in God's Word.

((2)) Descendants of the sons of Keturah. There were six sons born to Abraham and Keturah, his third wife. Each of these was the head of a small nation. One of these was the nation of Midianites, from Midian.

((3)) Spiritual descendants.

Abraham is called the father of the faithful.

(2) "I will bless thee."

((a)) Spiritual blessing—Gen. 15:6.

((b)) Temporal blessing—Gen. 13:14-17.

Lift up your eyes—northward—eastward—etc.

Gen. 15:18—Property (Protection).

Gen. 24:34, 35—Possessions.

The land of Palestine is one of the richest, and the Dead Sea contains chemicals worth billions of dollars.

(3) "I will make thy name great."

((a)) Abraham's name is next to the name of Christ, and occurs some 300 times in the Scriptures.

(4) "Thou shalt be a blessing."

He was a blessing to the people in his day; and through Christ, he is a blessing to the people of this day.

(5) "I will bless them that bless thee and curse him that curseth thee."

Other nations are mentioned only when they come in contact with the Jews—Matt. 25:40,41,46.

Nations who have treated the Jew well	Nations who have ill-treated the Jews
America has welcomed the Jew and has been blessed.	Russia and Turkey are modern examples of nations who have been cursed because they cursed the Jew.
This is also true of England.	Egypt was cursed by plagues because of her treatment of the Jew—Joel 3:19.
	Other nations are the Babylonians and the Saracens. Outstanding examples in Scripture, are Moab and Amalek—Zeph. 2:9-10. Edom, the Philistines, and Damascus were all judged because of their treatment of Jews.

God deals with the nations on the basis of their treatment of the Jews.

"In thee—(and in thy seed) shall all the families of the earth be blessed."

The Abrahamic are those who have come in contact with Abraham and his seed.

The non-Abrahamic are those who have not.

Abrahamic	Non-Abrahamic
Monotheistic group.	Also includes Pantheism and Idolatry. About 1,000,000.
Jews, Mohammedans, and professed Christians—about 800,000,000.	Includes Chinese, Mongolians, Tartars, Senegalese, Burmese, Siamese, Brahmans, Hottentots, American Indians, Bushmen, and all classes of degraded superstitious, warlike, human beings, such as the cannibals.
Includes English, Scotch, Welsh, Irish, Swedes, Norwegians, Danes, Dutch, Belgians, French, Germans, Swiss, Spanish, Portugese, Italians, Austrians, Greeks, etc.	

The covenant not only promised that great nations should come from Abraham, but also included a title to the land of Canaan—Gen. 13:14-17. This promise was made of a land in the possession of other nations, and to a childless old man.

The land belongs to the Jews by:

Gift or grant—cannot be duplicated, bought or sold.
Homestead—Deut. 32:8.
Conquest—Josh. 11:20,23.
Purchase—Needed cleansing by sacrifice—which was done in crucifixion. Christ holds the title.
Tenure—Lived on the land almost 1500 years.
Covenant.

(c) The sign of the covenant.
Circumcision of all males on the eighth day.
This set them apart as a marked people. It was a mark of distinction of separation, of purity, and of possession—Deut. 30:6; Jer. 9:25,26.

(d) Conclusion of the covenant—when the New Covenant was made.

5. The Mosaic Covenant.

Moses was the founder of a nation, not the father of a nation.

(a) Constitution of the Covenant.
A covenant made to the people of Israel, through Moses, who chose to serve the people of his nation, rather than to retain his position of honor as the son of Pharaoh's daughter.

(b) Contents of the Covenant.
(1) Commandments—the ten.
Moral law showing the righteous will of God, commanding condemnation and death. Matters of right and wrong in conduct. Ten commandments accompanied by 600 other laws that emanate from them.

(2) Civil law.
Judgments given to govern the social life of Israel.
Camp life—sanitary laws, etc.

(3) Ceremonial law.
((a)) Ordinances covering the religious life of Israel.
((1)) Given to the high priest who was to represent the people with God, and to make sacrifices for the sins of the people.
((2)) Not given at the same time as the Commandments were given. The Commandments were given first, and the people broke them before seeing them; so the ordinances were given because they needed atonement for their sins. In their act of breaking the first law, they broke them all. Moses' act of breaking the tables of stone was a testimony to this fact.
((3)) Priests and sacrifices established by command. These were substitutionary sacrifices for sin; for through sinning, the people deserved death, but God allowed the blood of the animals to be substitutionary.

(4) Spiritual laws.
The whole law is deeply spiritual. It is based, as Christ taught, on love to God and man.
Love to God inspires the first three commandments; love to man, the last seven.
The fourth commandment, Christ tells us, belongs to the human side of the law—Mark 2:27.
Rom. 7:14—Law is spiritual. Christ and apostles based the gospel on the law.
Don't condemn the law!

(c) Conditions of the Covenant (IF).
(1) Promise of blessing if they would obey the law—Ex. 19:5,6; Lev. 26:3; Deut. 28:1-4; Deut. 29:9.
(2) Promise of punishment if they disobeyed His commandments—Lev. 26:14-26; Deut. 28:15-68; 11:10-17.

Other Remarkable Fulfillments Showing How The Jewish Nation Has Been Persecuted As God Foretold.

1. Deut. 28:49-50,53—Most solemn chapter of Bible. Rabbis read each of five books of Pentateuch each year in synagogue, and when they come to Deut. 28 they read very slowly and solemnly.
Their cities were to become waste and desolate, and they were to be scattered among nations. They would become so desolate in the time of famine that they would kill and eat their own children. They would be crushed, and besieged,—and brought to the most awful extremities through famine. They would be sold into other lands, among their enemies, and they would find no rest for their heads.

   1800 years later the enemy came. This was the Roman army, and they were swift as eagles, and as fierce. An eagle was their emblem. They spared neither age nor sex.

2. Deut. 28:37.
"Thou shalt become an astonishment, a proverb, and a *byword* among all nations, whither the Lord shall lead thee."

This name is "sheenie" and it is an interesting word, and no two dictionaries give the same derivation for the word. One says it came from the word "Sheen-Shaddaiah," but Robert Dick Wilson, a man who has studied languages, believes in the inspiration of the Bible and is an authority on the subject, says there is no doubt but what it comes from the word Sheninah or Sheenah (Heb.—"Sheenaw"), which means a *byword*.

3. Deut. 28:63b.
"And ye shall be plucked from off the land whither thou goest to possess it."

The first plucking came when Northern Israel was carried into captivity by the Assyrians under Sargon. The enemy did not take all at this time, however, but carried away only the best. Part of Judah also was taken into Babylonian captivity, but the larger portion was left. Forty years after the rejection of Jesus Christ, they were plucked completely off the land by the Roman nation. On August 5, 70 A.D. Jerusalem was destroyed, 1,000,000 people were killed, and 97,000 taken captive. In 135 A.D. the Jews arose in rebellion against the Roman ruler Hadrian, in a war that lasted 3½ years. 580,000 Jews were killed, and all Jews were expelled from the land and forbidden to return on pain of death. Hadrian tried to blot out the remembrance of even the name of Jerusalem by building another city on the site, and giving it another name.

Many Jews were sold into captivity as slaves, and the country was completely cleared of its inhabitants, so that people from all the nations went in to live there. Jews did not dare to be found in the land of Palestine. Even as late as the 12th century, a Spanish Jew visited the country and found only about 200 Jews; and this was 1000 years after Rome overthrew Jerusalem. 3600 years ago God said Israel would be plucked off the land if she disobeyed, and it has been literally fulfilled.

4. Deut. 28:64.
"And the Lord shall scatter thee among all people, from the one end of the earth even unto the other; and there thou shalt serve other gods . . . . ."

In the old days when a conqueror subdued a land, he would transplant people from that land to another which he had conquered, and would bring people from the other land back to the first, thus mixing the two peoples. This was what happened in the case of the Samaritans; they are a mixture of Jew and Gentile. However, no foreign peoples were taken into Judah when the country was conquered by Babylon; for from that section was to come Jesus Christ, the Lion of the tribe of Judah. The Jews were not carried just into the conquering country, however, but they are everywhere. It is not so with any other people. No country on the face of the earth is without its Jews. They are citizens of the world, without a country; nothing has terminated their wanderings. There is nothing in the history of the world that can be likened to the dispersion of the Jews.

5. Deut. 28:65-68.
They were to have no rest, no peace, but were to live in constant fear.

This did not refer to the captivities; for they were not severely persecuted then. Since their dispersion, history bears witness to the completeness of the fulfillment of this prophecy. No other nation was ever treated like the Jews. It would take days to tell the history of the suffering of the Jews, to tell of the tortures, spoliations, and degradations, and this was all done by people under the name of Christianity. Several Jewish histories have been written; one of these is called "Valley of Tears." All the people of the earth are one in their hatred of the Jews. The Jews are surrounded by hatred and scorn.

(d) Conclusion of the Covenant.
This covenant merges with the Palestinian Covenant, and ends with the restoration of Israel and the new heavens and new earth.

(e) The sign of the covenant—Sabbath Day.

(1) This was given to Israel and never to the Gentiles.
Rom. 2:12-14
Exod. 31:12-18; 20:12,20
Deut. 5:12-15.

(2) Was given as a remembrance of the marvelous deliverance of Israel, but it would be wise for all nations to make an application and to rest one day in 7.

(3) The Sabbath day of the Pharisees was not pleasing to God—Christ did not change the Sabbath; it has passed away.

(4) Constantine did not change the Sabbath, but in 316 A.D. made a decree that all Christians observe the first day of the week. The early church observed the first day of the week. They spent the day in service to the Lord as Christ did. The Lord's Day is not one to be spent in idleness, in riding, in religious entertainments, and discussion of worldly things. It should be a day of worship, of service, of Bible reading, teaching, and Bible living.
The Sabbath came to an end 1900 years ago when the Dispensation of Grace began. Laws of state have called Sunday a civil Sabbath.
The Sabbath was a part of the law which is done away with in Christ. The Sabbath was not changed, but was displaced by the Lord's Day.
Col. 2:16—To speak of the Christian Sabbath is confusion.
Rev. 1:10—Lord's Day.

"Sunday" or the "Lord's Day" is a weekly celebration of the resurrection of our Lord from the dead.

(5) Christians rest not in a day, but in a Person.

6. The Davidic Covenant.

(a) The Constitution of the Covenant—II Sam. 7:8-19.
It was made with David, thru the prophet Nathan, 500 years after the days of Moses. Ps. 89 is a repetition of the covenant.

(b) The Contents of the Covenant.
Provided for a Davidic house.
This did not mean that David was to build a house, as God had told him thru Nathan not to do this. This referred to a political house—to David's posterity in the sense of an earthly kingdom thru his son.
Provided for a Davidic throne—Davidic house V. 13
Chapter 7—Royal authority, for the Messiah.
Provided for a Davidic kingdom—Vs. 16.
God has in mind, *not* Solomon, but Christ, of Whom Solomon is a limited type—II Sam. 7:14; Heb. 1:8.
This was an amazing revelation to David.

(c) The Sign of the Covenant.
(1) The Son of David—Luke 2:11,12.
"For unto you is born this day, in the city of David, a Saviour, which . . . . ."
((a)) Promises concerning the Son.
((1)) David would have a perpetual throne and a perpetual Son on that throne.
((2)) Added revelation—This Son was to be a Man of two natures. He would be God and Man in one Person; would be David's Son, but God would be His Father—Psa. 2:6,7; 45:6,7; 110:1.
((3)) David's Son would have two remarkable experiences. He would have a perpetual throne but—
He must go thru the experience of rejection, suffering, death, and resurrection before He would rule.
((4)) David's Son would have two thrones—Heavenly and earthly.
He will occupy His Father's throne until the time comes for the overthrowing of His enemies. At that time He will take His own throne on earth—Ps. 68:18; 110.
((5)) David's Son was to have a two-fold sway—a priestly, as well as a kingly sway—Ps. 110:4. *Not* a priest of the Levites, but after the order of Melchizedek.
David was not a priest, and could not be one, being of the tribe of Judah. Christ's priesthood is a heavenly one, and His sway is over happy hearts as well as happy nations. The Priesthood in Hebrews is Christ on the throne.
((6)) Kingdom of the Son to be set up by a two-fold act:
Descent of the Lord from heaven.
Judgment upon His enemies.
He will govern Israel and have dominion over the land of promise. This present spiritual kingdom is not the kingdom spoken of here.
((7)) Kingdom has *two-fold aspect*.
The coming of the King to earth will mark the introduction of this kingdom—Psa. 96:9,10; 98:9.
He will rule the Jewish nation, and also will have universal rule.—Ps. 78:8-11.

(d) Condition of the Covenant—II Sam. 7:14.
It was unconditional! God said, "I will."

(e) Conclusion—forever.

7. The Palestinian Covenant.

A continuation of the Mosaic covenant.

(a) The Constitution of the Covenant—Deut. 30:1-10.
Established in view of the world-wide dispersion of the Jews. (Because of disobedience) Vs. 1.

(b) Contents of the Covenant.
(1) Promises return of the Lord, following the repentance of the people.
(2) Promises regathering of the people from among the nations, and their restoration to their own land, after the return of the Messiah—vs. 3.
(3) Promises conversion of Israel.
(4) Promises judgment upon the nations which persecuted Israel (See Abrahamic Covenant).
(5) Promises great blessing and prosperity for Israel.

(c) Conditions of the Covenant.
   The repentance of scattered Israel, "IF"—V. 10.
(d) The conclusion of the Covenant.
   Ends with the new heavens and the new earth.

8. The New Covenant.

Resurrection—eternal completeness—Jer. 31:31 and Heb. 8:8. Made with the House of Israel, a continuation or a repetition of the Mosaic Covenant. It is in contrast with the Old Covenant.

(a) Constitution of the Covenant—Jer. 31:31-34.
   (1) Written or predicted by Jeremiah, the weeping Prophet. God not only promises judgment, but also restoration and inward renewal; and this is in connection with the new covenant—Matt. 26:27, 28; Heb. 8:6-13; Gen. 15.
   (2) The blood of Christ is the blood of the new and everlasting covenant. "This cup is the New Testament (covenant) in my blood." The covenant is made strong through the blood of Christ.
   (3) It is made with Israel, as was the Old Covenant.
   (4) The first one came at Sinai; the second at the death of Christ on the cross—Heb. 7:27; 9 and 10.
   (5) Israel has no priest, no temple, no sacrifice, and has been perplexed for 18 centuries, because she does not understand that the Old Covenant has been set aside.

(b) Contents of the New Covenant.
   It was made with Israel and Judah, and is further explained in Heb. 8:8-12.
   (1) Promise of Sanctification.
      ((a)) There is a great difference between the law written on tables of stone, as in the Mosaic Covenant, and that written on the heart. The Old Covenant commanded obedience, but gave men no power to do or not to do. The law never gives the power to obey.
      ((b)) In the New Covenant the law is written in the heart of man, and there will naturally follow a heart of obedience. A man will do under grace what he never will do under law.
   (2) Promise of the knowledge of God.
      ((a)) Not necessary to teach men, because all shall know God, from the least to the greatest. This knowledge is the greatest need in the world.
      ((b)) In the first chapter of Romans men knew God at the beginning, but did not want to know God. In order to do God's will, one must know Him. To know God one must study His Word. The living Word is the manifestation of God; the written Word is the revelation.
      Christians enjoy all the fullness of the new covenant, but it was made with the Jews—Eph. 2:11-20.
      We come into the blessing through union with Christ, Who is the High Priest and Mediator of the covenant.

(c) Conditions—none.

(d) Conclusion—Runs beyond millennium to new Heaven and new earth.

CHAPTER FOUR

The Ethnic Division Principle

III. ETHNIC DIVISION PRINCIPLE (Pertaining to Races of People).

a. Definition.

This is the principle by which the Word of Truth is rightly divided in relation to the three classes of which it treats, e.g., the Jew, the Gentile and the Church.

1. Learn I Cor. 10:32—"Give none offence, neither to the Jews, nor to the Gentiles, nor to the Church of God."
   (a) God, while not a respector of persons, is a respector of classes.
   (b) Three is the number of completeness.
       (1) There are 3 in the Godhead—Father, Son and Holy Ghost.
       (2) There are 3 places—Heaven, Earth and Hell.
       (3) There are 3 classes—Jews, Gentiles and Church of God.

2. Explanation.
   (a) The greater part of the O.T. has to do with the Jews, separated from the rest of mankind and entered into a covenant with God.
   (b) The Church is the "called out assembly," and has a distinct relation to God, having received definite promises.
   (c) Gentiles not so often mentioned, but are found in both Old Testament and New Testament. Sometimes called the heathen, or the nations.
   (d) In the beginning, from Gen. 1:1 to 11:9 we have the united race, one people, one language. From Gen. 11:10 through the Gospels we have the Jews primarily, with the Gentiles mentioned. In the New Testament we find the book of Acts, the book of transition, with both Jews and Church in view. In the Epistles, the Church is in view, and the Jews temporarily set aside. In Revelation the Jew is in view, with the Gentiles mentioned.

b. Questions which one must ask in dividing truth:

1. Who said this?
   (a) An apparent lie in the Bible.
       Gen. 3:4 "Thou shalt not surely die." God is here recording the lie of Satan. Satan said this.
   (b) The book of Job—It is made up of the words of Job and his friends, and at the end of the book God said, "These men spoke without knowledge." Bildad was having a kind of spiritual nightmare. Be careful in taking a text from Job.

2. To whom was it said?
   In many old editions of the Bible, you will find headings on the pages in which are the blessings "Spoken to or about the church;" all the unpleasant or bad things—"Spoken to or about the Jews." Isaiah addressed his book to the Jew, and did not write concerning the Church, yet many of the blessings are attributed to the Church.

3. Under what circumstances was it said?

4. This concerns whom?
   (a) The Psalms were written for the comfort and blessing of all people, but there is a difference between interpretation and application.
   (b) There are some things in the Old Testament which you cannot apply to yourself because they are opposite to the truth given to the Church. For example, we do not sacrifice the lamb as the Jews were commanded.
   (c) Every part of the Bible was written concerning one or the other of these three divisions. Sometimes one book will concern one group, sometimes all three, e.g., book of Romans.
       Romans 8—believers in Christ, the Church.
       Rom. 11:21,22—Gentiles.
       Rom. 9—Jews.
       Rom. 8—To his brethren in the Spirit.
       Rom. 9—To his brethren in the flesh.
       Rom. 11:11—Position of the Gentiles.
       Rom. 11:13-25—Warning concerning separation for Gentiles.

    (d) A tree in the Bible is a type of Israel.
        (1) Fig tree—Israel's national privileges in the world.
        (2) Olive tree—Israel's religious privileges.
        (3) The vine—Israel's spiritual privileges and blessing.

c. Origin of the three classes.

  1. The Jew traces his ancestry to Abraham through Shem. This nation was called out and set apart by God.

  2. All other nations are Gentiles. The Gentiles are descended from Japheth.

  3. The third class (the Church) is the result of the work of the Lord Jesus Christ. From the beginning of man, all were a united race—including both Jew and Gentile. The Jewish race was separated from the Gentiles at the time of Abraham.

  4. The Church is neither Jew nor Gentile, but a new creation formed out of both—through belief in Christ and Calvary's Cross.

  5. Ancestry of each division.
    (a) Jews traced to Abraham.
    (b) Gentiles traced to Adam.
    (c) Church traced to Christ, the last Adam.

  6. The Jews are the chosen race through which all nations are blessed.

d. Comparative position of Jews, Gentiles, and Church.

  1. The Jews—Rom. 9:4, 5.
  The book of Romans considers first the whole race—the Jews, the Gentiles, and the Church, giving information about each.
    (a) To the Israelites pertains the adoption.
    This means Israel in the O. T. adopted as God's people from among all the other nations. They became God's peculiar people, and sometimes are called "His Son," meaning the whole nation.
    (b) To them belongs the Glory.
        (1) The Shekinah cloud of glory led them out of Egypt. No other nation can claim such direction of God.
        (2) The glory was found only in the tabernacle of Israel.
    (c) Also the Covenants.
        (1) The greatest covenants were made with Israel and they still have these covenants—Abrahamic, Mosaic, Davidic.
        (2) Eph. 2:3—the Gentiles are strangers to the covenant. God gave the law to Israel, not to the Gentiles—Rom. 2:14.
    (d) The Law.
    The law which God gave to Israel set them apart from all other peoples and became a partition, a wall of separation. The Sabbath was the sign to Israel that God was their deliverer.
    (e) The Service.
    No other nation had a tabernacle, and no other nation had a Day of Atonement.
    (f) The Promises.
        (1) The promise of a Saviour was to the Jews.
        Christ came to the circumcision. He was a Jew, and appeared as a Jew.
        (2) Isaiah said, "Unto us a child is born, unto us a Son is given."
        Child—meaning His humanity, was born.
        Son—meaning His divinity, was given.
        (3) Jonah said, "Salvation is of the Jews."
        (4) The promises were given to Abraham, the father of the race—Heb. 7:6. He was promised a seed, meaning one.
    (g) The Fathers.
    Abraham, Isaac and Jacob belong to the Jews. No other nation has such divinely appointed leaders.
    (h) The Son, the seed of David—Rom. 1:4.
    He was the seed of David, but He was also the Son of God.
    (i) Salvation—John 4:22. Salvation is of the Jews.
    (j) The Oracles of God—Rom. 3:1, 2.
    (k) Reasons for God's choice of the Jews.
        (1) At the time of the confusion of tongues God dispersed a company of idolators. He called Abraham and his descendants, that they might witness to the other nations of the living God.

In establishing the boundaries of the nations, He placed Israel in the center of the world so that they might witness.

(2) That they might be writers of the Scriptures.
The Word of God came through the Jews. In Gen. 9:27 God said Japheth should dwell in the tents of Shem (other races). We have today the book of Japheth printed in the language of Shem, in the midst of Shem.

2. The Gentiles.
   (a) God in prophecy always deals with the Jews, and includes the Gentiles only as they come in contact with the Jews.
   (b) The result of this contact has been a cursing or a blessing, depending upon treatment of the Jews.
   (c) Daniel is the only exception.
   This is a book of Gentile politics.
   (d) Condition of the Gentiles—Eph. 2:11-13.
   "Without Christ, aliens from Israel, strangers to the covenants, having no hope, and without God."
   Afar off from God—Eph. 4:17, 18. Rom. 1.

3. The Church.
   (a) The body of Christ, Who is the Head—Eph. 1:22, 23.
      (1) The body is not known in the O.T.
      (2) The Jews are called a nation, not a body.
      (3) Began on the day of Pentecost, and will conclude with the Rapture.
      (4) The church has been given a great honor, the greatest bestowed by Him. He will use the church to demonstrate His mighty grace and the magnificence of His grace—Eph. 3.
   (b) Formed of the two classes, Jew and Gentile—Eph. 2:14, 15. The wall, barrier, or partition of the law has been broken down between these two.
   (c) Position of the church—Eph. 5:29-33.
      (1) Members of the Body of Christ by the baptism of the Holy Spirit. *Baptism* has to do with the Body of Christ; *Spirit-filling* has to do with the individual members.
         ((a)) There is no baptism of the Holy Spirit in the Old Testament, or in the Gospels.
         ((b)) John the Baptist said, "When he cometh he will baptize you with the Holy Spirit."
         ((c)) Baptism means introduction into a new sphere.
   (d) The church is promised a spiritual blessing—Eph. 1:3.
      (1) All of God's blessings in the Old Testament were to the nation of the Jews, and related to the earth.
      (2) God's promise to the church is that all who live godly shall suffer persecution.

4. Contrasts between the church and Israel.

Israel	*Church*
Gen. 12:1-3; 13:15. Promise of a nation, a land, a citizenship in Canaan.	Phil. 3:20. Promise of a citizenship in heaven.
Deut. 8:7-10; Psa. 37:25. Promise of great blessing and satisfaction of physical needs for reward of a godly life.	I Cor. 4:11, 12. Promise of great physical need, as reward of a godly, service-filled life.
Ps. 137:8, 9. Jews shall delight in wholesale slaughter of their enemies as revenge for captivity.	Rom. 12:19, 20. Church exhorted and commanded not to take vengeance. Avenge not—the Lord will repay.
Deut. 7:1, 2; Deut. 20: 16, 17; Josh. 6:21. Commanded to use carnal weapons.	II Cor. 10:4. Commanded to use weapons of warfare not carnal, as the Sword, the Word of God, and the Shield of Faith—Spiritual weapons.
I Sam. 15:33. Samuel used carnal weapons for correction of his people, even killing a man.	II Tim. 2:24; Gal. 5:22, 23. Preachers to lead the people with gentleness, love, etc. Fruit of Spirit.
Gen. 12:2; 13:2; 23:6. Abraham a man of God, blessed materially, was very rich, a mighty prince among men. The faithful man, a mighty prince.	Rom. 12:16; I Cor. 4:16; I Cor. 4:12, 13; I Cor. 1:26. The faithful apostle should mind not high things, but will become the offscouring of all things.
Ex. 21:23-25. Law says: Return evil for evil.	Eph. 4:32. Love says forgive.
Ex. 25:8, 22. Worship had to do with a place. Jews cannot worship now, as before, because the place is thrown down.	Eph. 2:18; I Cor. 12:13. Worship has to do with a person, any place. Where two or three are gathered, He is in the midst.
Lev. 18:5; Gal. 3:10. Life is a thing earned by a certain line of obedience.	Eph. 2:8, 9. Saved by faith, not through works.

Luke 1:31-33; Acts 15:14-16.
House of David to be restored.
Rom. 11:1, 11, 22, 24, 26.
Isa. 11:11-12; 14:1. Jer. 23:5, 6; 32:37, 38; Zeph.
3:14, 15. Promise of the restoration of Israel is an earthly blessing.

I Thess. 4:16, 17. Future of the church has to do with Heaven, and heavenly blessing. Phil. 3:20, 21; I John 3:2. We shall be like Christ.

Feasts

Lev. 23. Passover, Unleavened Bread, Firstfruits, Pentecost, Atonement, Trumpets, and Tabernacles. All in the first 7 months.

No feasts in church, but ordinances—such as *Baptism* and *Lord's Supper*.

Food and Drink

Ex. 12:20—nothing leavened.
Lev. 3:17—neither fat nor blood.
Deut. 14:3—no abominable thing.
Lev. 11:—diet God gave His people.

Col. 2:16; 3:17—Let no man judge you in what you eat or drink.

Choice

Neh. 9:7; Deut. 7:6.
Chosen in Abram, a special people to the Lord.

Eph. 1:4—Chosen in Him before the foundation of the world.

Time of Choice

Matt. 25:34. From foundation of the world.

Eph. 1:4—before foundation of world.
II Tim. 1:9—before world began.

Purpose

Gen. 12:2; Num. 23:9.
To be a great blessing, a great nation, and to dwell alone.

Eph. 1:22, 23; Col. 1:18; Eph. 4:12.
To build the Body of Christ, the Church.

Supremacy

Isa. 60:12.
Universal dominion—nations that do not serve her will perish.

Eph. 1:22, 23; 3:10. Her supremacy is in heavenly places.

Calling

Gen. 17:5, 6.
Called to the land to be many when one (multiplication).

Rom. 8:28; Eph. 1:18; 4:4. Yet to be called on high, called to unification (when many, called to be one).

Revelation

Gen. 12:1.
God tells Abraham.

Eph. 3:3,4; Col. 1:25.
God tells Paul.

Relation of Christ

Matt. 1:1; Zech. 14:9, 16, 17; 9:9.
King of Israel.

John 12:12-15; Eph. 1:22; 5:23; Col. 1:18. Head of the Church.

Inheritance

Gen. 14:9; Psa. 24:1.
Earthly.

Eph. 1:20-23.
Heavenly.

Blessings

Deut. 28: Conditional.

Unconditional.

CHAPTER FIVE

The Discrimination Principle

IV. THE DISCRIMINATION PRINCIPLE.

  a. Definition.

    1. That principle by which we should divide the Word of Truth, so as to make a distinction where God makes a difference.

    2. Failure to do this leads to confusion.

  b. Divisions.

    1. The difference between the creatures and the children of God.

      (a) Failure to make this difference leads to error, and results in the preaching of the brotherhood of man and the fatherhood of God. All men are not brothers, and God is not father of all men.

      (b) All men are the creatures of God, but all men are not the children of God.

      (c.) We became creatures of God at the creation of Adam, as the head of the race. The whole race was created in Adam. In creating Adam, God created each one of us. Every human being came from Adam.

      (d) Men become children of God through regeneration, re-creation, or the new birth. We are not *born* Christians.

      (e) Creaturehood goes back to creation, but childhood goes back to regeneration. The process is different. God created one man and gave him the power of propagation, but never has created a man since. Since Adam, men are born by the process of human propagation.

      (f) A creature of God is under sin; in Adam all men fell and came under the power of death and came into ruin. This is true of each son of Adam; a sinful man cannot beget a sinless son or a sinless daughter.
He is sinful, disobedient, sensual, devilish, begotten of the flesh, having a mind at enmity to God.

      (g) A child of God is the offspring of God, partaking of His nature; no longer linked to Adam of the natural race, but linked to Christ and the spiritual race. He is not under the wrath of God, but under the favor of God.

      (h) Adam was the head of all creation; Christ is the head of the new creation. When a creature of God believes in Christ, he becomes a child of God.

      (i) God is the God of all men, but the Father only of saved men. He is the Creator of all men.

      (j) Nicodemus called Christ a teacher, not recognizing His deity. Jesus did not answer his question but gave him what he needed, which was the gospel.
In His conversation with Nicodemus, Christ was not talking about another natural birth, but about the *new* birth; and He expected Nicodemus to know about this, because it had been written in Ezek. 36:25-27. As a teacher in Israel, Nicodemus should have known and understood.

      (k) Man is not saved by *church* membership, nor by *conduct*, nor *creed*, nor *character*, nor by anything except through *Christ*, and faith in Him.
Titus 3:5—"Not by human merit nor work nor any other thing." The only character which a man ever possesses is the godliness which comes from God. We can have fellowship with God only through the new nature, which He bestows upon us at the new birth; not through human merit, self-effort, or works.
John 3:16; Rom. 8:17; II Pet. 1:4. By nature we are creatures of God and members of a race that has gone away from God. Not one single thing man can do can make him a Christian.

      (l) When a creature of God becomes a child of God, he becomes a member of a brotherhood—Gal. 6:10—the household of faith. This is a spiritual brotherhood, and is the only *real* brotherhood on the face of the earth.

    2. The difference between being accepted and being acceptable.

      (a) In general.
        (1) All believers are accepted by God, but all believers are not acceptable to God—Eph. 1:6; II Cor. 5:9.
Eph. 1:6 refers to heavenly position—accepted in Christ. II Cor. 5:9 has reference to our daily walk or our condition—acceptable or well-pleasing in daily life.
        (2) It is a difference between position and condition.

      (b) Accepted in Christ—Eph. 1:6.
        (1) Representation—the beloved.
Christ is our Representative. He hung on the cross for us.

II Cor. 5:21—He bore our sins for us. He represents us today before the face of God. He took our sins; we take on His glory and righteousness.

(2) Identification.
His experiences are reckoned as ours—Gal. 2:20; Rom. 6:6; Rom. 6:6-8:11. We are to reckon the old man dead and make no provision for him.
Rom. 6:4, 5—We are buried with Him.
Col. 3:1—We are raised with Him.
Eph. 2:6—We have ascended with Him and sit in heavenly places in Christ.
Rom. 8:17, 30—We are glorified with Him.
Christ is *all* in Christianity—the center and circumference. We see God in Christ; God sees us in Christ.
Our position is perfect; our condition is not. Salvation is the way to perfect position and is through faith in Christ.

(3) Acceptability.
We are accepted in the beloved but we should live an acceptable life; it is our responsibility to do so.
We are accepted by faith, but we labor to be acceptable—II Tim. 2:15; II Cor. 5:9 (approved or accepted).
Christ was always well-pleasing to God. This should be a *constant* effort on the part of the believer, not spasmodic. We should try with all our hearts to be well-pleasing by the lives we live.

(4) Some warnings.
((a)) It is possible to be saved and yet suffer great loss—I Cor. 3:14, 15.
We are accepted in the Beloved. That does not mean that we can do just as the old nature desires, but we are to live and serve in a way well-pleasing to Him.
((b)) It is possible to be saved and yet become a "castaway"—I Cor. 9:27.
Castaway—disapproved.
A servant who does not run the race well, or fight the battle well may be set aside or thrown on the rubbish-heap. We must exercise diligence.
((c)) It is possible to be saved and still receive chastisement—Col. 3:25.
((d)) It is possible for a Christian to so live as to receive back in himself the results of his wrong living—Gal. 6:7, 8.

(5) Our acceptance is once for all; it is finished and instantaneous. Many people live for years without being acceptable to God. Acceptance is forever; but how few are the moments of our *acceptability*.

3. Difference between faith and works.

(a) Both are of divine appointment, and both are needful to the true believer. Without faith one is not a believer. Without works there is no evidence of faith. *Both* are found in the life of the true believer.

(b) Faith means belief, or dependence upon Jesus Christ and the truth written in God's Word, for salvation.
Faith includes the idea of receiving a testimony, which God gives concerning His Son.
Eph. 2:8-10—created in Christ Jesus unto good works.
verse 8—by Christ we are saved.
verse 9—not of works.
verse 10—unto good works.
Faith holds the supreme place in the Christian life; it is the means and cause of the victorious life and Christian experience.
Difference between Christian religion and other religions, which are man-made. Man-made religious works and then salvation. The religion of God says salvation, and then works—Titus 3:5; 2:14.

(c) Summary of Scriptures concerning faith.
(1) It is absolutely needful. Without faith it is impossible to please God.
(2) Faith is believing God, or taking Him at His word.
Saving faith is the faith that receives the testimony concerning God's Son.
(3) Faith is the means of spiritual life and every spiritual blessing. There is not a blessing that God has for man that is not bestowed upon this foundation of faith.

(d) Summary of Scripture concerning works.
Man is not saved by works, but faith—Eph. 2:9; Tit. 3:5.
Man is not justified by the deeds of the law, but by faith—Rom. 3:20; 5:1.
The law can give the knowledge of sin, but cannot save from sin; it has no love, brings no grace and brings no life.
It condemns man in sin; but cannot save.
Good works belong to a saved man, and give evidence of his salvation—Eph. 2:10; Tit. 3:8.
Good works will be rewarded when our Lord comes—II Cor. 5:10; II Tim. 4:8.

4. Difference between salvation and rewards.

(a) This might be called Present Blessing and Future Blessing.

The sinner is saved, and the believer is rewarded.

The sinner is never rewarded. Salvation to the sinner, and rewards to the saint. There is no reward for the sinner, for God will not recognize the sinner's works. Nothing awaits him except judgment, condemnation, and death.

(b) Salvation means emancipation from sin and from the wrath of God.

(c) Rewards are compensation for faithfulness, for labor, and for suffering.

(d) Salvation is a *gift* bestowed by God. Rewards are earned.

Salvation is a present gift, and rewards are a future attainment.

(e) Summary of Scripture concerning salvation.

   (1) It is wholly of the Lord.

      God is the source of salvation.

      Jesus Christ is the Saviour.

   (2) Salvation is all of God's grace, love, and mercy—Eph. 2:8, 9; II Tim. 1:9; Tit. 2:11.

   (3) Salvation is received by faith—Acts 16:31; Rom. 1:16; Eph. 2:8, 9.

   (4) Salvation is a present possession—something the believer has now—John 3:16; 5:24; 6:47; II Tim. 1:9.

(f) Summary of Scriptures concerning rewards.

   (1) Rewards are earned by works and by faithful service—I Cor. 3:11-13; 9:24, 25.

   (2) Rewards may be forfeited through carelessness, faithlessness, and compromise—I Cor. 3:12-15.

   (3) Rewards will be given when Christ returns.

   (4) Rewards are promised by God as a means of inspiration and encouragement.

   (5) Rewards are promised that the believer might be weaned from the pursuit of earthly riches and pleasures, and kept interested in the things of heaven.

      ((a)) Are to inspire us to a loving ministry, encourage us when in suffering and persecution, and to incite us to faithfulness in duty—Col. 3:17-25; II Tim. 4:8.

      ((b)) The crowns promised in God's Word are symbols of spiritual blessings.

         ((1)) Crown of rejoicing—for soul winners—I Thess. 2:19.

         ((2)) Incorruptible crown—for one who keeps his body under (temperate in all things) —I Cor. 9:25.

         ((3)) Crown of righteousness—telling of His coming—II Tim. 4:8.

         ((4)) Crown of glory—faithfulness in ministering—I Pet. 5:2-4.

         ((5)) Crown of life—enduring testing—James 1:12.

5. Difference between the believer's position and walk.

There is nothing that will add more joy to the Christian life and service than the realization of the truth concerning the position one has in Christ, and the relationship of that position to his walk.

(a) The believer's position or standing in the sight of God is one of absolute perfection in Christ. We are accepted in the Beloved. Nothing can be added to, and nothing can be taken away from our position.

No matter how holy a life a man may live, he cannot add to his perfect position in Christ.

It is unchangeable, unreversible, permanent, continuous, and eternal.

When God looks upon us, He sees us in Christ, and sees all the perfection in Christ as ours.

We see God in Christ, and God sees us in Christ.

It is not our perfection, but the perfection of Christ.

Eph. 1:4—Holy, without blame, before God.

Realization of this fact will work in you mightily, encouraging a desire to be perfect in the sight of men as well as in the sight of God, and it will cause you to pay more attention to your walk.

(b) The walk of the believer.

Positionally there is no difference between believers, but there may be a great difference in the walk of the various believers.

The walk of a Christian is the result of his spiritual state. If he is controlled by the flesh, he will be carnal, and will not enjoy full communion with Christ. The position of the believer is the result of the work of Christ.

(c) Summary of truth given in the Word of God concerning the way we ought to walk.

   (1) Walk in the Spirit—Gal. 5:16, 25.

   (2) Walk in newness of life—Rom. 6:4.

      ((a)) To cast off the former sinful habits and walk in Christ's resurrection power so that the spiritual nature will show in the daily walk.

      ((b)) Know, reckon, yield—Rom. 6:6; 6:11; 6:13.

         ((1)) *KNOW* all about your position in Christ.

         ((2)) Following that knowledge, *RECKON* yourselves to be dead to sin.

         ((3)) *YIELD* all your members to the One Who dwelleth in you, not to the old man.

(3) Walk circumspectly (accurately)—Eph. 5:15.
(4) Walk worthy of the Lord unto all pleasing—Col. 1:10.
Walk so as not to bring reproach upon the name of the Lord, or bring the contempt of the ungodly on Him.
(5) Walk in love—Eph. 5:2.
To be ruled and controlled by love to both God and man.
When we love God supremely, we love our fellowmen.
(6) Walk in wisdom and prudence—Col. 4:5.
To walk tactfully, so as not to cause any unsaved person to stumble.
We should never do those things which will keep men away from Christ. We ought to make Christ attractive to people by our lives. We ought to be samples of the Lord Jesus Christ.
(7) Walk in Truth—III John 4.
Walk according to the principles of God's Word, not according to the world or sentiment.
(8) Walk in Christ—Col. 2:6.
We are to walk as He walked—I John 2:6.
If you talk, walk. If you don't walk, don't talk.
Walk as He walked. God-dependent.
(9) Walk with God—Gen. 5:24; 6:9.
Means separations—we cannot walk with God and walk with the crowd.
Agreement—Two do not walk together except they be agreed. Two who are not in agreement will not walk together—Amos. 3:3.
Fellowship means that our minds are on each other. He loves you, and you love Him. He thinks of you, and you think of Him. You long to do something for Him; He longs to do *all* things for you.
(10) Walk before God—Gen. 17:1; 24:40.
El Shaddai means almighty and all-sufficient God. If we long enough for a perfect life, we will find our sufficiency in Him. We are to walk as if God were behind us and looking at us continually. We are to do all things in His sight—"Thou, O God, seest me."
(11) Walk after God—Deut. 13:4.
Means to walk after God, to do His will, to enjoy His way, to walk in His footsteps, to keep our eyes upon Him. He's our example.
(12) Walk in the light—I John 1:7.
To walk in the knowledge of His will. To seek and understand what is His will and to walk in it.
(13) Walk in good works—Eph. 2:10.
Means that as we walk through this life, we are constantly to be doing good deeds—After salvation.
(14) Walk honestly—Rom. 13:13.
Always walk and do that which pertains to the day.
(15) Walk by faith—II Cor. 5:7.
Walk by faith and not by sight, in utter repudiation of self-thought and self-judgment.
(16) Walk worthy of the vocation to which we are called—Eph. 4:1.

6. Difference between a possessor and mere professor.

This is a difference between the man who is a believer in the Lord Jesus Christ, and the man who merely makes a profession and knows nothing of the indwelling of Christ. There are many children of God who are unsettled and who are robbed of their assurance and happiness because they do not understand the Scriptures. As a result of this, they do not know whether or not they have eternal safety. They are in doubt and fear. All this trouble comes from the fact that they do not make a distinction where God makes a difference.

(a) In interpreting Scripture, never take a doubtful passage and use it to contradict clear and positive passages. There are no contradictions in the Bible.
  (1) Passages may seem to be dark, and may seem paradoxical, but they do *not* contradict.
  (2) Illustration—Heb. 6:4-8.
  This is a favorite passage with the Arminians. They believe that a man may be saved one day, lost the next, and saved again.
    ((a)) This was written to the Jews at a time when many, because of persecution, were giving up the Christian faith and returning to the old Judaistic faith.
    ((b)) It was written to the Jews when the temple worship was still going on. Judaism crucified Him. These Jewish believers who were going back to Judaism were crucifying Him afresh. It says nothing about being lost.
  (3) Illustration—Phil. 2:12—"work out your own salvation."
  God works salvation in and then we must work it *out*.
    ((1)) Some may say there are those in the church who give every evidence of being saved, and then turn away and become deniers.

((2)) We are not to judge the Word of God by the experiences of man, but to judge man's experience in the light of God's Word.

((3)) Eternal life never can be lost; if it could be lost then it would not be eternal. God's Word is true. When He says a man is saved, then he is saved.

(b) The difference between a possessor and a mere professor is a difference in character.

POSSESSOR	*PROFESSOR*
A man who possesses the nature God bestowed upon him.	A man who has no divine nature.
Is right in the sight of God.	Has never been right in sight of God.
One who depends upon Christ.	A mere imitator of a Christian.
Is Christ-centered.	Is self-centered.
Is a child of God.	Is a creature of God.
Has a living vital relationship with God.	Has no relationship with God. May be cultured, beautiful, moral, amiable, and religious, but still lack spiritual life.

(c) Scriptures concerning a true believer.
(1) He is saved—Eph. 2:8-10.
(2) He has eternal life—John 10:28.
(3) He is free from judgment for sin—John 5:24.
(4) He is saved from wrath through Christ—Rom. 5:9.
(5) He is a child of God—Gal. 3:26; Rom. 8:15.
(6) He is identified with Christ—Rom. 6:4,5,6.
(7) He is under God's favor—Rom. 5:1,2.

(d) The mere professor or imitator.
(1) Is a religious hypocrite.
(2) Is one who has been brought under the influence of the truth and Christianity, and being brought under that influence has assumed a religious appearance, but lacks true Christianity.
(3) He may be an apparently successful Christian worker, but he does not bow to God's will—Matt. 7:21-23. He may do marvelous things, may proclaim the name of God, yet after it is all done, in that day when he stands before the throne, the Lord will say, "I never knew you."
(4) A mere professor may be intellectually reformed, but not saved.
(5) A mere professor in the church is just as truly lost as the greatest sinner in the world. The man who is a mere professor does not like to be told he is a sinner. (Every sinner is a sinner in the sight of God, and one is no more lost than the other).
(6) The trouble with the church is too much unreality.
There are many hypocrites and there is unreality.
This unreality is demonstrated in our worship. Worship is adoration and contemplation of God because God has done something for us—Ps. 107. There is unreality in testimony. There should be reality in testifying of Christ if it is to impress others.
There is unreality in prayer; contrast the length of private and public prayer.

7. The difference between law and grace.
(a) Present-day religion is a kind of mixture of law and grace, although they really can not be mixed any more than oil and water. When you introduce law, you do away with grace, and vice-versa. They are in opposition to each other.
(1) Law is that system instituted by God on Mt. Sinai through Moses, the mediator. It is the law of the covenant, a legal system.
(2) Grace is an expression of God's kindness and favor, under the New Covenant, with Jesus Christ as Mediator.
((a)) It is unlimited and unmerited favor. It is bestowed by divine favor apart from any human merit or effort.
((b)) Grace is divine help for the helpless, apart from any and all human effort. Nothing you have ever done or can do, helped to give you salvation.
((c)) Grace means everything for nothing.
All the poor sinner needs for eternity is bestowed upon him, by God, as a gift.
(b) We must never get a wrong view of the Law.
(1) Law is not a great enemy, but the greatest friend we have. It is holy, just, and good—Rom. 7:12; Ps. 19:7, 8.
If a man is going to be holy, just, perfect, and good, he must obey the law. The law therefore tells men they are unholy, imperfect, and evil. Law was designed to show man what he should be and do. It shows man what he really is. It proves that he is carnal, has evil tendencies, and is utterly unable to do what he knows is right.
The law was added because of transgressions—Gal. 3:19.
Where no law is, there is no transgression—Rom. 4:15; 5:20; 7:7, 13. The law was added that sin might have the character of transgression. There was sin in the world before the law was

given, but the law was given that man might be made conscious of that sin. Under law, sin became transgression.

(2) The law shows man that he is a natural sinner, not a cultivated sinner.
Everyone has told lies, and we did not have to go to school or be educated in lying. Neither did our mothers teach us to lie. We do not take a course in lying; it is natural.

(3) Law shows man that all men are sinners.
The Seventh Day Adventists say that if you keep the law it proves you are holy. If the Seventh Day Adventists would put themselves under the law, the law would prove them sinners. We say a man is a sinner because he does something wrong. Law says he does wrong because he is a sinner. That is the difference between man and God. Man says, "This man did something wrong, and that makes him a sinner." God says, "He is a sinner and he will do something wrong." Wrong-doing is an expression of sin.

(4) The Law reveals the heart of man; Grace reveals the heart of God. Law reveals the heart of man with all its sin; Grace reveals the heart of God with all His love.

(5) Law shows how crooked we are; Grace makes us straight. Law reveals the dirt, but Grace makes us clean. Law was given that the offense might abound. In the last few verses of Rom. 5 we find the source of Sin and the source of Grace. Offense means Adam's sin.

(6) Grace came to save us from our sin, and to save believers from a life of sin. Abiding in Jesus and resting in the Spirit, we are to live godly and not to fulfill the lusts of the flesh.

(7) Law was given that sin might be revealed.
How can the Law being good, bring death? If you declare that the law brings death, you speak without knowledge. *Sin* brings death, and Law merely shows sin in its true light. Sin is rebellion against the authority of God, and so the condemnation is declared to be just. Since the Law is already perfect and good, then Sin is against all that is perfect and good.

(8) Grace can make the exceedingly great sinner white as snow; Law makes nothing perfect. Law has the power to say, "Be perfect," but has not the power to *make* a man perfect.

(9) Moses was probably a man as nearly perfect as a man could be. Twenty-one times it is said of Moses that he was faithful, yet he was unfaithful once, which showed that he was a sinner. Law could not make him perfect; he failed once and this shows that he was imperfect.

(10) Law is the schoolmaster to bring us to Christ.
The law of God, which reveals sin and leads to Christ, is the best friend a man may have.
Gal. 3:23-27. If a man will not be taught by this schoolmaster, then he will come under condemnation; if he is willing, he can be taught.

(11) A believer is not under Law but under Grace—Rom. 6:14. A believer is not to live a life of disobedience, and continue in sin. We are to abide in Christ and to walk as He walked—to live lives that will bring evidence of the fruit of the Spirit, and to bear one another's burdens. Against the fruit of the Spirit there is no law. If everybody loved everybody else, then we would need no law.

(12) God wants the righteousness of the Law fulfilled in us. We fill (fulfill) it through love. What we need to do is to walk in dependence upon the Spirit of God and in yieldedness to Him. Then the righteousness of the law will be fulfilled in us. God wants us to live in perfection.

(13) The Jew, in order to live a perfect life, looked at the Law. We should look at Christ and if we look at Him we will be bound to fulfill the law.

(14) We are not under the Law. So far as we are concerned, God should be able to abolish the Law. "I am not under the Law, and I object to anyone putting me under the Law." But I am not lawless. I am not going to do those things to which God says, "No."

(15) No one can say, "Thou shalt not," to the believers. The Scripture says, "Let no man judge thee in any of these things."

(16) Don't let the devil trip you up. There are many temptations for a preacher to lie.

(17) Peter recognized the inability of man to keep the law, when he said (at the meeting in Jerusalem), "Our fathers were never able to keep the law, why should we expect the Gentile Christians to do so?"

(c) The abundance of the grace of God.
If grace is almost undefinable, then abundance is inexpressible and inconceivable.

(1) Riches of grace—Eph. 1:7, 8.
This is a wealth that has no limit.

(2) Abounding grace—Rom. 5:15.

(3) Exceeding grace—II Cor. 9:14.

(4) Manifold grace—I Pet. 4:10.

(5) Exceeding riches—Eph. 2:7.

(6) Unsearchable riches—Eph. 3:8.

(7) Exceeding abundant—I Tim. 1:14.

(d) Summary
People are inclined to look upon the Law as an enemy.
To the disobedient man the Law is condemnation and death.

This is true of the unsaved man particularly. A lawless man hates law. When we become believers in the Lord Jesus Christ, then through love for Christ we learn to love the Law. There is blessing for us through the Law.

We need to understand that the Law is often misinterpreted and misapplied. For the unbeliever to try to be saved through Law is only a means of that unbeliever becoming deeper in condemnation. Attempting to keep the Law demonstrates a knowledge of the standard by which he is convicted. If the believer thinks that by keeping the Law he can be pleasing to God, he is demonstrating a knowledge of the divine standard, by which he is judged, and is putting himself under the law. Trying to keep the Law is adding condemnation to condemnation. Victory over sin never came through keeping the Law. The believer who puts himself under the Law, thinking to have victory, is putting himself under sin. In trying to keep the letter of the Law, he is forgetting and ignoring the spirit of the Law. He will try to have things all right on the outside, but he may have everything all wrong on the inside.

8. The difference between the Kingdom of Heaven and the Kingdom of God.

(a) The word "Kingdom," as used in the Scriptures, really means sovereignty rather than territory. It refers to a sphere, rather than extent—King-dom—the King's dominion. You will find in Scripture the two terms "Kingdom of Heaven" and "Kingdom of God."

   (1) The Kingdom of Heaven is from heaven and under the heavens upon the earth, and the Kingdom of God is in heaven over the earth, existed eternally and extends to the whole universe.

   (2) The Kingdom of Heaven has the Messiah for its king.
(The personal, millennial, earth-rule of Christ set up at His second coming.) The kingdom of God has God for its ruler, and is the all-embracing rule of God over every being, subject to the will of God in every place and tongue.

   (3) The Kingdom of Heaven is political in its sphere; the Kingdom of God is spiritual in its sphere.

   (4) The Kingdom of Heaven is Jewish, the kingdom which God promised to the nation of Israel in the Old Testament, and is a literal kingdom with a literal king upon a literal throne.

      ((a)) The kingdom of God is inclusive in character, including:
         ((1)) All who in any period believed God.
         ((2)) The seed of Abraham.
         ((3)) The Church.
         ((4)) All who believe after the tribulation.
      ((b)) The kingdom of God is from the beginning. Abel, Noah, Abraham, and David were in the kingdom of God.
      ((c)) When the Lord Jesus gives up the Kingdom into the hands of God, then the Kingdom will be supreme.

   (5) The Kingdom of Heaven is national in its aspect; the Kingdom of God is universal in its aspect.

   (6) The Kingdom of Heaven is limited in its scope to the earth; the Kingdom of God is unlimited.

   (7) The Kingdom of Heaven is dispensational in its duration, being limited to a time of 1000 years. The Kingdom of God is eternal and not dispensational, and will never come to an end.

   (8) Summary.
God has but one Kingdom—the Kingdom of God.
There are different phases of this one Kingdom. In the beginning of the Bible we have the Kingdom of Jehovah—that is one phase of the Kingdom of God. The Kingdom of Israel shows the people in close relation to God and is a part of the Kingdom of God. During that time, Israel was the only way of access to God. In Daniel we have mention of the Kingdom of Heaven which is a phase of the Kingdom of God. Today it is the Kingdom of the Son of His love—another phase of the Kingdom of God—Col. 1:13.

CHAPTER SIX

The Predictive Principle

V. THE PREDICTIVE PRINCIPLE.

There is a difference between prophecy and prediction. We have in the Bible the definition of the office and function of the prophet—Ex. 7:1, 2. Aaron's office as a prophet was to be the spokesman of Moses. The message of God was to come from Moses through Aaron to Pharaoh—Ex. 4:15, 16. Aaron was the spokesman of Moses unto the people. He was to speak the words that Moses gave him.

a. Definition. A prophet was essentially God's spokesman, and his sole mission was to speak the Word of God and only the words which God gave him to speak. God said to Jonah, "Go and preach what I bid thee."

1. Prophecy does not necessarily mean the unusual. Our trouble when we speak about prophecy is that we think it has to do with the unusual, the spectacular, with signs and visions, such as the beast coming up out of the sea, etc. If you speak of prophecy, people expect you to explain all these things.

2. A prophet is God's spokesman. He is not only a FORETELLER, but a FORTHTELLER of the Word of God. We always think of a prophet as one who foretells the future, but primarily a prophet was not a foreteller, but he forthtold the Word of God. Foretelling is only a small part of the prophet's work. A prophet is one who speaks for God, whether by way of instruction, reproof, correction, judgment, etc. A man is God's prophet when he speaks forth the Word of God.

3. Reason for not having prophets now.
There is no office of prophet in the church today as there was in the early church. Before the Word of God had been written, so that everyone could have it, there were special gifts given by the Holy Spirit, and prophecy was the greatest. To the man who had this gift, God revealed His will and His Word. We do not need the prophets, as we have the word and will of God in the Bible. In that day they were dependent upon the prophets. When the Church came to the place where information from God was needed, the Holy Spirit gave it to some man, who proclaimed it to the people—Acts 13:1; I Cor. 12.

4. Prophecy and predictive prophecy.
Prophecy is speaking forth the Word of God. Predictive prophecy is speaking forth the Word of God which has to do with the future.

5. A prophet—by Dr. Scofield. "A prophet is a man whose function primarily is that of a revivalist and a patriot, speaking on the behalf of God, to the national conscience, striving to bring faith in Jehovah, purity of worship, and patriotism among the people."

6. Why the prophets came to Israel. A prophet always came in a time of apostasy and declension. Whenever you find a prophet in Israel, you know there is something wrong. In the beginning when God established the priesthood, He made no provision for the prophets, and there would have been no prophets had there been no failure on the part of the priests.

7. What prophecy concerned.
Prophecy had to do primarily with the moral and religious condition of the people of the prophet's own time. The exhortations are local and Israelitish.

8. The prophet was appointed.
The priests and kings had their offices by right of birth; but not so the prophet. He was called especially, and given a special message to be given to the people at a divinely appointed time.

9. Why predictive prophecy came to be written.
Some of the prophets were also foretellers of future events. When it became evident that the sin of Israel would necessitate the withdrawal of God's presence, resulting in the dispersion of Israel, it also became evident, that this would result in the cessation of prophetic utterances. God wanted to proclaim that in some future day the Messianic Kingdom would come, and so prophecy must be preserved for future generations.
Predictive Scripture in the main has to do with the Gentile—only as he comes in contact with the Jews. Daniel is the one exception.

10. Chart of Subjects Covered by Prophecy. (See page 38)

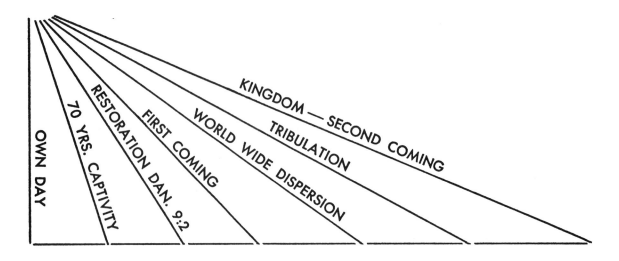

(a) The prophet spoke the Word of God concerning the moral condition of his own people, and his own time.

(b) The 70 year captivity refers to the Babylonian captivity. In this prophecy the time also is stated. It was to last 70 years—Jer. 25:11.

(c) Restoration—Jer. 29:10; Dan. 9:2. Daniel was instrumental in bringing about the restoration of Israel. Having studied the prophecies, he found that the 70 year period was nearly up, and so he went to Cyrus the King and showed the prophecy in Isaiah which said that Cyrus would restore the people of Israel to their land. The Word of God presented to the king by the man of God worked effectively in the heart of the king.

(d) First coming of the Messiah—Isa. 53.
The first prophecy in Gen. 3:15 speaks of both the first and second comings. The bruising of the heel of the seed of woman comes in the first coming, and the crushing of the serpent's head, will come in the second coming. We also have the resurrection in this verse, because a man cannot crush the one who bruised him until there is a resurrection. The seed of the woman was the seed of Abraham, of the line of Isaac, of the house of Jacob, of the tribe of Judah, of the stem of Jesse, of the house of David. We have picture after picture of the way in which this servant of Jehovah would be treated. Isaiah gives a marvelous picture of the first coming in Isa. 53, which really begins with 52:13. Here we find that He would be so marred in His humiliation that men would be astonished, and His exaltation would be so marvelous that kings would close their mouths in astonishment. He had no form nor comeliness. The Jews saw all these things come to pass, and yet that blind nation thought He was being smitten for His own transgressions, not realizing that it was for their own.

(e) World wide dispersion of Israel.
Prophecy not only speaks of the captivities and the restorations, but also speaks of the world-wide dispersion of the Jews.
God says He will bring them back from among all the nations—Amos. 9:9; Ezek. 36:24-28; 37:14. There is a great mass of predictive prophecy which speaks of this world-wide dispersion.

(f) The time of Jacob's trouble.
Called the tribulation, the great one—Jer. 30:4-7; Dan. 12:1.

(g) The Second coming of Christ.
Christ is the Messiah King—Isa. 11. Practically everything in the Word of God that is of a predictive nature will be found on this chart. God goes over and over these, as will be found; for the best plan to follow in getting the teaching into men's minds is repetition. Not all of these have to do with Israel, but the predictive prophecies apply to the Gentiles only as they come into contact with the nation of Israel.

(h) Classification of Prophets.
(1) *Pre-Exile prophets*

Jonah	Isaiah	Jeremiah	Joel
Amos	Micah	Habakkuk	Obadiah
Hosea	Nahum	Zephaniah	

(2) *Exile*
Daniel   Ezekiel   — both of Judah.

(3) *Post-Exile*
Haggai, Zechariah, Malachi
Malachi is known as the seal of the prophets.
No man knows what's going to happen in the future. Only God can know.

(i) Conclusion
Man could not write the Bible if he would, and would not if he could.

b. Notes from a lecture by Dr. A. T. Pierson on the predictions in Scripture.

1. The Bible points to prediction as an absolute proof that God is speaking. God makes that claim Himself, that when He utters these predictive statements, they can come from God and God alone—Isa. 42:9; 44:6-8; 45:21; 46:9, 10. The difference between the idol of man, and God, is that the heathen carries his god and God carries His people. John 13:19; 14:29—The proof of a prophet—the things that he utters are fulfilled.

2. The Bible challenges other religions to foretell future events—Isa. 41:21-29; Deut. 18:21, 22.

3. The Bible is a Book of prediction.

   (a) There is a great deal of prediction in the Bible.
   There is so much prediction in the Word of God that there can be no honest doubt about this book being the Word of God.

   (b) The writings of other religions are obscure, and if they do make a prediction it usually fails, but there are always excuses made for such errors.

4. Criteria by which to test prophecy.

   (a) Remoteness of time.
   In order that there shall be no possibility of an efficient agency on the part of the one who predicts it to bring a thing to pass, it is necessary that there be remoteness of time for the fulfillment of a prediction. The prophecy must be uttered sufficiently before the time for it to come to pass so that the prophet cannot make it come to pass through his own power.

   (b) Minuteness of detail.
   The particulars of the prophecy should be so many and so minute that there could be no possibility of shrewd guesswork for the accuracy of the fulfillment. 33 prophecies were fulfilled within several hours at the crucifixion.

   (c) Novelty of combination.
   There should have been nothing in previous history which would make it possible to forecast a like event in the future.
   There must be something new, something fresh, startling, original, in the prediction and the method of its fulfillment to prove divine intervention.

   (d) Mystery of contradiction.
   There should be something in the prophecy when examined carefully, which is apparently contradictory and paradoxical—an apparent contradiction that makes it impossible to understand the prediction fully until history has supplied the key.

   (e) Clearness of forecast.
   No ambiguity, no cloudiness of statement—a clearness of forecast to make the meaning obvious.

c. Application of the Predictive principle tests.

1. Prophecies concerning Christ.
He was to be the seed of woman, seed of Abraham, of the line of Isaac, house of Jacob, tribe of Judah, family of David, born of a Virgin. There are the predictions of the cries from the cross, His working of miracles, the last days of His life, betrayal by His own, the selling of Christ for thirty pieces of silver, details of the crucifixion such as: His death and burial in a rich man's grave after His grave was appointed with wicked men, His intercession for transgressors, third-day resurrection, incorruptible body, and ascension into heaven.

   (a) Remoteness of Time.
   400 years elapsed between the writing of the last book of the Old Testament and the birth of Christ. Besides this, some of the details written about Him were written as long as 4000 years B.C.

   (b) Minuteness of detail.
   There are hundreds of prophecies in the Old Testament concerning Christ, and the details are very minute, such as have to do with the drink given on the cross, and the gambling over the single garment of the Lord at the foot of the cross.

   (c) Novelty of combination.
   There never was anything like this before—a human child who was also a divine son. In the Old Testament an individual relationship with God was absolutely unknown; the Jew never called God "Father." Jesus introduced something new, when, in the Lord's Prayer, He addressed God as Father.

(d) Mysteries of contradiction.

Prophets wrote of the suffering and glory of Christ. They couldn't understand it then.

(e) Accuracy and clearness of forecast.

(1) Prophecy declares that Jesus must be born of some of the families of earth. Every time a family of a certain line brought offspring into the world, God picked out one who would be in the line of Christ.

(2) He must be born in a certain place.

Of the three known continents—Africa, Asia, and Europe—Asia is chosen; and of the countries of Asia, God chose the small country—Syria. Of the three districts—Judea, Samaria, and Galilee—Judea is taken; and out of the many small villages, the village of Bethlehem.

(3) He was to be born at a certain time.

It might be any century, any year. God did not tell Eve when this Seed of Woman would be born. God alone knew, and He foretold the exact year.

((a)) Sir Robert Anderson, head of the Scotland Yard detective Agency, was not a preacher, but a student of the Bible. He has figured out from prophecy that Christ came on the exact day of the year as prophesied.

((b)) In Gen. 49:10, the season is given. This is a prophecy uttered by the dying patriarch, Jacob. He gave a prophecy which was true of each son, and also true of the tribe which came from each. God says these are true of the last days. Jacob said, "the scepter shall not depart from Judah till Shiloh come." Shiloh is the Old Testament name for Christ. When Christ came we find that Judah was still in authority with a great deal of power in her hands, but her power was waning.

2. History must be taken into consideration in the fulfillment of prophecy—Rev. 11:9, 10.

Until the present day men have skipped over this prophecy, for in no other day could the whole world have rejoiced together for three days the message could not have been received in many places for months and years afterwards. Today a message can be flashed around the world in just a few seconds.

3. The Mosaic Covenant.

Nobody but God could make the statements made in connection with this covenant. When Israel entered into the land of Canaan God said He would bless them if they continued to obey Him, but He prophesied four punishments which would befall them if they disobeyed.

Would be plucked off the land,

Scattered among all the nations,

Persecuted as no other people;

Yet would be preserved; for God said He would bring them back.

d. There is a great deal of difference between speculation concerning prophecy and interpretation of a prophecy.

1. The vision of Daniel—Dan. 8.

The place of Shushan referred to here, has recently been excavated, and everything found there verifies the Word of God.

If God does not give light on this prophecy, then no one knows what is meant by these two beasts. We can only speculate, and then will miss the meaning.

God explains this vision in the last part of the chapter—Dan. 8:20-25. If a prophecy has not yet been fulfilled, history will fulfill it, and it will be filled full.

2. The dream image of Nebuchadnezzar.

It is not necessary to speculate on this, for God tells us what this is—Dan. 2. It is a forecast of the "Times of the Gentiles"—Luke 21:24.

The times of the Gentiles is that period of time in which Jerusalem is politically in the hands of the Gentiles.

Jerusalem fell into the hands of the Gentiles 2500 years ago, when taken by Nebuchadnezzar, which was the beginning of "the times of the Gentiles."

Jerusalem went down and Babylon came up. Jerusalem became politically a cipher, and Babylon politically the center.

3. This vision was striking, terrible, and so fearful that "his sleep brake from him." Immediately he sent for the wise men to interpret the vision. This they were willing and eager to do; but first he must tell them what he dreamed. The king, however, had forgotten what it was, except that it had frightened him and it was terrifying. Since they could not reproduce the dream and give its meaning, the king ordered them all to be executed.

Now Daniel was a wise man, and when the soldiers came to him, he thought they were getting a little "previous" and he asked to see the king. Daniel was conducted to the palace, and brought before the king, declaring that he could tell the dream and interpret it—not because of any superior knowledge—but because he was a servant of Jehovah. The dream and its interpretation are given in Dan. 2:31-45.

4. These four metals composing the image were symbolical of four world empires:

  (a) Head of Gold—Babylon.
  Babylon under Nebuchadnezzar. He was the only absolute monarch (one person—no vote of the people) the world ever saw. God gave it into his hands—Isa. 14:4. Jer. 51:7. Babylon was the *golden empire.*

  (b) Breast and arms of silver—Media-Persia, Dan. 5.
  This passage is one that the critics like to criticize. Secular history proves that Belshazzar was a king. His name has been uncovered. This has stopped the mouths of critics who based their criticism of this chapter on the fact that no such name had been recorded in secular history.
  Now Belshazzar was the second ruler of the kingdom. Nebuchadnezzar was his grandfather, and Nabonidus was his father and the first ruler. While Belshazzar's father was away from the city on business, he decided he wanted to show off, so he ordered the feast.
  The occasion for the "showing off" was when the enemy, the Medes and Persians, were encamped outside the city. But the king, Belshazzar, was so sure of the safety of the city, that he chose to ignore the danger. The walls were too strong to be broken down, and too high to climb over, and they felt safe.
  In the midst of this revelry there appeared the fingers of a man's hand that wrote on the plaster of the wall. The words written were, "Mene, Mene, Tekel, Upharsin."
  Belshazzar didn't understand, but he was so scared his knees shook. Then, like his great ancestor, he sent for his wise men, who were just as ignorant as those of Nebuchadnezzar's day—Dan. 5:8, 9. That scared them more than ever, and they made so much noise the queen's mother came down to see what the trouble was—Dan. 5:10-12. At her suggestion Daniel was sent for and offered gifts which he refused—Dan. 5:16. Before telling the meaning of the writing, he chided Belshazzar because he had not profited by the experience of Nebuchadnezzar, who had been punished by God for becoming filled with pride. Daniel then told the meaning of the words (Dan. 5:25-28); but Belshazzar, not greatly impressed, went on with the banquet.
  That night Belshazzar was slain, and Darius the Mede took the city. This was the *second* world empire, the Medo-Persian empire as given in Daniel's interpretation in Daniel 5. The *silver empire* is a good term for this second one, for the soldiers of the Persian army wore silver corsets of armor. It was a silver army.

  (c) The belly and sides of brass—Greece.
  In Dan. 8, Daniel states that the ram is Persia and the he-goat Greece. Greece, therefore, was to take the place of Media-Persia. We read that the ram went north, south, and west (three directions) and began to grow so that nothing was able to stand before it. Persia was a world monarchy, with 127 provinces under her rule. When the ram had become great, there appeared in the west a he-goat with a horn. That horn was the first king, Alexander the Great, the great general who never lost a battle. At twenty years of age he was the ruler of a petty empire, and at thirty he was the ruler of the world. Alexander came from the west swiftly, and the goat Daniel saw came so fast that he seemed not to touch the ground. The army of Alexander moved in an almost miraculous way, so that men marvelled.
  The Greek army was a brazen-coated army, the brass army of the *brass kingdom.* When the first king of Macedonia consulted an oracle (wise person), he was told to follow a herd of wild goats. He did so, and where they stopped he built a city, calling it Aegea, the "City of goats." There is a body of water adjoining the country of Greece—the Aegean sea. The goat then, is a sign of Greece, in secular history; and God had told Daniel a long time before about the goats.

  (d) Legs of Iron—Rome—Luke 2:1.
  Caesar Augustus was the ruler of Rome.
  Rome was the *iron empire,* which made the world to tremble. One thousand years is a long time, but one thousand years after God made this revelation to Nebuchadnezzar, it came to pass.

  (e) The ten toes of iron and clay.
    (1) Here we have not metal or mineral, but something foreign, clay or mud in the feet of the image. This is something that does not belong in this image at all, and does not unite with the other ingredients. From the context, we find that the clay stands for just the opposite of monarchy. It is the *rule of the people* (democracy). As the iron and clay will not mix, so monarchy (rule by one) and democracy (rule of people) will not mix. The feet of the image are not stable.
    The image is top-heavy. There is not clay in the head. The rule of the people comes-not at the beginning—but at the end. With the rule of the people we have Socialism, Anarchy, etc. In all countries today the rule of the people is the popular government.
    (2) In the revival of the old Roman Empire the two divisions are to become ten, and there will be both iron and clay in them.
    (3) God told Nebuchadnezzar that after him should come a kingdom inferior to Babylon. Silver is inferior to them all. e.g. Nebuchadnezzar was an absolute monarchy, but the silver monarch was bound by the laws of the Medes and Persians. If Nebuchadnezzar didn't like the laws, he made new ones.

(4) We are prone to say of our plan of government that it is best, but the best is that of an absolute monarchy. That is the way Christ will rule.

(5) These ten kingdoms will spring up in the old Roman Empire. There will be, in this revival, a group of subordinate kings under one king. We are on the verge of these ten kingdoms right now. God is working it out—Dan. 7:23-25.

(f) The Mountain.

  (1) A Mountain in Scripture speaks of a government, a rule, or kingdom—Ps. 30:7. The mountain here is the kingdom of Judah. The stone, or rock, is the Lord Jesus Christ. In the Word, both stone and rock are used to represent Christ in many instances.

  (2) The stone Nebuchadnezzar saw cut out of the mountain of Judah was Christ—I Pet. 2:4, 8. It was cut out without hands, in a supernatural way. Man had nothing to do with the cutting of it. Christ was supernatural in His first coming, and will be in His second coming.

  (3) The stone falls on the feet of the image—not on the head nor on the thigh. When it smites the image it is crushed to dust. That is the catastrophe coming. The falling of the stone will bring the end of "the times of the Gentiles." God will set up His kingdom under His Son, and the stone will become a mountain that fills the earth. The Kingdom of Heaven will be the world empire then. God declares the meaning of this over and over.

  (4) Some prophecies in the Bible God does not explain, so we know nothing about them. Many of the prophecies in the book of Revelation cannot be explained. There are some Scriptures which will never be understood until history fulfills them. The prophets themselves did not understand them, because the fulfillment must come with the passing of time.

e. Symbolical prophecy.

1. Ezekiel, the writer of symbolical prophecy.

  (a) In Ezek. 1 the vision of which he wrote is also explained in the same chapter. He saw the cherubim —highly figurative.

  (b) Ezekiel 5.
Ezekiel was the man with long hair and a long beard. God said to him, "Shave it all off. Take the balances and weigh the hair and divide it into three equal parts. Take one part and throw it into the fire; take another part and smite it with the sword, and take the third part out and throw it to the winds. Take a few hairs and tie them in your skirt."
God explains it in the same chapter.
One-third of the inhabitants of Jerusalem shall die with famine, pestilence and burning.
One-third shall fall by the sword.
The remaining third shall be scattered among all nations.
The little bunch tied in the skirt is the faithful remnant—Jer. 52:16.

  (c) Ezekiel 4.
Ezekiel was told to go on a diet. He was to weigh his food and measure the water he drank.
God said that He would bring a famine upon Israel and they would weigh their food and measure the water in that time, even as Ezekiel was doing.

2. Jeremiah.

  (a) The linen girdle—Chapter 13:1-5. All the orientals wore (and still do wear) girdles. Those of higher rank, such as the kings, wore theirs about the breast; and those of lower rank wore the girdle about the loins.
Jeremiah was commanded by God to get a new linen girdle and wear it. Of course a new girdle would be of importance and would be noticed by everyone. After Jeremiah had worn it for some time, God said, "Take the girdle and bury it down by the Euphrates." Jeremiah did so—Jer. 13:6-11. The girdle was a symbol of service. The people of Israel had an important and honorable part in God's service for the salvation of the lost, and just as a man will wear a new girdle for honor and praise, so they were for God's praise. But just as this new girdle had lost its beauty and usefulness down by the Euphrates, so they will be marred and will lose their beauty and usefulness down by the Euphrates.

  (b) Jer. 16—The sign of the unmarried prophet.
God told Jeremiah to abstain from marriage, from mourning, and from mirth. This is symbolical. Jeremiah was not to marry, not to have a family, not to go into the house of mourning, not to feast at the time of feasting.
When the people wanted an explanation, he was to tell them, "The reason why I am not married is because I dare not bring a family into the world, since they would fall into evil ways and judgment." The reason for not mourning—the time is coming when they will be under the judgment of God, when they will need consolation and there will be no consolation. The reason for not feasting— the time is coming when there will be no mirth.
This is predictive prophecy, in which God uses everyday events in life to preach His truth.

f. How one may misinterpret predictive prophecy.

1. Ezek. 37. Vision of valley of dry bones.

(a) How this has been misused and misinterpreted!
People picture the Church as a valley of dry bones. There is a great deal of encouragement here, because these bones all come alive again.
(b) The Church is the Body of Christ, and not a valley of dry bones. There are a lot of dry bones in the organization, it is true.
(c) This has no reference to the Church at all. So many people when reading this, do not finish it. We know it does not refer to the Church.
(d) There is no Church clearly revealed in the Old Testament; this is reserved for the mystery in the N.T.
(e) Ezek. 37:11-14. We know what the bones are, because God tells us. This figure is prophecy concerning a national resurrection of Israel. There it will be a restoration of all the twelve tribes.

g. Rules for the interpretation of prophecy:
1. Let the prophet give his own interpretation.
   (a) The Ram and the He-goat—Dan. 8:20, 21.
   Ram—2 horns—Medo-Persia (one horn higher).
   Goat—king of Greece.
   (b) Valley of dry bones.
   (c) We do not know who the two witnesses are in Rev. 11:3-12. God does not clearly tell us—Mal. 4:5.
   (d) The trees, grass, sun, moon and stars in Revelation are just what they are; not (as one man said) the nobility, the common people, a walled city, an unwalled city, and the population of the city.
   (e) Jerusalem is Jerusalem, and not Sodom. Jerusalem is guilty of the same sins, and is spiritually called Sodom.
   (f) Jer. 18:1-10—Israel is like a vessel marred in the potter's hands, and God will make it anew.
   (g) John 2:19-22—Jesus prophesied concerning the temple, and gave His own interpretation.
   (h) Matt. 13:18-23—This is a predictive parable of the sower which the Lord interpreted.

2. Facts in history may give the interpretation.
   (a) City of Tyre—Ezek. 26:
   (b) The Flood—More than a century before the flood God predicted it. Before that, man had never seen rain. It took history to fulfill it.
   (c) Joseph's dream—The sun and stars, and the sheaves of wheat were explained and fulfilled in the course of history.
   (d) Many of Daniel's statements and prophecies are known now through the fulfillment of history, e.g., Dan. 2.

3. Other inspired Scriptures may give the interpretation of prophecy.
   (a) Psalm 16.
   This was mysterious to men in bygone days. A man who will not remain in the place of death, and whose body will never decay. Other inspired Scriptures tell us all about it.
   (b) Isa. 29:14 and Habakkuk 1:5.
   This is the work that is to be wondered at. The Messianic import is given in Acts 13:40, 41.
   (c) Psalm 41:9—
   This refers to Judas, but we would not know this without Acts 1:15-18.
   (d) Nebuchadnezzar's dream image.
   See discussion in notes.
   This is found in Daniel 2, and other Scriptures needed to complete the interpretation are Daniel 5 and Daniel 8.

4. The resemblance of things compared will help in interpretation.
   (a) A great many prophecies compare Christ to a Lamb. Where Christ is set forth as a lamb in Scriptures, see what they have to say concerning a lamb, and the resemblance will aid interpretation.
   (b) He is also called the Lion of the tribe of Judah. This shows another characteristic of Christ.
   (c) Gen. 49—This is a good example of the rules. Many striking comparisons are made here. A study of these beasts will prove an aid—e.g.—
       (1) Benjamin is ravenous as a wolf. (Only tribe which took up archery.)
       (2) Naphtali is a hind in the mountains let loose.
       Naphtali, like the deer, was wild and lived in the mountains.
       (3) Issachar is like an ass, bearing a double burden.
       Issachar today is lowly, slow, like an ass. Not anxious to go, and would rather let someone put a double burden on his back than take two steps to get out of the way.

5. Proper recognition of figures of speech.

6. Proper interpretation of symbols and types. You know nothing about prophecy if God does not give the meaning somewhere in Scripture. Speculation is not interpretation.

CHAPTER SEVEN

The Application Principle

VI. THE APPLICATION PRINCIPLE.

a. Definition.

1. The principle by which an application of truth may be made *only* after the correct interpretation has been learned.

   (a) This means that when you study the Bible you must first seek the proper interpretation of the text, the exact meaning always, and the literal meaning. You ought never to take a text and preach on it without examining the words of the text. Discover—

   (1) Why that passage was given.
   (2) What was the original purpose of God in writing the Scripture.
   (3) What was in the mind of God when He caused it to be written.

   (b) When the meaning is learned, then you may apply it to the life of an individual, of a community, etc., but first of all discover the real meaning of the text. There is a great difference between application and interpretation. There is much confusion in the church today because men have taken the Word of God and made application without any true reference to the interpretation.

   (c) All Bible students should be agreed as to the interpretation. There may be many applications, but there is only one correct interpretation.

   (d) Things necessary for interpretation:

   (1) Common sense—the ability to discover harmony in things that agree and differences in unlike things.
   (2) Faith in Scripture as the Word of God.
   (3) Mental perception.
   (4) Other things that help:
       ((a)) Obedience.
       ((b)) Knowledge of Bible geography, people, etc.
       ((c)) Knowledge of contemporary history.
       ((d)) Purity of life.
   (5) II Tim. 3:14-16; Eph. 3:3, 4; Col. 4:16; I Thess. 5:27.
       The Scriptures were to be read and understood by all.

   (e) Hindrances in interpretation.

   (1) Desire for the applause of the world.
   (2) Vanity and flattery may lead to blindness.
   (3) Study without regularity and without system.
   (4) Studying only favorite portions.

   (f) Methods which prevent proper interpretation.

   (1) Mystical. It originated in heathenism. It goes back to the study of the priesthood. Here is a belief that those only who are divinely appointed by God can properly interpret.
   (2) Allegorical. This method treats the Bible as though it were made up of combination of metaphors or comparisons. It *adds* to the Scripture.
   (3) Rationalistic. This is a method of unbelief. Nature is the standard, and reason is the guide. All must harmonize with man.
   (4) Apologetic. Absolute perfection of every statement in the Bible is the claim. There is a swing from the rationalistic to the other extreme.
   (5) Literal. This takes everything in Scripture literally.

b. Interpretation and Application of Texts.

1. David and Mephibosheth—II Sam. 9.

   (a) Interpretation.
   Kindness shown by David and his faithfulness to his covenant with Jonathan.

   (b) Application.
   This is a beautiful picture of salvation by Christ.
   David is now king and wishes to show the kindness of God to the house of Saul because of his covenant with Jonathan, Saul's son.
   David now had the upper hand, and no one would have found any fault with him if he had rounded up the members of Saul's family and killed them all, but David's throne became a throne of mercy rather than of judgment because of another (Jonathan). We may draw a comparison here and show that through the blood of Jesus Christ the throne of God is a throne of mercy today because of An-

other, God's Son. But this throne will some day become a throne of judgment because of those who reject Christ.

Verse 3 tells us that Jonathan had a son whose name was Mephibosheth and was lame on both feet. Mephibosheth was lame because of a fall. His nurse had dropped him when fleeing with him from the enemy. He had fallen at the hands of another. Sinful man has fallen at the hands of another, who was Adam. Every son of Adam is lame on both feet. Now where was Mephibosheth? He was in the house of Machir, in the land of Lodebar. That was an interesting place, and that is just where the sinner is. Machir means "sold." Mephiboseth was living in a house of bondage. We are all sold under sin in a house of bondage—a slave of sin and a slave of Satan.

The land of Lodebar means "no pasture." Where there is no pasture there is no satisfaction. No pasture means "no peace."

We read later that David sent and fetched him. Mephibosheth did not go, he was not seeking David, and he did not fetch himself, but David sent and fetched him. When we were sinners, God sent and fetched us.

When Mephibosheth came to David, he fell on his face. He feared David. This is a picture of the sinner in fear on that great judgment day. But Mephibosheth was to be shown kindness for the sake of another. God, for Christ's sake, will save the sinner. God did not save you for your own sake, but because of another. Mephibosheth went to live in Jerusalem, which means "Peace." He came from Lodebar, no pasture, to Jerusalem, the "city of peace." Here is an opportunity to tell the sinner to leave Lodebar and move down to Jerusalem. God is all ready to fetch him out of Lodebar and over to Jerusalem.

The end of the story is—"so Mephibosheth did eat continually at the king's table; and was lame on both of his feet." The fact of the matter is, that when Mephibosheth came from Lodebar to Jerusalem, he brought his lame feet right along with him. When we came to the King's house and ate at the King's table, and became members of the family of God we brought our lame feet with us.

2. Naaman and Elisha—II Kings 5.

(a) Interpretation.

This has to do with a Syrian captain and the Jewish captive.

Here was a little girl who believed that the prophet could heal Naaman of his leprosy.

(b) Application.

Someone has said that there are two million physical lepers in the world. We are not certain as to that number, but we do know that there are many times that number of spiritual lepers. Spiritually, every man is a leper until cleansed in the blood. This story gives the gospel plan of salvation.

(1) Leprosy is a symbol of sin. Men are lepers in the sight of God, when in sin.

((a)) In the nation of Israel lepers were excluded from worship in the temple of God, by the command of Jehovah. This was not true in any of the other nations, for lepers were allowed to mingle with the rest of the people. Sin, like leprosy, breaks out in the most loathsome forms. You can see it on all sides. Sin, like leprosy, makes every one hideous. Sin, like leprosy, brings separation. In the nation of Israel the leper could not come into the camp with the others. When anyone came near he must shout, "Unclean, unclean!" If the moral lepers of today had to shout, "Unclean" there would be a terrific racket. Sin, like leprosy, cannot be cured by man. A sinner is a death-doomed man and no one can cure him but God. It seems that no one could cure leprosy but God, in the Scriptures. We mention here that there are some ways in which the sinner and a leper are not alike. A leper never makes light of his leprosy, but a sinner does make light of his sin. The leper knows he is a leper, but the sinner fails to recognize that he is a sinner.

(2) When a sinner is awakened to his sin he will be miserable, as was Naaman. With all of his good things, Naaman was not happy.

(3) The gospel of cleansing came to Naaman through a little girl—not a great woman; but she had a great message. She had a humble position. Though she was a servant of Naaman and his wife, she was also a servant of Jehovah. Here is a lesson. The thing necessary to get Naaman into touch with God was the testimony of a servant. When this little girl started to testify, things started to move. Naaman moved, and the king moved, and then Naaman moved over into Israel.

(4) The law of Assyria did not bar Naaman from society, but in Israel God's law said a leper must be separated. When Naaman came into Israel, then Elisha treated him as a leper should be treated. The trouble today is that the world is trying to make sin respectable, and God will not have it so. You should treat the sinner as a sinner and put him in his place. You can never save a man by patting him on the back and then feeding him cream puffs. When the sinner takes a sinner's place, then he will be saved. There is too much fellowship with sin, and compromise with sin. Naaman had to take the leper's place before he was cleansed. The sinner must take the place of the sinner.

(5) Naaman was willing to go far and do much, but he wanted to do things his own way. The sinner is much like Naaman, for he is not satisfied with the remedy prescribed. He will say it is too

easy. A sinner never does like God's plan, and the reason is—God's plan strips the sinner of all his righteousness. It brings all sinners on the same plane.

(6) Naaman dipped 7 times. 7 is the number of God. 6 is the number of evil and of man. There is no cleansing for man until 6 is submerged in God's 7. In Adam we are marked with 6, but in Christ we are marked with 7.

3. The Prodigal Son—Luke 15.

(a) Interpretation.

Now notice the setting.

The Lord Jesus is surrounded by the publicans and sinners. The Pharisees and Scribes are murmuring, "This man receiveth publicans and sinners and eateth with them." He spoke this parable to the Scribes and Pharisees and it is for them. By interpretation this parable belongs to that dispensation, and if it is to be understood it must be treated dispensationally. The publicans and sinners were Jews as well as the others, and they were all in covenant relationship with God. That sacrifice taken into the tabernacle every year cleansed all of them. The publicans and sinners were wayward children of God. The parable teaches a great love of God for the children in covenant relationship with Him. This was a national covenant.

(b) Application.

If any application is to be made to this present dispensation it must be made to people who are in covenant relationship with God. In other words, the prodigal son is not a lost sinner but a saved sinner. He is a son. The lost sheep, the lost coin, and the lost boy all apply to the backslider. The one hundred sheep were saved; the coins were saved; the two boys were saved. It was a sheep that was lost, not a goat. It was a real coin that was lost, not a counterfeit. It was just as good as the rest of the coins on the string. The boy that was lost was just as much a son as the one who stayed at home. This boy was a son, and nothing could unmake him a son. He was a son in the home, and a son when he left the home, and a son when in the field feeding swine. If he had died in the far country he would have still been a son. This boy was a son even when he brought shame to the family. The parable teaches the everlasting love of God for His own. The son could waste and spend all that he had (save his father's love) but he could not spend that; and when he returned home his father met him with outstretched arms.

4. Light in our dwelling—Exod. 10:21-24.

There is a darkness in Egypt.

(a) Interpretation.

The people of God are in slavery, and God is going to free them.

(b) Application—the sinner in slavery unto Satan and freed by God.

(c) Comparisons of interpretation and application.

(1) They were freed by judgments; this is the ninth—darkness. It was leveled against the sun god (ra) of the Egyptians. The judgment came in Egypt because Pharaoh would not let God's people go. Today there is spiritual darkness because the world doesn't recognize God.

(2) The children of Israel had light in their dwellings.

(3) It was not a natural light, but supernatural. Truly there should be light in our dwellings in the midst of the darkness of the world. We are children of light; there should be a light in our home which is a supernatural light.

5. Book of Ecclesiastes.

(a) Interpretation.

(1) Eccl. 7:16—"Be not righteous overmuch."

(2) Eccl. 7:17—"Be not overmuch wicked."

(3) Eccl. 2:24—"Nothing better for a man than that he should eat and drink."

(4) Eccl. 3:4—"There is a time to dance."

We must remember that Ecclesiastes is the book of the natural man (of the unsaved man). "Vanity of vanities" is used 28 times. It means emptiness of all life aside from God. We could probably translate it "soap bubbles." The key to the book is 6:12.

(b) Application.

In chapter one there are three parables:

(1) The sun riseth and goeth down in the same place. Things of the world always come to the same end or place—Verse 5.

(2) The wind goes, but always comes back, and will come back continually. This is a picture of the unsaved man—Verse 6.

(3) All rivers run into the sea, yet are not full; take all the streams the world has to offer and pour them into the soul, and man is never full—Verse 7.

6. Achan and Ai—Josh. 7, 8.

(a) In chapter 6 we have the fall of the city of Jericho—a city given to Israel by the power of God.

(b) Chapter 7—defeat comes.

Joshua proceeds in the same way as at Jericho. God was to receive the wealth of Ai, but Achan took some of the spoil and hid it in his tent.

Until sin is purged, God's hand is withheld. There is need of judgment in the church today. We would have more power if we would exercise more discipline.

Achan's sin was a sin committed in a moment of victory, and led to defeat. It was a sin of sacrilege. He took something that belonged to God. Sin robs God. It was a secret sin, but God knew. God knows everything—I Chron. 28:9.

7. Rahab—Josh. 2.

    (a) Interpretation.

        (1) Joshua was the greatest General on the pages of history, because he followed the Lord.

        (2) Rahab asked for salvation for herself and family.

        (3) A woman saved when Jericho was appointed for utter destruction—here is the gospel.

    (b) Application.

        (1) Rahab dwelt in a condemned city. Jericho is a type of the world under the curse of God.

        (2) Rahab was a bad character—a condemned person.

        There was nothing in her to commend her to God. There is nothing in man to commend him to God—Rom. 3:10.

        (3) Faith of Rahab.

        Because she had heard—she knew.

        (4) Rahab's salvation.

        The men said: "Our life for yours." Here is substitution as portrayed at Calvary.

The Typical Principle

VII. THE TYPICAL PRINCIPLE.

a. Definition—A type is a divinely appointed illustration of some scriptural truth.

   1. Reasons for neglecting the study of types.

      (a) Called fanciful because of ignorance.
Sir Robert Anderson said, "The typology of the Old Testament is the very alphabet of the language in which the doctrine of the New Testament is written; and as many of our great theologians are admittedly ignorant of typology, we need not feel surprised if they are not always the safest exponents of the doctrines."

      (b) It is called uninteresting because difficult. This is pure laziness. The study of types takes time, work, prayer, and sweat.

   2. Reason for studying types.
Col. 2:17—"Which are a shadow of things to come; but the body is of Christ."
You can never have a shadow without a body to cast that shadow. In the Old Testament you have the shadow preceding Christ, and in the New Testament you meet with the body which cast the shadow.
Types are pictures or object lessons by which God taught His people concerning His grace and saving power.

b. The type in scripture.
Our English word "type" is derived from the Greek word, "tupos," which occurs sixteen times in the New Testament. It is translated twice, "print" (John 20:25); twice, "figure" (Acts 7:43; Rom. 5:14); twice, "pattern" (Tit. 2:7; Heb. 8:5); once, "fashion" (Acts 7:44); once, "manner" (Acts 23:25); once, "form" (Rom. 6:17); and seven times, "example" (I Cor. 10:6,11; Phil. 3:17; I Thess. 1:7; II Thess. 3:9; I Tim. 4:12; I Pet. 5:3).
The Greek word is very striking and has many shades of meaning. The original significance is the effect of a blow, an impression or stamp, mark, pattern, form, or mould.

c. Classification of types.

   1. A person—One whose life illustrates some great principle or truth of redemption.
Rom. 5:14—Adam.
Heb. 5:6—Melchizedek.
Heb. 7:11—Aaron.
Gal. 4:28—Isaac.
There are many others such as Sarah, Jonah, Joseph, etc.

   2. An event—
I Cor. 10:11—experiences of Israel.
Deliverance from Egyptian bondage.
The wilderness journey.
The conquest of Canaan.

   3. A thing.
Veil of the tabernacle—Heb. 10:20.
Brazen serpent—Num. 21.

   4. Ritual types.
This includes the offerings, the priesthood, the tabernacle and its furniture, and the passover.

d. Interpretation of types.
A true type, to be such in reality, must be:

   1. A true picture of the person or thing it represents or prefigures.

   2. Of divine appointment.

   3. A picture which prefigures something future.
A type must never be used to teach a doctrine, but only to illustrate a doctrine elsewhere explicitly taught—John 3:14; I Cor. 5:7.

e. How to use types in Bible study.

   1. The Passover Lamb—I Cor. 5:7.
This is typical of Christ and it is divinely authorized. This takes us back to Ex. 12. It is a most remark-

able chapter and contains one of the most astounding types of the Bible. Israel is in Egypt—in bondage. Here we have the judgment on the land, and the deliverance of Israel by the Passover Lamb. That night Israel was led out of bondage.

From Ex. 12 we go to John 19:36—"A bone of him shall not be broken." John the Baptist had it revealed to him that Christ was the lamb. No one is ever called the Lamb of God except Christ—John 1: 29. God never had in mind any lamb save the one Lamb. In spite of the slaying of thousands of lambs, you never read of Passover lambs, but "the Passover Lamb." On the night of the Passover, there were possibly thousands of lambs slain, but God did not say "Kill them," but, "Kill it." All divine sacrifices are embodied *only* in the Lamb slain from the foundation of the world. Calvary culminates, down to the minutest detail, the slaughter of innumerable lambs.

(a) One thing that stands out in Ex. 12 is the fact that Israel was in bondage—in slavery. Their burdens had become so great that they were almost unbearable—Ex. 2:23. This slavery is typical of the slavery endured by the sinner who is the bond-slave of sin. This bondage is worse than the slavery of the Israelites.

(b) They were in sin. We are inclined to think of these people as martyrs, but they deserved just what they endured. They were not only slaves, but also sinners as well. They were as sinful as the Egyptians; in fact, they were worse than the Egyptians, for they had light that the Egyptians did not have. They had contact with God and had such promises and enlightenment as the Egyptians had never had. Israel was worshipping the Gods of the Egyptians—Ezek. 20: 33-38. Israel was so contaminated, and so headstrong in her idolatry, that God thought to destroy her. This is a picture of man outside of Christ.

(c) They were delivered through the lamb.
It was God's purpose to bring these people out of Egypt—to deliver them. But, before He could set them free, before they could know the blessing of Jehovah dwelling in their midst, before they could walk with God, the sin question must be taken care of.
God will not associate Himself with sin; God is Holy. It was God's plan to deliver them after the question of their sin was settled. God settled that question by passing the sentence of death against the first-born in the land of Egypt.
Exodus 11:4, 5—That included the first-born in the Hebrew homes as well as the first-born in the homes of the Egyptians. God brought the judgments against the gods of the Egyptians, and so against those who worshipped the gods.
God singled out in every case, the household's pride, the first-born, the heir of the family, the one in whom the hopes of the house were centered. This first-born is representative of the family and of the family's guilt. The whole family is under condemnation, a condemnation that rests upon Jew and Gentile. "All have sinned," and "The wages of sin is death." That is what Christ received on the cross, the wages of sin. They were wages He had not earned, because He was sinless; but He received them anyway.
The condition then, is this: Here is a people, sinful slaves under condemnation. When God said, "I am come down to deliver them," that is grace.
Moses was not going to deliver them, but was merely an instrument in the hands of God. God was the Deliverer. Another Deliverer came 1900 years ago; Christ, the same "I AM," came down to deliver men — that is grace. God came down, incarnate in Christ, in order that slaves might be delivered. What has been said concerning the people of Israel is true of man today. Romans 3— There is no difference. All have not committed the same kind or the same number of sins, but all have sinned. There was no difference between Israel and Egypt, but God put a difference between them—there was the lamb between.

(d) Concerning the lamb.
  (1) Specifications—Exodus 12:3.
      One lamb is always sufficient, and Christ is always sufficient. The lamb must be a perfect specimen, a first-born male, without outer defilement and inner wrong—I Pet. 1:19; Heb. 7:26.
  (2) The lamb must be slain.
      A live lamb would not save the first-born in the home.
  (3) The blood must be sprinkled on the two sides and above the door. Something must be done with the blood. Some say that if Jesus died for the world, the world must be saved. They forget that the blood must be applied. It takes more than the shedding of blood to save a sinner. There must be a personal appropriation. The blood must be put on the door in the form of a cross.
      Blood in the Lamb—Incarnation.
      Blood in the basin—Death.
      Blood on the door—Application.
      Christ living cannot save. "Except the Son of man to be lifted up"—John 3:14.
  (4) The lamb must be put into the fire.
      It not only had to be slain, but it also had to be roasted as well. There might be some cross-pieces to hold the limbs apart.

Thus the lamb was literally crucified. This gives us a picture of Christ crucified. He was hung before the open fire of God's wrath, and the flames of God's wrath enveloped Him.

(5) It must not be eaten raw.
The carcass had to endure the fire until the roasting was complete or until the action of the fire was completed. Christ said, "It is finished." He had endured it all. The lamb must not be soaked with water, because water would resist the action of the fire. Nothing was to be done to alleviate the sufferings of Christ on the cross.

(6) They were to eat the lamb.
The eating of the lamb would strengthen them for their journey. There are Christians today who haven't fed on the lamb, and so have not strength to get out of the land of Egypt.

(7) What was left must be burned.
If any of the flesh of the lamb was not eaten, it would spoil and decay, and become corrupt. But this lamb is typical of Christ, and anything that savors of corruption must be destroyed.

(e) Concerning the blood.
The blood was sprinkled for God. It was for God's eye, not for the eye of the first-born. The blood spilt on Calvary we have never seen, but God saw it.

(f) Result of the Passover.
When the Passover was over, there was death in every home in the land of Egypt. In the homes of the Egyptians it was the death of the first-born. In the homes of the Israelites it was the death of the first-born lamb. There was a first-born dead in every home.

(g) The feast of unleavened bread—Ex. 12:15.
This was instituted also. They were to put leaven out of their homes, and for seven days were to eat unleavened bread.

(h) The time of the Passover.
The lamb was slain at three o'clock in the afternoon; judgment came at midnight. Between three and midnight there was time for the sprinkling of the blood, but after midnight no blood could be sprinkled; it was too late.
Christ was crucified 1900 years ago. That was at three in the afternoon. There is a midnight of God's judgment coming, but before that time men must come under the blood, to be saved.

(i) The New Year.
In Exodus 12 we read that God changed the calendar of the Israelites. They were at the beginning of of the seventh month, but God changed it to the first month. Six is the number of man, failure and sin. Six months had passed, and the seventh had come, and the seventh was to be the new beginning based on the Passover. The old six is blotted out.

2. The Brazen serpent.

This is one of the types of the cross which is pointed out by the Lord. It is as if He did not want us to miss this type—John 3:14, 15. This takes us back to Numbers 21. The Israelites were sinful, and were murmuring against God. As judgment, fiery serpents were sent among them. When the people cried to Moses for aid, God instructed Moses to construct a serpent of brass and lift it up on a pole. All that was necessary was to look—"Look and live." It is this case of physical healing in the Old Testament that Christ took as an illustration of spiritual healing in the New Testament. This case of healing in the physical realm is typical of healing in the spiritual realm.

(a) Condition of the people.
Death was among them—"Much people of Israel died." This was caused by the bite of the fiery serpent. There is no man or woman living who has not the poison of the serpent-bite. We are sinners, and under the sentence and shadow of death. The poison of the serpent is the poison of sin.

(b) Remedies and results.
In Israel, God gave them the serpent on the pole. It was God's remedy, not man's.

(1) Destroying the serpents.
When the Israelites began to die they cried to Moses, "Pray to the Lord that He will take away the serpents." That was man's method, God's method was to lift up the serpent.

(2) Work for your salvation.
God didn't say, "Forget all about yourself and go out and help some of the other poor fellows who have been bitten."

(3) Fighting for salvation.
God did not say, "Go out and fight the serpents." It is not fight that saves, but faith.

(4) Bargaining for salvation.
They were not told to make an offering to the serpent.

(5) Looking to the law for salvation.
They were not told to look at Moses. Such people do not recognize—Titus 3:5.

(6) They were not told to look at themselves.
All you see when you look at yourself is a snake-bite. Don't look at your own wounds, look at His. A victorious life is not to be lived by looking at yourself, but by looking at Christ.

(7) Trusting in reform.

God did not say, "Shake off the snakes." He does not say today, "Quit drinking or dancing."

(8) Looking to God.

Do not look to God, but to Christ. Believing there is a God does not make you a Christian.

(9) Looking at the pole.

We are not told to look at the pole, but the serpent on the pole. Look! At what? Not at the pole, not at Moses; not at themselves, but at the serpent.

(c) The serpent was made of brass.

Brass in Scripture is typical of judgment. So the serpent of brass speaks of judgment. Christ was judged in our stead. The serpent on the pole stands for judgment. The anti-type gives us judgment, for Christ on the cross was judged.

(d) It was a serpent.

That serpent on the pole was made in the likeness of that which brought death. In other words, Christ took upon Himself the form of that which had done the mischief.

(e) It was a serpent in which there was no poison.

There was no sin in Christ. He had no sin, He knew no sin, He did no sin.

(f) It must be lifted on a pole.

The Saviour must be put on a cross. No other execution would do. The Jewish method of execution was stoning; but Christ stoned to death would not save.

(g) The command.

Look and live! Look and be saved! You are not saved because you understand, but because you look. You don't have to have an education to look. Any fool can look.

(h) The cure.

A look at the serpent on the pole brought life. The serpents brought death, but the look brought life. A sinner under condemnation who looks, receives a new life. Sin and Satan are not taken out of the world, but the one who *looks* has a new life. A simple remedy—look and live.

(i) Reason for failure.

Suppose someone said, "That is foolish to think that a person can be healed that way." If you will not look, you will not live. There are people today who say, "Christ crucified is foolishness." If they will not look, they must die. Sin will not argue; the poison will not argue. Sin kills.

(j) One class could not be healed.

There was one class of people to whom the uplifted serpent was useless. They were those already dead.

3. The Two birds.

This is a double type, and had to do with the cleansing of the leper—Lev. 13 and 14:1-7. These two birds are typical of the death and resurrection of Christ, and speak to us in a beautiful way of our salvation through His work.

(a) A leper is typical of a sinner. Leprosy is one of the great types of sin in the Bible.

We have in this thirteenth chapter the thought of leprosy in its beginning. The beginning may be in a very small spot, but it works on and on until finally it touches the whole body of a man. That is the way sin works. The man with just one little sin in his life reveals the fact that he is a sinner just as truly as if he committed ten thousand sins. One little white lie reveals sin just as truly as the committing of a terrible crime.

(b) The leper was a man condemned by the law.

It was God's command. The sinner is condemned by the law also. There is not a person who has not failed to break—not only one—but all of the commandments in the spirit of the law. Man is condemned by the Law.

(c) When a leper was discovered, he was separated from the people of God, and from the house of God. He was cut off from man and from God; his was a living death.

(d) The leper's hope was God. The sinner's hope is God. The leper was considered by Israel to be judicially dead.

The sinner is judicially dead in trespasses and sins; he is without life. Apart from Christ there is no physical life, no spiritual life, no judicial life, and no eternal life.

(e) The cleansing of the leper.

(1) Choosing the sacrifice.

The priest goes out to where the leper is—the leper can't come in; so Christ came to the sinner. The priest led the man to living or running water. He must take two birds, and in the taking of the two birds you have the type—the two birds.

(2) Two birds represent the two natures of Christ.

He was both man and God; both of the earth and of Heaven. The birds were to be clean. One of the birds was to be killed outside the camp. That was where the Lord Jesus was killed. The bird must be slain before the leper was cleansed, and the bird was slain by the command of God. It was in obedience to the Word of God that Christ went to the cross.

The bird was slain in an earthen vessel. God took on humanity for the purpose of death, that He might die for us.

The bird was slain over running water, or rather "living" water, fresh from a running stream. So the bird was killed over an earthen vessel, or in an earthen vessel, in which was living water. There were two streams which met, blood and water—just as John saw the blood and water coming from the side of Christ. Water in the Scripture is typical of two things: the Spirit of God, and the Word of God. The Word of God is living and pure, and the Spirit of God is living and pure.

After the first bird has been slain, the living bird is taken and dipped into the blood of the dead bird. The living bird dipped into the blood of the dead bird, was marked with the stains of death. That is typical of resurrection. It is the living bird that bears the marks of death.

The Lord came from the tomb bearing the marks of the death of the cross.

That living bird with the marks of death, was taken out into the open field and set free to fly up into the heaven. So when the Lord broke the bands of death, He was free. Out in the field when the living bird was set free, it ascended into heaven, and so did Christ.

(3) The cleansing of the leper.

The blood of the slain bird was sprinkled on the leper seven times. It was applied with hyssop, a weed that typifies faith.

After sprinkling, the leper is pronounced clean and has a living witness to the fact that he is clean. After an application of Christ's blood the sinner is clean. The leper then took his place in the camp of Israel. He was like one coming back from the dead. Our salvation is life from the dead.

4. The Red Heifer—Numbers 19.

(a) Every Old Testament sacrifice is typical.

This is proven typical in Heb. 9:13, 14. It is typical of the person and work of Christ. It is only found in Numbers, but is given as a perpetual statute—Num. 19:21.

(b) The sacrifice.

It was to be a red heifer without spot or blemish, which had never worn a yoke. It was delivered to Eleazar outside the camp. One slew it and the blood was sprinkled seven times toward the tabernacle. Then it was burned and the ashes were used, mixed with water, to purify the defiled.

Numbers 19:11-16—Defilement came by touching the body or bones or grave of a dead body. The body, bones and grave represent the things of death, and death represents sin ("the wages of sin is death").

Sin spreads defilement. This sacrifice is to maintain fellowship with God, rather than to obtain salvation. They had salvation. They had been brought out from Egypt and saved from the Red Sea, yet defilement separated them from God. Whether the act was intentional or not, the defilement separated them from God.

5. Jacob's ladder—Gen. 28.

(a) The word "ladder" really means stairway.

(b) Jacob is in the land of Luz. He is fleeing because of his fear of Esau and because of his trickery in getting the blessing.

(c) He saw a stairway and angels ascending and descending. There is no other ladder in scripture.

(d) Typical character explained in John 1:45-51.

(e) The ladder reached to God.

This indicates the future of Israel; she will return to the land. Jacob is a picture of the nation. They were promised blessing in the land. Jacob is Israel in the past.

(f) Christ is the anti-type.

(1) He is the ladder by which God came down to man. God was on earth 1900 years ago in Christ. If there is no Virgin Birth, then God didn't come down. If He had a human father there was sin in Him and He needed to be born again, and there was no Saviour.

(2) He is the ladder by which man went up to God.

Christ is a man in heaven. He is in heaven as a man, high priest, intercessor and advocate. The incarnation is perpetual.

(3) It indicates the greatness of the separation between God and man.

Man is here with his head on a stone and God is in heaven.

The two are separated by sin. Christ is a white rose in a bed of scarlet poppies.

(4) The ladder indicates a mediator, even as Christ is a Mediator.

A mediator must be the friend of both man and God.

(5) The ladder indicates salvation—"I am the way" (I am the ladder). He is the way from man's sin to God's glory, from the wrath of God to the love of God.

(g) Jesus could love you from Heaven, but He couldn't save you from there. The ladder touched earth and Heaven. It was set up first on earth—Virgin Birth; and then it touched Heaven—ascension. We can never enter Heaven in any other way than through His death and resurrection. How do we get up? We mount by faith. Jacob's experience at the foot of the ladder was the same as that of many at the cross. "Surely the Lord was in this place and I knew it not"—V. 16.

6. Manna—Exodus 16; type in John 6:30-58.
(a) The manna itself.
    (1) The wilderness food of Israel.
    (2) Egypt is behind and Canaan before—they didn't have it in either place.
    (3) It came every morning for forty years. Sabbaths were expected.
(b) Christ is the Anti-type.
(c) Series of comparisons.
    (1) Manna came down from heaven; Christ is the bread which cometh down from Heaven.
    (2) Manna came from the first heaven by gravitation; Jesus came from the third heaven by incarnation.
    (3) Manna is miraculous and mysterious; Jesus is supernatural and mysterious.
    (4) The word Manna comes from the word meaning "What is it?" (Man-Hu) They used the same word to ask of Jesus, "Who is this?"
    (5) They didn't have to understand the manna; all they had to do was eat. All we have to do is accept Christ; we don't have to understand.
    (6) Meaning of the four descriptive words.
        Small —indicates His humiliation.
        Round—indicates His Deity—all heavenly bodies are spherical. Roundness is the symbol of eternity.
        White —indicates purity. From cradle to cross His path was unsullied.
        Sweet —indicates peace and satisfaction that comes through Him.
    (7) Manna descended in the dew; dew is typical of the Holy Spirit who brings Christ to the sinner.
    (8) We see the Gospel in the manna, though not as easily as in some types. Manna came in the night time; Jesus came in the night of sin in the world to take our place. He suffered from the injustice of man and the justice of God.
    The making of manna into bread indicates the suffering of Christ on the cross when He faced the wrath of God.
    (9) Manna had to be gathered and beaten in a mortar, indicating the bruising of Christ.
    (10) Manna was exposed to fire; Christ was exposed to the fire of God's wrath.
    (11) Manna lying on the earth was lifted up in a golden vessel and taken into the presence of the Lord—indicating the resurrection. The golden pot indicates deity.
    (12) Manna rested on the earth only a little while; the thirty-three years of Christ's life are brief in the face of eternity.
    (13) Manna came then and has never come since; Christ came once and has never come since.
    (14) We've never seen the manna, and we've never seen the Lord with the physical eye.
    (15) Manna gave physical life; the Lord brings life to body, soul and spirit.
    (16) The thought of man's appropriation is involved. Man had to go on and get the manna; so we must appropriate Christ.
    (17) Manna was a free gift of God, and it couldn't be bought; Salvation was God's free gift through Christ.
    (18) Manna was provided for all, within the reach of all, but if man didn't want it, he didn't have to take it; so, salvation is provided for all, and if man isn't saved it's because he doesn't take it.
    (19) God gave manna because He loved the children of Israel. He gave salvation and His Son because He loved us.
    (20) The children of Israel murmured: We are filled with murmurings, and complain when we should be rejoicing in Christ.

7. Jonah.
Matt. 12:40—"For as Jonah was three days and three nights in the whale's belly; so shall the Son of Man be three days and three nights in the heart of the earth."
Dr. John R. Sampey says: "Our Lord referred on two different occasions to the sign of Jonah the prophet (Matt. 12:38-41; Luke 11:29-32; Matt. 16.4). He speaks of Jonah's experience in the belly of the fish as parallel with His own approaching entombment for three days, and cites the repentance of the Ninevites as a rebuke to the unbelieving men of His own generation. Our Lord thus speaks, both of the physical miracle of the preservation of Jonah in the body of the fish, and of the moral miracle of repentance of the Ninevites, and without the slightest hint that he regarded the story as an allegory." J. Kennedy well says that if the narrative were an allegory, "the man who wrote it was guilty of a gratuitous insult to the memory of a prophet, and could not have been inspired by the prophet's Master thus to dishonor a faithful servant."

(a) Jonah was sent upon a mission—Jonah 1:2. Christ was sent upon a mission—Matt. 1:21. Jonah was to preach to the Ninevites, condemning the great city for its wickedness. His message was repentance. The mission of our Lord was to save the lost. He came to seek and save the lost. We never sought Him—He sought us. He came not merely to preach a gospel but that there might be a gospel to preach—the message of death and resurrection, the two aspects of His saving work.

(b) Jonah voluntarily gave himself up—Jonah 1:9, 10, 12; 2:2, 3. Christ voluntarily gave Himself up —Matt. 26:50; II Cor. 5:21.

The men on board knew that Jonah had fled from the Lord and rebuked him for it. Jonah offered himself that the others might be saved.

Christ voluntarily gave Himself to save a lost world. Compare Jonah 2:2, 3 with Psalm 88:6, 7. God's wrath was poured out upon His Son who was obedient unto death, even the death of the cross. His life was laid down. No one could take it from Him. He who knew no sin was willing to be our substitute. Jonah deserved death because of disobedience—his own sins. Our Lord was delivered for OUR offenses. He received what *we* deserved.

(c) Jonah was preserved—Jonah 2:7. Christ too was preserved in a miraculous way—Matt. 12:40.

For three days and nights, Jonah was preserved in the belly of the great fish. Our Lord had reference to this in Matt. 12:40 and Luke 24:6, 7. The prepared fish could not hold and digest Jonah. Nor could the grave hold the Giver of eternal life. The VICTIM on the cross became the VICTOR in the resurrection.

Jonah was raised in order that he might proclaim a saving message. Christ was miraculously resurrected that we might preach the gospel story; for Christ on the cross will not save. We preach *not* a dead Christ, but a living Saviour. If Christ be not raised from the dead, our preaching and faith are vain.

(d) Jonah, a Jew, brought good tidings to the Gentiles—Jonah 1:9; 3:4, 10. Christ, a Jew, brought salvation to the Gentiles—Luke 2:32. Acts 9:15.

It was through Abraham's seed that all of the families of the earth were to be blessed. We must never forget that we are indebted to the Jews for the Scriptures; and that because of a Jew, we have been offered salvation. Jonah, as Peter, was a patriot and neither could understand why any Gentile should be included in salvation. Peter had to be rebuked by the words ,"What God hath cleansed, that call not thou common" Acts 10:15.

8. The Cities of Refuge—Num. 35; Josh. 20:1-6.

We cannot help believing that the writer of Hebrews has reference to the cities of refuge in chapter 6, verse 18, "Who have fled for refuge to lay hold upon the hope set before us." Isaiah said, "We have a strong city; salvation will God appoint for walls and bulwarks." The Psalmist said, "God is our refuge and strength, a very present help in trouble."

(a) The cities of refuge were easily accessible. The description of the cities of refuge (three on each side of the Jordan) is clearly given in Numbers 35. Any one could be reached in one day from any part of the country. They were not in the valleys but on the hills, visible to all. Our Lord was lifted upon the cross as the sinner's substitute. A look at the Saviour Who is near now, will save anyone who is willing to trust.

The gates of each city were always open. This is the day of grace and mercy for the sinner. The call is, "whosoever will," as the gates of mercy stand wide open.

(b) The cities were appointed and selected long before they came into use. They were appointed in the wilderness before the land of promise was reached.

God promised a Saviour, in His Son, Jesus Christ. When man sinned, God promised a Saviour— Gen. 3:15. But provision had been made before this—I Pet. 1:20; Rev. 13:8. When the proper time came, God was ready. He is always on time—Gal. 4:4, 5.

(c) The cities provided safety. The innocent man was kept within the walls until the high priest died. Then he was free to return to his loved ones. Death can never claim our High Priest. The redeemed in Christ are safe forever. There is no condemnation to those in Christ Jesus. The priesthood of the Old Testament was only temporary. Our Lord's priesthood is perpetual. To become a living Priest or Intercessor for us, He must taste of death—Heb. 9:16, 17.

(d) The refuge was sufficient and perfect as seen in the meaning of the names.

(1) Kadesh—"sanctuary," or "righteousness." Christ is our righteousness. We exchanged our filthy rags for His robe of righteousness. God's righteousness is that righteousness which His righteousness requires Him to require. There was nothing in us that He could require, but Christ is made unto us righteousness.

(2) Shechem—"shoulder." This speaks of strength and the place of burden. The high priest carried upon each shoulder the six names of the tribes of Israel when entering the Holy of Holies. It is the place where the shepherd carries the lost sheep which has been found. Christ is our perfect burden-bearer. The arm that upholds the universe will uphold the weakest blood-bought saint.

(3) Hebron—"fellowship." This is typical of the fellowship which is restored in and through Christ after the break in the garden of Eden. Our Lord came to be friendless that we might have a friend.

(4) Bezer—"fortress." Christ is our Fortress. We are secure and safe in Him. Satan is mighty but our Saviour is Almighty.

(5) Ramoth—"exaltation." Christ became lower than angels, even as a worm (so says the Psalmist), that He might be exalted and lift us above the angels. Our mediator is now seated at the right hand of His Father.

(6) Golan—"joy." He is our exceeding joy. "In his presence is fulness of joy."
Truly, after summing up these cities and their meanings, we discover that our Lord is sufficient. He is the El Shaddai—the Almighty God—the God Who is ENOUGH.

9. Solomon contrasted with Christ (Antithesis).

"A greater than Solomon is here"—Matt. 12:42.

Who was Solomon? In some respects he was the greatest of the Kings of Israel. He was the first of Israel's monarchs that sought to go beyond the boundaries of the land of promise and cultivate the friendship of other nations.

SOLOMON'S ADMINISTRATION—He reigned over all kingdoms, from the river Euphrates unto the land of the Philistines, and unto the border of Egypt.

SOLOMON'S ACCUMULATION—His provision for one day was 300 bushels of fine flour and 600 bushels of meal, 10 fat oxen, 20 oxen from the pastures, 100 sheep, 40,000 stalls for horses and 12,000 horsemen.

SOLOMON'S EDUCATION—His understanding excelled the wisdom of all the children of the east country, and all the wisdom of Egypt. He was wiser than all men. The Queen of Sheba came from afar to prove him. Solomon satisfied her with his answers, and she was overcome with his greatness. In appreciation she gave him—"one hundred and twenty talents of gold, and of spices very great store, and precious stones."

SOLOMON'S VERSIFICATION—He spoke three thousand proverbs and his songs were a thousand and five. People came from far and near to hear the wisdom of Solomon.

YET—He possessed no satisfaction. Listen to him as he reasons about life: "Vanity and vexation of Spirit . . . I hated life."

AND—His heart was turned from the Lord. He married many strange women with the result that he had to please them and permit them to worship their false gods. Solomon was just another creature who declined after the eyes of the world had been focused upon him as Public Figure number One.

SO—Christ warns us, concerning Solomon. His glory was artificial. It couldn't even be compared to the meanest flower. "Solomon in all his glory was not so well arrayed."

BUT—Speaking of Himself, Jesus declares in Matthew 12:42—"A greater than Solomon is here."

Solomon allied himself to paganism for political advantage; Christ allied Himself to the world for the sinner's advantage.

Solomon's heart was hardened because he loved luxury; Christ's heart was melted because He loved the sinner.

Solomon came into the world, destined to be rich; Christ came into the world, destined to be poor.

Solomon heard the voice of admiration; Christ heard the voice of accusation.

Solomon made a maxim and disobeyed it; God made a law and Christ obeyed it.

Solomon came into the world to be a pleasure-seeker; Christ came into the world to be a soul-seeker.

Solomon expected respect and honor; Christ accepted disrespect and dishonor.

With the coming of Solomon, a new world of thought was to be opened to the Israelites. With the coming of Christ, a new experience of salvation was to be offered to the world.

A change came into the nation through the world which Solomon opened.

A change came into men's hearts through the abundant grace which Christ offered.

Solomon was tempted by the wicked and fell; Christ was tempted by the adversary and overcame.

Solomon offered the sacrifice of animals for his sins; Christ offered the sacrifice of Himself for our sins.

Solomon stood surrounded demanding National Defense; Christ stood alone experiencing National Offense.

Adam, by one offense, became guilty and transmitted his guilt to mankind. Adam's sin is our heritage. We cannot be a pedagogue and lecture to our first father. When we speak of him, we speak of ourselves. We are heirs to all the sin his fall produced.

10. Melchizedek—Psalm 110:4.

(a) Mentioned in 3 portions: Mosaic—Gen. 14:17-24; Davidic—Psa. 110; Pauline—Heb. 5-8.
Described as: King of Salem—King of Righteousness—Priest of the Most High God ("Melchi"—King; "Zedek"—Righteousness).
Christ and Melchizedek are the only two who have filled the two offices of King and Priest.

(b) Heb. 7:4—declares He is a man.
Heb. 7:3—some say this is positive proof that this man must be Jesus Christ. "Without father or mother." Because of these words they thought he must be Jesus. But Jesus had a mother.

(c) Melchizedek was a priest by the decree of God. He was without father and mother because they weren't in the priestly line. A priest was a priest by right of birth. He is the only priest in this order. Things that are true of Melchizedek are true of Jesus. He had no father or mother in the priestly line; no descendants.

(d) Melchizedek was the only one in history who combined the offices of priest and king. Christ was the only One in prophecy Who combined the two offices—Zech. 6:9-14; Jer. 23:5; Zech. 3:8; Isa. 4:2.

(e) Christ's priesthood is not after the order of Aaron, but after the manner of Aaron. He has taken us from the pit; out of darkness into light. He will never be interrupted by death as were the Levitical priests.

(f) Melchizedek is king of righteousness and king of peace. The Lord Jesus Christ is our Righteousness and our Peace. We will never know peace on earth till He comes to reign.

(g) Abraham was met by the two kings of Sodom and Salem (world and God). His testing came at the very hour of victory. When we stand we should take special heed lest we fall.

(h) Melchizedek blessed God. He was a mediator between Abraham and God.

(i) Melchizedek blessed Abraham. This is characteristic of Christ blessing us. He blesses with outstretched hand over His own.

(j) Abraham gave tithes to Melchizedek. He refused wealth from one and gave tithes to another.

11. Feasts of the Lord (Holy Festivals) Lev. 23:

(a) General information.
   (1) They are: Passover, Unleavened Bread, Firstfruits, Pentecost, Trumpets, Day of Atonement and Tabernacle.
   (2) There are: three in the first month, one in the third, and three in the seventh.
   (3) Jehovah is the Host and the people are the guests.
   (4) A change made when the passover was instituted.
      ((a)) First passover celebrated in the seventh month.
      ((b)) God remade the calendar and made the seventh month the first month of the year.
   (5) They are religious feasts.
      ((a)) They are set feasts in that they occurred at an appointed time.
      ((b)) They were instituted after the Israelites came out of Egypt and while they were in the wilderness.
   (6) Calendar of feasts:

1ST MONTH	14th Day	15th Day 7 Days	After Sabbath	2ND MONTH	3RD MONTH	50 Days After	4TH MONTH	5TH MONTH	6TH MONTH	7TH MONTH	1st Day	10th Day	15th Day
	Passover	Unleavened Bread	Firstfruits			Pentecost or Weeks					Trumpets	Atonement	Tabernacles

   (7) There are three outstanding feasts: Passover, Pentecost and Tabernacles. Tabernacles was a great time of rejoicing.
   (8) The Jews measured time as follows: the first month had 29 days, the second had 30, the third 29, the fourth 30, etc. To make up the necessary time they added a month every third year.

(b) Passover.
   (1) Lev. 23:4,5. I Cor. 5:7—Christ our Passover.
   (2) First given in Egypt. Exodus 12 shows the type.
   (3) Throughout the Word no one is called the Lamb save Jesus Christ. Always mentioned in the singular because God had in mind one Lamb.
   (4) Condition of the people—were enslaved, under a taskmaster. They cried out and the Lord heard. They were sinners. Here is a picture of the unsaved man—a slave. Rom. 6:16—slaves unto death. Before slaves can be freed, the problem of sin has to be settled. God said, "I am come down to deliver." That's grace—to deliver the sinner. 1900 years ago, Christ, the same "I am," came down to deliver us—grace!
   (5) This is the way in which He delivered:

((a)) He put the sentence of death on all first-born, man and beast. First-born is a symbol of man in Adam.

((b)) Before deliverance can take place the sin question must be settled.

((c)) Death sentence on all, declared there is no difference in relation to sin. Yet there was a difference—the difference of a lamb. There is always that difference (a lamb) between the saved and unsaved. Cain and Abel; Publican and Pharisees; two malefactors in Luke.

((d)) Qualifications of the Lamb:

((1)) Lamb never too little for the household.

((2)) Lamb must be perfect.

((3)) The person of Christ must be represented by a male.

((4)) Must be a first-born.

((5)) Must be slain.

((6)) Lamb must be roasted with fire.

((7)) Lamb to be eaten—not raw nor sodden with water—nothing done to stop action of fire. Typical of our Lord's suffering.

((e)) There must be an application of blood for salvation and so with the appropriation of Christ.

((1)) Blood placed on the door to save from judgment.

((2)) Death in every home. In the home of the Egyptian, the death of the first-born child. In the home of the Israelite it was the lamb.

((3)) Lamb meant absolute safety.

((4)) Judgment came at midnight. Lamb was slain at three. Any time between those hours the blood could be sprinkled, but at midnight it was too late.

(c) Feast of Unleavened Bread—Lev. 23:6-8.

(1) Feast.

((a)) Immediately after the Passover—Lev. 23:6-8; Exodus 12. Lasted seven days.

((b)) Seven days speaks of a complete cycle.

((c)) Limitations.

((1)) Only the Jews (born ones and bought ones) could eat this feast.

((2)) Only those born of God and bought by God can live pleasing to Him.

(d) Feast of the Firstfruits—Lev. 23:9-14.

(1) Time.

((a)) While the Feast of Unleavened Bread was in progress.

((b)) Always on the first day of the week.

(2) Conditions.

((a)) Could not be observed until Israel was in the land.

((b)) Had to come into the land and reap the harvest.

((c)) Had to pass through the wilderness before they could reap the firstfruits.

(3) The Feast.

((a)) Sheaf—they were to reap and take a sheaf (the first taken out of the field).

((b)) This was to be presented to God.

((c)) It was to be waved (to and fro) before Jehovah.

((d)) The sheaf was a sample and pledge of the coming promise.

((1)) The Jew pledged to God one-tenth of the harvest.

((2)) God pledged to the Jew the rest of the harvest.

(4) Application.

((a)) I Cor. 15—Christ the firstfruits.

((b)) Christ is the first great sheaf of the resurrection and the others are to follow.

((c)) It has reference to the resurrection.

(e) Feast of Weeks or Pentecost—Deut. 16:10-16; Lev. 23:15-22.

(1) Seven weeks between the time of firstfruits and Pentecost.

(2) Typical significance:

((a)) Passover—death of Christ.

((b)) Firstfruits—resurrection—God holds to the first day of the week. First day is the day of resurrection.

((c)) Weeks—fulfillment of the descent of the Holy Spirit, to form the church.

(3) Feast.

((a)) Two loaves baked with leaven.

((b)) In the harvest they were not to glean the corners.

(4) Application.

((a)) This has reference to the people. Two loaves because the Jew and Gentile are blessed and brought into union in Christ, through the descent of the Holy Spirit.

((b)) In the harvest there is blessing not for the Jew only. They were to leave the corners and gleanings for the poor and strangers.

So the blessing of Pentecost—the Holy Spirit—comes to the Jew, Samaritans and Gentiles.

((c)) Two things happened on the day of Pentecost.
((1)) Men were baptized with the Spirit. This is not mentioned in Acts 2, but prophesied five times. I Cor. 12:13 shows the purpose of baptism—to unite into one Church.
((2)) Men were filled also for service. The Spirit is not measured, but the gifts. "He giveth not the Spirit by measure."
((d)) The Spirit came because it was fifty days after the resurrection.
((e)) There is no feast from Pentecost to Trumpets. This indicates the interval of the present dispensation. The first four feasts look back; the last three look forward.

(f) Feast of Trumpets—Lev. 23:23-25.
(1) Feast was on the first day of the seventh month.
((a)) Israel was ordered about by trumpets. A trumpet called them to war and worship; a trumpet ushered in the year of Jubilee (year of liberation and restoration).
((b)) Trumpets represented the voice of God to Israel.
((c)) Trumpets were made of silver. Silver is the type of redemption.
(2) Typical.
((a)) It looks forward to the regathering of Israel.
((b)) It refers to the Messiah's coming—Matt. 24:30,31; Isa. 11:11; Isa. 27:12,13; Amos 9:15; Ezek. 37 (Valley of dry bones—national restoration).
(3) Application—to the Church.
We too are to be gathered together with Him—I Thess. 4:16. The trump shall sound and call us—I Cor. 15:51,52.

(g) Day of Atonement. Tenth day of the month—Lev. 23:26-32.
(1) Feast.
((a)) Leviticus 16 gives the ritual. Lev. 23 gives the day in connection with the set feast.
((b)) The whole service is in atonement—separation and expiation for sin in the highest and fullest sense possible in those days. For *all* the iniquities, *all* the transgressions, and *all* the sins of Israel.
((c)) Shows the holiness of God and the sinfulness of man. Man must not penetrate the veil without the blood of sacrifice.
(2) Application.
((a)) It is a real labor day.
((1)) The High Priest did all the work, no one helped him.
((2)) When Christ came no one helped Him; no one could—not even the Father in heaven.
((3)) No one can share in the service but we share in the results.
((b)) Aaron laid aside the garments of beauty and glory, and put on plain linen garments. He didn't wear his high priestly robes. After he had finished he put back on the garments of glory. It speaks of the Lord. When He came to earth He put aside the robes of glory and put on the white robes of sinless humanity until after the cross.
(3) Contrasts.
((a)) Cleansing.
((1)) On the day of Atonement Aaron had to cleanse himself—complete washing expresses the thought that the High Priest who does the work must be pure and clean.
((2)) Christ needed no cleansing.
((b)) Sacrifice.
((1)) Aaron must offer a sacrifice for himself; he was a sinner and needed atonement. God couldn't have found a better man than Aaron, and yet he needed atonement —taken from among men.
((2)) Christ did not offer a sacrifice for Himself. If that had been necessary He never could have been sacrificed for others.
((c)) Number of sacrifices.
((1)) Aaron offered sacrifices.
((2)) Christ offered one sacrifice, once for all.
(4) Ritual of two goats—Lev. 16.
((a)) Represent Christ in death and life, or death and resurrection.
((b)) This ritual is peculiar to Israel.
((c)) Both goats presented to the Lord. A bullock is offered as a sin offering and then one goat is killed as a sin offering and the blood is carried to the mercy-seat. On the cross Christ settled the question of sin and sins.

((1)) The first goat was killed for the people; his blood was shed for the people, for atonement. So Christ shed His blood for our sins.
((2)) The second goat was not killed; the priest laid his hands on the head of the goat and confessed the sins of Israel and the goat was led out into the wilderness.
"Behold the Lamb of God which taketh away the sins of the world."
Remission means bear away. The second goat was sent away in liberty to the land of forgetfulness.
((d)) Speaks of future cleansing for Israel.
(h) Feast of Tabernacles. Fifteenth day of the seventh month—Lev. 23: 33-43.
(1) The feast.
((a)) Was a kind of harvest home celebration—thanksgiving to God for His goodness.
((b)) Came at the end of the harvest season.
((c)) Lasted seven days.
((d)) It is the last great feast of the year.
(2) Application.
((a)) Points to the millennial days and even to the golden age that will follow—Zech. 14:16, 17.
((b)) Israel is cleansed for her Messiah.
((c)) People will dwell out in the open.
((d)) It looks to eternity—Eph. 1:18.

12. Tabernacle in the Wilderness.

(a) General.
(1) Exodus 25:1, 8—"a sanctuary that I may dwell among them"—John 1: 1, 14. "Dwelt" means tabernacled.

(2) Tabernacle Old Testament.　　　　　　　　Tabernacle New Testament.
　　Where God dwelt.　　　　　　　　　　　　Where God dwelt.
　　Made of gold and silver and linen.　　　　 Made of flesh and blood.

(b) Plan of tabernacle. Court is made of a fence of pure white, fine-twined linen.

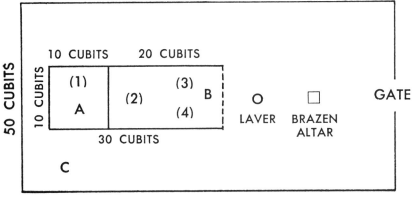

A. HOLY OF HOLIES

B. HOLY PLACE

C. OUTER COURT

1. ARK OF COVENANT

2. ALTAR OF INCENSE

3. TABLE OF SHEWBREAD

4. CANDLESTICK

(1) Called a tent, though it really refers to the outer covering. Tent suggests moving or pilgrimage.
(2) Names:
((a)) Tabernacle—Gives the thought of settling down.
((b)) Sanctuary—Exodus 25:8—in the sense of sanctified or separated place—a holy place.
((c)) Tabernacle of the congregation—Exodus 29:42-44. Place where the congregation of Israel met God.
((d)) Tabernacle of testimony—Num. 1:50-53. Where the testimony of God or the law was kept. It was a witness of God's holiness.
((e)) Jehovah's pavilion—Psa. 27:5. Where God's people come in time of trouble.
((f)) Jehovah's palace.
((g)) The place where the Lord dwells between the cherubim—Psalms 80:1; 89:1.
((h)) House of the Lord—Psa. 27:4—place of fellowship.
(c) Pattern of the tabernacle—Heb. 8:2, 5; 9:24; Exodus 25:9.
(1) Apparently after a model given to Moses.
(2) The reality of the tabernacle is in heaven. This is a shadow.
(d) Purpose of the tabernacle—Ex. 25:8, 22; 29:45, 46.
(1) "That I may dwell among them." God wants a sanctuary that He may dwell among men.

(2) God desires to be in fellowship with man, but sin came between—as sin always puts one **far** away from God.

(e) Prophecy of the tabernacle.
    (1) Was a prophecy of the Incarnation when God would take a tabernacle of flesh to dwell **among** men—John 1:14.
    (2) God is the actor—Heb. 2:14, 16. Man is excluded and has nothing to do with it. Fulness of the Godhead is in Christ. The living Word reveals the invisible thoughts of God. Jesus is **God** manifest in the flesh.
    (3) Messages:
        ((a)) The message of the builders—Ex. 31:2-6; 35:30-35. Men who were Spirit-filled. In order to be workers today we need men divinely endued. God Himself is the Architect and Moses was the overseer. The people were the real workers and the work was approved by God.
        ((b)) Four colors:
            Blue—color of heaven—Son of God.
            Purple—color of royalty—Christ, the Messiah.
            Scarlet—blood color. The Lamb, Who was a sacrifice for sin.
            Linen curtain speaks of Him Who is the only righteous Man.
        ((c)) Veil was to be embroidered with cherubim.
            ((1)) In the Holy of Holies we have the mercy-seat and over it the cherubim.
            ((2)) Speaks of the presence of God—always connected with the throne of God.
            ((3)) They could not look upon the golden cherubim in the Holy of Holies, but they could look on the image on the curtain. Christ is the image of the Father.
        ((d)) Veil had man on one side and God on the other. Artificial light on one side and **the** Shekinah glory on the other.
        ((e)) Purpose: it shall divide—Ex. 26:33.
            ((1)) Did not permit access to God; it prevented access to God.
            ((2)) Not saved because Christ lived. His life would keep us from God forever. We are saved because He *died*.
            ((3)) It tells us that the only kind of humanity that can stand in the presence of God is the sinless humanity of the Son of God.
            ((4)) The veil barred man out, but there's a way in. We can't praise, pray, work or buy our way in. The only way is substitutionary sacrifice and blood in the basin. The blood sprinkled on the veil and then the high priest enters. No man ever went in except by blood.
        ((f)) Matt. 27:50, 51.
            ((1)) Veil speaks of incarnation.
            ((2)) Rending speaks of death.
            ((3)) Completely and supernaturally done.
                From top to bottom—God rent it.
                Tradition says two teams of oxen couldn't rend it. It was rent from above.
            ((4)) Completely rent from top to bottom makes us think of the words, "It is finished." Man doesn't have to do anything but believe.
            ((5)) Told of the end of the old ritualism.
                The Shekinah Glory hidden for centuries by the veil, is now open to everyone. **We** enter by faith.
                We have the Holy of Holies in heaven. Christ is there and we go there by faith— through the blood.
                While He lived, His perfect life was a barrier to our ever entering in unless **He** died.
                We enter by His sacrifice.

(4) White fence around the tabernacle.
        ((a)) Directions.
            ((1)) 100 cubits x 50 cubits.
            ((2)) Open to the sky—no roof.
            ((3)) Linen wall hung on 60 pillars of brass. 20 on each side. 10 on each end.
            ((4)) Pillars rested on brass sockets and were connected with silver rods.
                Each socket weighed about 100 pounds.
                Fillet—means connecting rod.
            ((5)) Secured by cords of linen and tent pegs.
            ((6)) Tops of the pillars were overlaid with a silver ornament.
            ((7)) Curtains were hung to the pillars with little hooks of silver.
            ((8)) The gate was twenty cubits wide and hung on four pillars.

((b)) Typical significance.
((1)) Linen means Righteous One—Jesus.
The perfection of Christ shuts men out. God accepts only perfect righteousness. Gives the idea of mediation. The wall is between sinful man and a holy God— Rom. 1:18. So Christ is both human and divine.
God is law as well as love—He is not lawless and can't permit His love to violate His law. The requirements of a mediator are judgment and redemption.
((2)) Brass always a symbol of judgment.
((3)) Silver is always the symbol of redemption.
((4)) Pure linen hung on the pillars of brass and was set in sockets of brass, but was held together with rods of silver hooks.
The brass of judgment and the silver of redemption.
((5)) He could have come down from the cross but He wouldn't have saved us if He *had*. He *wouldn't* come down—*not* couldn't.
Our redemption held Him there (silver hooks of redemption held the linen to the brass).
((6)) He takes the white linen of His righteousness and wraps it around us— I Cor. 1:30.
((7)) The ornaments on top were for beauty. They speak of the beauty of the Lord. He is the fairest of ten thousand.
((8)) Silver over brass. Redemption over judgment.

(5) Framework of the Tabernacle—Ex. 26:15-30.
((a)) General directions.
((1)) 10 x 30 cubits. Tabernacle proper.
((2)) Made of shittim wood overlaid with gold, standing on a foundation of silver.
((3)) 48 boards—20, 20, 6, 2.
((4)) Two sockets of silver under each board for a firm foundation. 100 in all. Four sockets under veil pillars.
((5)) Held by bars covered with gold. Five bars on each side.
((b)) Typical significance.
((1)) Shittim wood.
Resists the effects of weather and attacks of insects.
It is called "incorruptible wood"—symbol of Christ's humanity.
Desert wood. The only wood available. Christ is a root out of dry ground.
Prepared boards — prepared humanity.
Incorruptibility. No salvation through His life, but through His death. He is unique—sinless perfection. He was not *liable* to death, but *capable* of death.
((2)) Wood overlaid with gold.
Gold—deity.
Wood—humanity.
((3)) Dual nature.
Two materials—equal one board.
Two natures equal one body—a mystery but also a divine fact.
((4)) The boards were to stand up in silver. Silver speaks of redemption—Ex. 30:11-16 —given at the time of numbering.
((5)) Everyone had to give the same amount—one half shekel. The same standard of redemption for all and salvation is individual. God is no respecter of persons— Acts 20:28; Heb. 2:9; Jn. 10:11, 18.
((6)) Boards had been cut off from the trees. He was cut off from men and even from God in His last hour.
((7)) The two boards are typical of two truths; Christ died. Christ arose.
((8)) The bars held the boards together. There is no length given. They were wood overlaid with gold. They were held to the boards by rings of gold. The whole tabernacle was held by bars.
Col. 1:17—The five bars on each side equal the grace of God in giving His Son.

(6) Coverings.
((a)) General directions.
There are four in number.
First—curtain of fine-twined linen, scarlet, purple, blue, and cherubim embroidered.
Second—goat's hair.
Third—ram's skin dyed red.
Fourth—badger or seal skin.
((b)) Curtain of linen—Ex. 26:1-6.
((1)) Directions. Made up of ten curtains sewed into two breadths of five each. 40

cubits x 28 cubits. 30 cubits over the top and 10 down the back. 2 curtains were linked with 100 loops of blue and 50 hooks of gold.

((2)) Typical significance.

Linen — righteousness. Of pure white, the finest piece of material ever woven from flax. Christ is the finest personality Who ever walked the earth. Colors all came from the death of animal life.

The same is true in the veil. Scarlet from the cochineal bug; blue and purple from shellfish.

40 cubits long speaks of the testing of Christ.

((c)) Curtain of goat's hair—Ex. 26:7-13.

((1)) General directions.

Six in one and five in the other. 100 loops and 50 taches of brass. The eleventh curtain hung down in front.

It is made from goat's hair and scripture teaches goats are black—Song of Solomon 6:5. Tents of the Arabs today are black, and made of goat's hair according Atchinak of Palestine.

((2)) Typical significance.

Black is the color of sin and comes from the goat—type of sin.

11—equals sin; goat—equals sin; black—equals sin.

We have enacted in the erection of the tabernacle—the Gospel.

White curtain—Christ.

Black curtain—sin.

The black on the white—our sins on Christ—"Laid on Him the iniquity of us all."

He died for all our sins—past, present, future.

((d)) Curtains of ram's skins dyed red—Ex. 26:14.

((1)) General directions—Exodus 26:14.

((2)) Typical significance.

The black of our sins brought about His sacrifice.

The ram is the sacrificial animal used at the consecration of Aaron and his sons. It speaks of dedication—"I have come to do thy will." It was used as the substitute for Isaac.

It means His consecration to the Father's business led Him to the cross.

Skin—not hair—the sacrifice of the life of the animal.

((e)) Badger skin or sealskin—Ex. 26:14.

((1)) General directions.

Dull blue, gray, or dark brown. Not very pleasing to the eye. No form given. No definite measurements.

((2)) Typical significance.

"He hath no form nor comeliness."

People outside could only see the outer covering.

To see the linen you had to be inside.

The world sees only His humanity not His deity—"He was in the world and the world was made by Him and the world knew Him not." The world only sees Him as a man, an outcast, homeless, and a wanderer.

From inside one sees purple, scarlet, blue, gold and silver. Get in Christ and see His beauty.

(7) Brazen altar.

((a)) General directions.

5 x 5 x 3 cubits. Made of brass and wood. Four horns. Half way down a network of brass is put in where the sacrifice is made. All utensils are made of brass.

((b)) Typical significance.

((1)) Typical of Christ on the Cross. The thought is judgment.

((2)) Why use wood in an altar on which fire is burning continually?

It shows wood charred and marred for us.

The charred wood of the altar speaks of charred humanity of Christ as the fire of God's wrath flowed over Him.

The altar spoke of judgment and the wood of sacrifice.

((3)) The altar is the largest article in the tabernacle.

Some say others could be put into it. Everything in the tabernacle is based on the work of Christ.

((4)) The altar is at the door.

Approach to God is only by way of the altar. No Israelite could approach until he came to the altar with a victim as substitute. There is now no approach apart from the cross.

((5)) Christ is the Lamb—the slain Lamb. He is not dead but living. The cross stands at the door of heaven. No other sacrifice would avail.

((6)) Blood is poured out at the foot of the altar. "The life is in the blood." Jesus poured out His life.

((7)) Fire burned continually. It was not of man's kindling; it came from the presence of the Lord. This speaks of judgment on sin. It is typical of God's judgment which was poured out on the cross. To be in the fire is awful. To be in God's wrath is awful, and that is where Christ went for us.

((8)) Ashes dropped through the grate and were removed by a brazen shovel, and put in a brazen pot and taken outside to a clean place. Their dropping through speaks of the finished work of Christ. The whole ceremony speaks of the accepted sacrifice.

(8) The Laver.
  ((a)) General directions—Ex. 30: 17-21.
    ((1)) It stood between the altar and the tabernacle.
    ((2)) It was made of brass. The brass was supplied by the gifts of the women.
    The women gave up their mirrors. These mirrors were of brass.
    ((3)) It was like a reservoir, in that there was washing by water, rather than in water.
  ((b)) Typical significance.
    ((1)) Speaks of cleansing—Eph. 5:26; Tit. 3:5.
    ((2)) It was made of brass and this speaks of judgment. The basis of all cleansing is the death of Christ.
    ((3)) The mirrors symbolized the Word of God. Looking into the Word is looking into a mirror.
  ((c)) Two-fold message from the laver.
  Regeneration.
  Sanctification.
  We have to come to the laver for regeneration and sanctification.

(9) The candlestick—Ex. 25:31-40.
  ((a)) General directions.
  It was beaten out of a talent of pure gold. Valued at $25,000 to $30,000.
  It had a base and a central stem. There were three stems on each side, a total of seven stems.
  These branches were ornamented with buds and blossoms and almonds. It was a little almond tree.
  It is a lampstand, not a candlestick. There were vessels on the ends of the branches with oil and a wick in each. Olive oil was used.
  ((b)) Typical significance.
    ((1)) Person of the Lord.
    Gold—Deity. The divine nature is emphasized. He is the true candlestick. If He were not God there wouldn't be any light in the world—"I am the light of the world"—John 8:12.
    Number 7—His perfection. Perfection marked Him. He was perfect—the only One against Whom no charge could be made.
    ((2)) Work of the Lord.
    Oil—Holy Spirit. It gave its light because of the oil; because it was filled with oil. This speaks of the relationship between the Son and Spirit of God and His work through the Spirit.
    His death.
    His work had to do with redemption. It was a piece of hammered-work. Every blow necessary was laid upon it. Christ suffered to the full satisfaction of God, and then cried, "It is finished." There were no unnecessary blows, but every necessary one was given.
    The Roman soldiers hammered Him on the face with their fists; they hammered His back with the scourge; they hammered Him to the cross. He was not only hammered by the hands of men, but hammered by the hammer of divine righteousness without mercy—"It pleased the Lord to bruise Him"—Isa. 53:10. He became the greatest piece of hammered-work in all time.
    His resurrection.
    Almond tree (Aaron's rod—dead stick made alive).
    Almond—means wakeful and hastener. It is the first tree to waken in the spring and is the firstfruits of all the trees.
    We see the resurrection in the firstfruit.
    We have fragrance (flowers) and fruit; the only One in Whom the fruit of the Spirit was fully manifested.

((c)) Application.

We see ourselves in the candlestick. We are the wick—"Ye shine as lights." Light must come through human instruments while Christ is not here.

((1)) To give light the wick must be in the oil.

((2)) Oil must be in the wick—"If so be that the Spirit be in you."

((3)) Fire. Fire burns and turns to ashes. "None of self and all of Thee"; that's ashes.

((4)) Wick must be trimmed. There were snuffers to trim the wick. If it is not trimmed it does not give much light and is smoky. The High Priest did the trimming and so does our High Priest.

Burnt wick is taken off today which gave light yesterday.

Past experience is the burnt wick.

Past service is the burnt wick.

Past testimony is the burnt wick.

The burnt wick will not give light today. We do not give light by what we did in the past, but by what we do today. When Paul boasted of the past he said, "I am become a fool."

((5)) The burnt wick was put in a golden snuff-box.

Our service is in the golden snuff-box of God's remembrance.

(10) Table of Shewbread—Ex. 25:23-28; Lev. 24:5-9.

((a)) General directions.

It was made of acacia wood. 2 x 1 x 1½ cubits.

It was overlaid with pure gold.

It was to have on it shewbread before the Lord always.

((b)) Typical significance.

Christ—the Bread of Life.

Christ—bearing the people in the presence of God.

(11) Golden Altar of Incense.

((a)) General directions.

It stood just before the veil.

It was made of wood overlaid with gold.

It was two cubits high. So far as we know it was the tallest article in the Holy Place.

It had horns and a crown of gold around the edge.

Incense was offered every morning and night.

((b)) Typical significance.

((1)) Materials.

Gold-deity.

Wood—humanity.

Gold over wood glorified the wood. The One Who was despised and rejected is now glorified.

((2)) Height and crown—glorification and exaltation.

((3)) Horn—stands for power.

Horns were probably four in number—Heb. 7:16. They give the thought of Christ constituted Priest "after the power of an endless life." We have a connection with the blood of the sin offering for it was put on the horns of this altar.

((4)) Incense burned.

Four sweet spices in equal proportion. Speaks of the evenness and balance of His life.

The result is fragrance. It is spoken of as pure and holy—typical of purity and holiness.

It could not be made to use as perfume—the punishment was death.

Incense was typical of prayer—Psa. 141:2.

Rev. 5:8—brings the message of intercession of our Lord.

Incense went up for Israel, the people of God, and for them only. The same is true of Christ; He prays only for His own—John 17:9.

Our prayers to the Father reach the Father through Christ.

The horns were marked with blood—our intercession is based on the cross. Without the cross He could not intercede for us.

Burning of incense continually foreshadows His continual intercession for us.

(12) The Ark of the Covenant.

((a)) General directions—Ex. 25:10-22; 37:1-9.

((1)) It was the furniture for the Holy of Holies.

((2)) It was a chest of acacia wood, covered within and without with gold.

((3)) It was 2½ x 1½ x 1½ cubits.

((4)) Around the top was a border of gold. There was a ring on each corner. It was carried by staves passing through the rings.

((5)) The staves were of acacia wood covered with gold and were never removed.

((6)) The covering was the mercy-seat.

((7)) The ark was prepared for the Law, and into it went the tables of stone.

((8)) It is called the ark of the covenant and testimony because it contained the Law.

((b)) Typical significance.

((1)) Acacia is incorruptible wood—which speaks of His sinless humanity.

((2)) Gold—deity.

((3)) One ark and two materials—suggest One with two natures.

((4)) The wood gave it form; His humanity gives Him form.

((5)) All you saw of the ark was the gold. As you study the Man in His life and death, His deity is obvious.

((6)) The ark had the Law hidden in its heart. This speaks of the Son. He was born under the Law and kept it perfectly in His heart.

((7)) In the tabernacle was the only place where the Law was kept unbroken. In Israel they could not be trusted to keep the Law.

((8)) Aaron's rod speaks of resurrection of the risen and triumphant Christ. It was a prophecy of the priesthood of our Lord, and a reminder of Israel's rebellion.

((9)) Golden pot of manna. The Lord says, "I am the bread." A reminder of the murmuring in the wilderness.

((10)) It contained all Israel's chief treasures. Christ contains all our treasures.

(13) Mercy-Seat.

((a)) General directions.

It was a cover made of pure gold with a cherub at each end. Their wings met over the center. Their faces looked down.

((b)) Typical significance.

((1)) The name means "covering."

((2)) "Covering" is not an adequate translation. It is the same word as is translated "atonement." In it we have the idea of propitiation. It is called in the Septuagint —propitiatory seat.

In the ark God placed the Law. That Law man had broken and it shows what man is, for the Law is holy, just, and good. By the Law God must pronounce judgment. Anybody who looks to the Law finds death, not salvation. Law knows no distinction among men.

13. The High Priest and his garments.

(a) The High Priest.

(1) Apart from the High Priest the tabernacle would be inaccessible.
He was the mediator between God and man.

(2) Two lines of priesthood: Aaron and Melchizedek.

(3) Aaron was a type or contrast.
Aaron was a priest on earth: Christ never was a priest on earth.
Aaron ceased to be priest when he died; Christ never ceases to be priest.

(4) The work of the High Priest didn't begin until after the death of the sacrifice took place.

(5) The priesthood had to do with Israel—God's own people. All believers are in heaven in Christ. Christ is our confessor in heaven.

(6) The priesthood was in behalf of the people. Christ our Righteousness is in heaven. There is finality to His work.

(b) The garments of the High Priest.

(1) General description.
Exodus 28—They were made of purple, scarlet, fine linen, gold, and precious stones. They were holy garments for glory and beauty—God-designed.

(2) Embroidered coat, and linen breeches—Ex. 28:3, 39, 42.
There was a coat with a long skirt and fine linen breeches. The breeches were undergarments that reached from the loins to the thigh. They speak of righteousness and purity. Aaron needed cleansing. The anti-type needed none.

(3) Linen girdle.
This is not the girdle of the ephod. It was wound around the body. It is the symbol of service— Phil. 2:7; John 13:4—servant. After regeneration there is need of daily cleansing.

(4) Robes of the Ephod.

((a)) General directions.
Blue from shoulder to feet. One piece woven without seam. There was a habergeon with

two holes for arms, and one for the head. The skirt was trimmed with pomegranates and embroidered in blue, purple, and scarlet. There were pomegranates and bells on the hems.

((b)) Typical significance.

Blue—the heavenly color showing the heavenly character of His ministry.

Bells speak of the tongue, showing the perfect speech of the Son of God. The bells speak of testimony.

Pomegranates speak of fruitfulness—fruit of many seeds.

Whenever there is testimony there is fruit.

When the priest went into the Holy of Holies, the people could hear the bells and so knew he was alive. How do we know Jesus lives in heaven? Because of the bells. On the day of Pentecost, there was the fulfillment of the ringing of the bells. Bells and pomegranates are never separated. Wherever there is a testimony you find a fruitfulness of the Spirit.

(5) Ephod.
((a)) General directions.

It was an outer garment made of blue, purple, scarlet, fine-twined linen and gold.

It was woven in two pieces—one for the front and one for the back.

They were joined with gold.

There was an onyx-stone on each shoulder. On each stone were the names of six tribes of Israel.

((b)) Typical significance.

He bore all Israel on His shoulders before God. So Christ bears us before God.

The shoulder is the place of strength.

(6) Breastplate.
((a)) General directions.

It is of the same material as the ephod.

It is foursquare.

There were twelve stones for the twelve tribes, on the breast.

The High Priest bore them on his heart as well as on his shoulder.

((b)) Typical significance.

We are always in the place of affection.

(7) Mitre.

It is the head covering and shows obedience to God.

(8) Golden plate.

It was the crowning piece. It was fastened to the mitre with laces of blue. On it was "Holiness to the Lord." Our holiness is in the presence of God.

(9) Urim and Thummim.

For wisdom. God spoke to His people through these. Probably they were two precious stones carried in the pouch of the breastplate. The words are Hebrew words meaning lights and perfection.

14. The Offerings or Sacrifices—Lev. 1:5:

(a) There are five of them: Burnt, meat, peace, sin, and trespass. It takes all five to present Christ's work. The first three are sweet savour. The last two are non-sweet savour; they have to do with sin—that is, they picture Christ as the sinner's substitute.

(b) Types of sacrifices used.

There were three kinds of four-footed beasts—oxen, sheep, and goats. There also were two birds of sacrifice—turtle-doves and young pigeons.

(c) All sacrifices were either such as were offered on the ground of communion with God (Burnt and Peace), or else as were intended to restore that communion when it had been dimmed (Sin and Trespass).

(d) Discussion of each offering.

(1) The burnt offering—Lev. 1.

((a)) Entire surrender unto God whether of the individual or the congregation. Thus it could not be offered without the shedding of blood.

This portrays our Lord's perfect submission to the Father. He was obedient unto death.

((b)) The sacrifice was always a male animal—indicating strength and energy.

((c)) Blood sprinkled on altar.

((d)) Animal cut in pieces and wholly burned.

(2) The meat offering—Lev. 2.

((a)) Really a meal offering since there is no flesh in it. It comes from the vegetable kingdom. No blood. It brings before us the products of the soil—that which represents the sweat of man's brow and labor.

((b)) There are three varieties of the sacrifice and all speak of Christ.
    ((1)) Fine flour. Ground and sifted. Speaks of evenness and balance of Christ. No excess or lack of any quality.
      The grain, ground between the millstones and exposed to fire, speaks of Christ's sacrifice.
      Frankincense. Frank means whiteness and speaks of purity. Incense speaks of prayer—"He ever liveth to make intercession." The fragrance speaks of the fragrance of His life. He is the Lily of the Valley.
    ((2)) Baked loaves. They are cakes mixed with oil. No leaven permitted. No decay or corruption in our Lord. No honey. Honey is a natural sweetness which stands for natural sweetness apart from grace. Honey causes and promotes fermentation. Salt was to be used, preserving against corruption.
    ((3)) Green corn. Dried by fire and beaten, pictures suffering of Christ.
      Full ears—excellence and perfection.
      The firstfruits of the harvest. The best, full, first, and finest ears.

(3) The peace offering—Lev. 3.
  ((a)) Speaks of happy fellowship.
  ((b)) Followed other feasts.
  ((c)) Either public or private.
  ((d)) Male or female.
  ((e)) Lev. 7 tells us that the "inwards" were waved before the Lord, along with "the breast" and "right shoulder." The purpose of the waving was to present the sacrifice to the Lord and then to receive it back from Him.
  ((f)) This offering is typical of Christ in relation to the believer's peace. Col. 1:20.

(4) The sin offering—Lev. 4.
  ((a)) Not like the trespass offering, which only atoned for one special offense. The sin offering symbolized general redemption.
  ((b)) This is the most important of all sacrifices.
  ((c)) Every spot of blood from a sin offering on a garment conveyed defilement.

(5) The trespass offering—Lev. 5.
  ((a)) Provided for certain transgressions committed through ignorance. Demands confession.
  ((b)) Prescribed in the cases of healed lepers—Lev. 14:12.
  ((c)) Blood thrown on the corners of the altars.

(e) Comparison of the offerings.

(1) Burnt offering (oblation). Through Christ's finished work we come into the presence of God for worship.

(2) Meat offering (Human perfection). Speaks of His unblemished manhood.

(3) Peace offering (conciliation). Christ our peace.

(4) Sin offering (expiation). Christ made sin for us.

(5) Trespass offering (satisfaction). Christ settles the question of sin.

Man is a guilty transgressor and needs forgiveness—(Trespass offering, Ch. 5).
Man is a sinner and needs atoning sacrifice—(Sin offering, Ch. 4).
Man has a heart alienated from God and needs reconciliation—(Peace offering, Ch. 3).
Man, fallen and depraved, needs a substitute—(Meat offering, Ch. 2).
Man is unworthy and needs to be identified with a Worthy One—(Burnt offering, Ch. 1).

CHAPTER NINE

The Principle of Human Willingness in Illumination

VIII. PRINCIPLE OF HUMAN WILLINGNESS IN ILLUMINATION.

a. Definition.

    1. It is the principle by which a knowledge of God's truth is guaranteed to souls willing to know the truth— John 7:17.

    "If a man will to do His will," might better be translated, "He that willeth to do His will." Whatever truth a man or woman knows comes because he or she is willing to receive the truth. This has reference to the saved man. "Will"—have an absolute mind to it.

b. Application—must be illumination.

1. You must be guided by the Holy Spirit.

    (a) Our understanding is darkened (God's Word reveals it, and such is man's experience); and God alone is able, through His Spirit, to open our understanding and to make us behold the glorious things in His Word. No human teacher can do this. Sin has veiled our understanding, so that it is easier for man to understand many other things than it is for him to understand spiritual things. He may be very ignorant concerning the latter. He may speak learnedly about the laws of nature, but be totally ignorant of how a man may become righteous.

    I Cor. 2:14—He who would learn the truth of God must be taught by God alone. Sometimes He lets us study and ponder for hours, days, and even months before giving us a complete revelation by the Holy Spirit. A flood of light comes upon that which has been dark and mysterious.

        (1) Matt. 16:16,17—No one but God could have shown this to Peter. He had spent many months with Christ but this knowledge came only by sudden revelation.

        (2) Matt. 11:25-27—The little child in the Spirit who comes to God through simple faith, will have revealed to him things which the wise and prudent could never see. What you get from the Scripture you must get for yourself. All any Bible teacher can do is to put you on the right path and start you off. The Bible is a mine, and you can never get anything out of it without digging for it. Sin will bring blindness.

        (3) Isa. 29:10-18 contains visions and prophecies. The learned and the unlearned man alike, untaught by the Holy Spirit, finds the Bible a sealed book which neither can understand, because the Lord has sent upon them a deep sleep.

        He has blinded their eyes and veiled their faces because of sin. Sin seals the Book. When you cling to sin, you will find difficulty in interpreting the Book. To the natural man the Bible is full of apparent contradictions. In proportion as a man loves his sin the Book will be sealed to him. And, if you cling to your sin, it will become not only a sealed Book, but a Book which you despise.

2. You must have intellectual honesty.

    (a) You must recognize that the Bible is the Word of God, and be ready to submit your opinion to it. Truth is not what you have been taught. If what a man has been taught is truth, then man, who has been taught Mormonism, Buddhism, Modernism, etc., has been taught truth. You may have been taught truth, but truth is not what you have been taught.

        ADMIT—the Word; SUBMIT—to the Word; COMMIT—memorize; TRANSMIT—tell it forth.

    (b) In studying the Word of God, we must dismiss from our minds what we have been taught, e.g.

        (1) The snake and the apple—Gen. 3.

        (2) Some say Cain was rejected because he was bad, and Abel was received because he was good. If Abel was good, why did he need a sin offering? They were both bad. God accepted Abel on the basis of faith, and rejected Cain on the basis of his unbelief.

    (c) What you have been taught in accordance with the Word of God is truth, and what you have been taught that is not in accordance with the Word is not truth. When you study the Word take the place of a learner.

        (1) Be like Mary who believed the Word, and not like Peter, who (when Jesus said He must go to Jerusalem to suffer) said, "Not so."

        (2) One of the hardest things to do is to unlearn what you have already learned.

        (3) People run off into fanaticism because they believe what they hear.

3. The supreme authority of the Holy Scripture must be impressed upon the heart.

    (a) This is the only safeguard against error and evil. Books written by men are perfectly worthless as to authority. There may be lots of good in them, but as authority they are worthless, no matter how interesting. We ought not to take human authority. Think yourself empty in the Book before you read yourself full.

4. There must be a willingness to obey the Book.

(a) The Bible student, to become a real Bible student, must obey every injunction in the Book which pertains to him. There will be no knowledge until we are willing to obey. After all, the real difficulty in the way of understanding the teaching of the Word of God lies in our refusal to obey the Word. Matt. 13:12—The people who opposed Jesus Christ had some knowledge, but they refused to make use of it and obey it, and it was taken from them. It is possible to spend a great deal of time in the Word of God and yet be ignorant of it.

(b) There are Scriptures which directly condemn some habits we have, and too often we turn away and will not read because we do not want to obey them, and we will not obey. Do you want to be controlled by God's will?

(c) God reveals His truth to those who are willing to walk in the light. You will never grow in grace save as you grow in the knowledge of the Lord Jesus Christ. We must study and then walk in the light gained thereby. If a man willeth not to do His will, then God will withhold the knowledge from him. He who will abuse the light, will receive only blindness.

(d) This is a universal test. If we live up to the light we have, God will give us more, and if we refuse to obey, we will have no more light. Universal sin is the reason for universal darkness. The universal disobedience of man accounts for the spiritual blindness of today. If you desire to be a Bible student, be careful how you approach the Word, and be sure you obey it.

CHAPTER TEN

The First Mention Principle

IX. THE FIRST MENTION PRINCIPLE.

a. Definition.

1. That principle by which God indicates in the first mention of a subject, the truth with which that subject stands connected in the mind of God.

   (a) Newton said, "I find in Scripture this principle of interpretation, which I believe, if conscientiously adopted, will serve as an unfailing guide to what was in the mind of God. This is the keystone of the whole matter."

   (b) Dr. A. T. Pierson—"This is a law we have long since noted, and have never yet found it to fail. The first occurrence of a word, expression, or utterance, is the key to its subsequent meaning, or it will be a guide to ascertaining the essential truth connected with it."

   (c) The first time a thing is mentioned in Scripture it carries with it a meaning that will be carried all through the Word of God. We find 13 in Scripture used in connection with rebellion. All through Scripture 13 is a number that has in it the note of rebellion against God. It foreshadows apostasy.

   (d) There is only one speaker throughout all Scripture, although there are many mouths. Only one providing, governing, controlling mind—Heb. 1:1. God spake through "holy men of old" in the past, but in these days He speaks through His Son. No matter when, where, or how, the message is given, God is the speaker, and since there is only one speaker, and since that speaker knows from the beginning what He is going to say, He can so shape the first utterances as to forecast everything that is to follow. He is able to do that.

b. Examples.

1. **The subtlety of Satan—Gen. 3:1.**
   This is the first time the serpent is mentioned, and the characteristic mentioned is subtlety. All through the Book you will find Satan to be subtle. Expect subtlety every time you meet him—II Cor. 11:3. In the beginning he attacked Eve. In Matt. 4 we see him testing the Lord.

   (a) The basis for the first testing is hunger. This is a most exasperating thing. Jesus had been in the wilderness forty days, and before He had gone into the wilderness at the baptism, God had spoken and said, "This is my beloved Son." Now He had been forty days without food, and Satan comes and says, "If thou art the Son." This is a subtle insinuation. "Did you really hear that voice from heaven? If you were the Son of God you would not suffer here forty days and nights. Do you mean to tell me that God would permit His Son to go hungry?"

      (1) Hunger is the most innocent and necessary of human desires. Man never gets hungry because of sin. Before the fall, man needed food. Hunger is a fulfillment of the divine plan. Man must have food to live. Hunger is a God-created sense, and to feed it is to satisfy His purpose. God intends that a hungry man should eat.

      (2) Satan knew when to come. He was subtle in his coming and in his insinuations—"I don't ask you to do anything wrong, but if you are the Son of God, and if it is all true, then you can get yourself some food." Here is the serpent's subtlety. It is not a sin to satisfy a legitimate craving, but it is a sin to satisfy it in the wrong way. So he suggested two things. Prove you are the Son of God, and satisfy your hunger.

      (3) Jesus Christ quoted the Word of God, because the Word of God gives the will of God. He was dependent upon God because He came as a man. He did not perform a miracle to save Himself, because God had sent Him and He was dependent upon God—"It is written."

   (b) Second testing—at the temple. Satan can also quote Scripture. "I wouldn't bring you to a holy place like this and tempt you to do evil. Come to the top of the temple. Now cast yourself down. For it is written, angels will have charge over thee. You profess you are the Man who is going to live by the Word, then throw yourself down." But Christ came back with, "It is written."

   (c) Third testing—kingdoms of the world. Here was the glory of Greece, the pomp of Rome, and all the islands of the sea. "They are all mine, and I will give them to you if you will worship me. Why did you come into the world? Didn't you come so that you could have the whole world as a possession? All you have to do (it won't take a minute) is worship me. No Gethsemane, no spitting in your face, no crown of thorns, no nails in your body, no agony. Just a minute, bow down and worship me." All this *did* belong to Satan. He is the prince of this world and the god of this age. But Jesus said, "I will take the long road to the cross, and the kingdom of God will be established." There is nothing more subtle in the Word of God than Satan's attack on the Lord Jesus, and this is indicated in the first mention of him, the serpent.

2. The business of Satan.

(a) This is indicated in the first words recorded. "Yea, hath God said"—Gen. 3:1. This is direct opposition to the Word of God, and Satan's business is opposing the Word. The special sphere of Satan's activities is not criminal nor immoral, but his sphere is the religious. He is busy in that sphere where the Word of God is attacked. He questions and contradicts the Word of God.

(b) His first words in the Old Testament were, "Yea, hath God said?" And in the New Testament he says to the Lord Jesus, "If thou be the Son of God." He questions the spoken word of God from heaven. Satan's sphere of influence is not in the police court, not in the theater, nor on the stage. Look behind the pulpit and listen to the sermon. False teaching is a denial of the Word of God, and will be preached in Satan's subtle way.

> When you find a man denying the Word, there is the mark of the serpent. Don't blame the devil for the things of the world and the flesh. When a saint slips and becomes intoxicated, people blame it on the devil, but it is a work of the flesh. When another saint goes to the theater, they blame it on the devil; but that is the fault of the world. But when you find a professor or preacher denying the Word, that is the fault of the devil. A modernistic sermon could be preached in four words, "Yea, hath God said?" It could also be preached in one word, "If."

3. The keynote of Christ's ministry.

(a) The first words recorded of Jesus were, "Wist ye not that I must be about my Father's business?"—Luke 2:49. No speech of Jesus Christ's is recorded until He was twelve years of age. Nothing He had uttered as a child was so significant. Nothing could be more simple or beautiful, or more complete and prophetic than this statement of His mission on earth. When they nailed Him to the cross, the last words He said were, "It is finished." His whole life was given to the Father's business. "Behold I come to do thy will, O God."

(b) When He entered upon His ministry the first thing He said was, "It is written." He said this three times; and His whole ministry was according to the Word of God.

4. Faith—Genesis 15:6.

"Abraham believed God and He counted it to him for righteousness." This is a principle which pervades the whole Book. Righteousness is always counted to a man on the basis of faith, and the principle is stated in the first occurrence of these three words. "Not by works of righteousness which we have done," nor "by the deeds of the law," but if you are righteous today it is because you are counted righteous by God on the basis of faith.

5. Holiness—Gen. 2:3.

What does it mean? Go back to this first reference and see—(Set apart).

6. Spirit of God—Gen. 1:2.

"Moved" means "brooded," as a bird broods over a nest of eggs. It is translated "moved" because when a hen broods over her eggs, there is a constant movement in the breast of the hen which creates heat. The hen broods to bring life out of death, to bring light out of darkness. So the Spirit broods to bring life and order out of chaos. The Spirit of God is called the brooding dove. He broods over the chaos of the sinner's life. As the Spirit brooded over ruined creation, so He broods over the ruined creatures. He broods and moves over every sinner saved, Luke 1:35. Under the divine brooding of the Spirit the miraculous birth of Christ takes place. He broods over us to give life. He brings life out of darkness.

7. The Son of Man—Psa. 8:4.

"Thou hast put all things under his feet"—Has to do with dominion over the earth and universal dominion under God's hand. Do not confuse the title, Son of Man, with a son of man. Ezekiel was a son of man, but Christ is the only, "the Son of Man." Hebrews 2 is a divine commentary on Psalm 8. First mention in New Testament is Matt. 8:20. It is a title never found in the Church Epistles. It is not a title that has to do with a Church relationship, but with a Kingdom relationship. It has to do with the world's relationship with Christ, and His rule over the earth.

8. The Day of the Lord—Isa. 2:11, 12. Revelation is the book of this Day.

(a) There are a number of *days* in Scripture, but not all are twenty-four hours in length. Today is the day of man, and at the end of this period called the Day of Man, the Church will be caught up with the Lord in the air. The Day of the Lord signifies the abasement of man and the exaltation of God. Today is a day in which man is exalted. He is IT. Apparently God has handed things over to man, and taken His hands off. In this day God is not called the Lord of all the earth, as in other periods, but He is called the God of Heaven. Apparently He has decided to permit man to see what he can do in the way of rule and religion. Man certainly has made a mess of things. Nobody knows what is going to happen tomorrow. Man bars God out.

(b) There are four great days in Scripture.
(1) Day of man—I Cor. 4:3—exaltation of man—present day.

(2) Day of Christ—Phil. 2:16—when the church is in the air.

(3) Day of the Lord—Isa. 2:11,12—takes a large place in Scripture—Millennium.

(4) Day of God—II Pet. 3:12.

(c) The Day of the Lord will be a day when man will be abased, and the Lord will be exalted. The book of Revelation gives a panorama of the events which take place in the Day of the Lord. In the first chapter of Revelation John says he was in the Spirit on the Lord's day. This does not mean the first day of the week, but that by the Spirit, he was carried out into the Day of the Lord—Joel 2:1-11; 28-32; Amos 5:18-20; Zeph. 1:15-18.

9. The city of Jerusalem. Judges 1:7-8.

Here is the first time Jerusalem is mentioned as a city. "The men of Judah smote it with the edge of the sword and set it on fire." We have the history of the city of Jerusalem right there. It is a picture of the city's future in miniature, and an epitome of all its subsequent history. Jerusalem was besieged twenty-seven times, and burned three times.

10. Babylon—Gen. 11.

The first mention of Babylon shows that it began with rebellion against God. "The times of the Gentiles" began with a king in Babylon. It was always rebellious against God. It was an idolatrous place. In Rev. 17 we see that it was a place of idolatry. That is why it is called a harlot and mother of harlots. It will be the seat of the anti-Christ. Idolatry is a satanic system which was introduced by Babylon. It was built by Nimrod—(Gen. 10:10), the rebel against God. The motive was self-glory, and it always means self-glory. Babylon is a Greek form. Invariably, in the Old Testament, the word is simply Babel, the meaning of which is confusion, and in this sense the word is used symbolically.

It is also an imitation. It was made of bricks instead of stone, and put together with slime instead of mortar. It will be in the future a mock kingdom with a mock ruler. The motive back of the building was self-glory, rather than the glory of God. What you find in Genesis concerning Babylon is true of Babylon all through the Word of God. Idolatry is a system introduced into the world by Satan at Babylon through the person of Nimrod.

The Progressive Mention Principle

X. PROGRESSIVE MENTION PRINCIPLE.

  a. Definition: That principle by which God makes the revelation of any given truth increasingly clear as the Word proceeds to its consummation.

    1. You will find that the Word of God is a progression. As you study, it will bring added details to truth that God has revealed in the beginning.

    2. There are two ways of studying Scripture:

      (a) Canonically: in the order in which the books appear—man's order.

      (b) Chronologically: in the order in which they were written, and the events occur—order of revelation.

        (1) There is a teaching in the Word of God in the very arrangement of the books. Romans is the foundation on which all the epistles rest. Thessalonians was the first written. The Holy Spirit put it in its place in the Bible because of its teachings.

        (2) Bernard has written a book, "The Progress of Doctrine in the New Testament," in which he says, "The reality of the progression is very visible, and more especially so when we reach the New Testament—the last stages of this progressive teaching. Glance from the first words of the Bible to the last: 'In the beginning God'—'Even so, Lord Jesus.' There is a progression from one to the other. There is a difference in the rates of progress—in the Old Testament the progress is protracted, languid, sometimes almost obscured, ending with an entire suspension for 400 years. After this, comes the New Testament, and here the progress is rapid. Before, it was centuries, *now* it is but years. The great scheme unfolds rapidly. Just as a plant grows slowly at first and is barely visible in growth, so is the truth in the Old Testament. But in the New Testament, the plant has budded, and soon the full blossom appears. The growth then is rapid. First the root, then the shoot, and then the fruit."

      (c) The thought of progress in Scripture ought to give to us one right method of Bible study, and that method lies right on the surface. The Bible was written by books, and was built up by books, so it ought to be studied by books. It is a Book of books. Follow a certain subject through Scripture. You will find that it becomes complete through a steady growth. There are great highways in Scripture, and we ought to travel them just as we travel other highways. We will thus accumulate knowledge. There are many speakers, but one mind.

  b. Examples of the growth of truth.

    1. Predictions that have to do with the Person of the coming One, the Saviour.

      (a) When sin came into the world, immediately God gave the promise of the Seed of the woman who would bruise the serpent. This promise comes with the fall of man—Gen. 3:15.

      (b) Several centuries pass, and then comes the man Abraham, with whom God makes a covenant—"In thy seed shall all the nations of the earth be blessed." In looking for a Satan-bruiser, then, we know he is to come from the man Abraham, as a descendant, not from just any family or any part of the earth.

      (c) The next detail given is the fact that of Abraham's two sons, Isaac is chosen.

      (d) Isaac has two sons, and the promise is made definitely to Jacob.

      (e) Jacob has twelve sons, and again the line is limited—this time to Judah.

      (f) Judah becomes a great tribe, numbering thousands. Where shall we look for the coming One? The family of David.

      (g) Not only of the family of David, but in the town of Bethlehem.

      (h) When He is to be born—Dan. 9:25.

      (i) Zechariah tells us that He will ride into the city of Jerusalem—9:9.

      (j) Malachi 3:1 tells of the fore-runner who is John the Baptist.

      (k) In Zechariah 11:12—He is to be sold for thirty pieces of silver.

      (l) Psalm 22—His heart is to be broken—description of manner of death.

      (m) Psalm 34:20—Not a bone of His body shall be broken.

      (n) To David, God reveals that when the Son is slain, He will not remain in the tomb. David sees the resurrection of Christ. He sees Him placed in the tomb, and yet with the path of life stretching out before Him. He also sees His ascension into the heavens.

      (o) To Isaiah is revealed God's part in Christ's death—Isa. 53:4,5.

2. Progression concerning prayer.

A failure to recognize this truth concerning progression will lead to misunderstanding, and will give incomplete truth.

(a) In the Old Testament we find David, Daniel, and other men praying three times a day, with their faces toward Jerusalem. If we do not recognize the law of progression, then we must teach that we must follow their example. God says more than this.

(b) In the Gospels (Matt. 6:6) God says to pray in the closets; but in the Epistles (I Thess. 5:17) He says to pray without ceasing. This does not mean to get down on your knees in the closet and pray night and day. It means that as a Christian, one must be in the spirit of prayer at all times, be in constant communion with the Father. It is not necessary to pray in words. You can pray while walking. Jesus prayed; His whole life was prayer. Before He did anything He prayed. Sometimes He prayed all night. T. M. Haldeman said, "Christ was the epitome, the incarnation of prayer."

3. The Whole of the Word of God.

Don't live in the Old Testament nor in the New Testament alone. The Old Testament is the kindergarten, and when you have finished with that, go on into the University of Scripture. We must have the Old Testament in order to understand the New. The Old Testament is the beginning. The first words of the New Testament take us back into the Old. You must know who David and Abraham were. You have to have Leviticus in order to understand the book of Hebrews. You need the whole Word of God!

4. The Trinity.

(a) In the Old Testament this was only intimated through the plural noun, Elohim, and the plural pronouns, us, our—Gen. 3:5; Gen. 1:26.

(b) A declaration is made in the New Testament where only an intimation is made in the Old Testament. At the baptism we have all three persons present—the Lord Jesus was in the water, the Father spoke from heaven saying, "This is my son;" and the Holy Spirit came from heaven to earth. This is the declaration of the mystery which no human being can explain.

5. The Holy Spirit.

There is a development of doctrine. In Genesis 1, the name signifies "A breathing;" and this comes to its fulness of progression in the New Testament. He is mentioned 88 times in the Old Testament, and many more in the New Testament. Study the books chronologically in order.

6. Law and Grace.

Law in the Old Testament. Grace in the New.

7. Rewards.

In the Old Testament they are material; in the New Testament they are spiritual and eternal.

8. Faith.

This is given as a foundation in the Old Testament. In II Peter 1:5-9 we have an addition to it.

9. God's dwelling places.

(a) Creation.

(b) Tabernacle.

(c) Temple in Jerusalem.

(d) The temple of Christ's body.

(e) In the believer—I Cor. 3:16; 6:19.

10. Satan—his characteristics.

(a) A liar from the beginning—Gen. 3:4. Denied what God said and misled the human race by a lie.

(b) A murderer from the beginning. He murdered the whole human race in that all are dead in trespasses and sin.

(c) The accuser—Job 1:11.

(d) The hinderer or resister—Zech. 3:1,2.
When Jesus said He must go to Jerusalem to suffer and die, Peter contradicted Him. Jesus said, "Get thee behind me, Satan."—Again the hinderer.

(e) The tempter.
　　(1) Gen. 3—tempted Eve.
　　(2) Matt. 4—tempted the Lord Jesus Christ.

(f) The betrayer, entered into Judas.

(g) Seducer of saints; instigator of lies—Acts 5:1-5.

(h) Incarnation—in man of sin—II Thess. 2:3,4. Incarnation in the man of sin, the son of perdition, the instigator of all lawlessness.

(i) Rebellion—Rev. 19. Goes forth to openly war against Christ and the saints.

11. The believer's armour against Satan—Eph. 6:13-17.

(a) Girdle of truth—protection against the liar.

(b) Breastplate of righteousness—against the accuser.

(c) Gospel boots—protection against the hinderer.

(d) Shield of faith—protection against the one who leads men to deny.

(e) Helmet of salvation—against the one who denies the Word. Be ever ready to say, "It is written."

12. The Lamb in Scripture. Found in the first and last books of the Bible. The story is woven through scripture.

(a) Gen. 4—Abel brought his lamb to the altar. We are not told that it was slain, although it undoubtedly was. All we are told was that Abel brought the firstling of the flock and the Lord accepted it. It was for a person.

(b) Gen. 22—We find a strange intimation that even Abraham himself did not understand. Isaac said, "We have the wood and the fire, but where is the lamb?" Abraham said, "My son, God will provide himself a lamb."

(c) Exodus 12—the lamb must be slain. Blood must be sprinkled on the door. For the first time the emphasis is placed on the slaying of the lamb and the shedding of blood.

(d) Leviticus 16—One kid died and the other lived. This indicates the two aspects of Christ's work. A dying Saviour and a living Saviour; death and resurrection.

(e) Isaiah 53—for the first time in Scripture we find that the Lamb is a person. He is slain for the whole world.

(f) John 1:29—the first distinct revelation that this person, the Lamb of God, is a man named Jesus— "Behold the Lamb of God."

(g) Acts 8—Philip is speaking to the eunuch and for the first time the Scripture states that the Lamb prophesied by Isaiah, is Jesus Who died on Calvary.

(h) I Pet. 1:18-21—here we have the foreordaining of Christ as the slain Lamb—the slain and resurrected Lamb. All threads gathered together.

(i) Revelation 5—the Lamb is identified with the Lion of the tribe of Judah, Who will reign on the throne of David. Revelation is full of the Lamb.

13. Animal sacrifice.

(a) It was instituted by God for only one reason. It is valuable only as being typical of the Redeemer.

(b) All Old Testament sacrifices are not only typical but also educational. They show the perpetual need of the people because of sin. But the sacrifice for a man must be a man. An animal could not satisfy God's wrath and hatred of sin. All Old Testament sacrifices pointed to Calvary. God is infinite and so sin has an infinite aspect, and as such, an infinite sacrifice is needed. A man was needed to take the place of a man and satisfy God's justice.

14. Atonement.

The great day in the history of Israel was the annual Day of Atonement.

(a) Atonement means covering. Noah covered the ark inside and outside with pitch. The Hebrew word is "KAPHAR."

(b) On the day of atonement, God covered the sins of Israel—"Blessed is the man whose sins are covered." On the basis of the blood of bulls and goats their sins were covered, looking forward to the blood that was to be shed on Calvary. There is a progression from the Old Testament to the New Testament. *Our* sins are not covered, but they are washed away. David's sins are not covered any more. Since Christ died, his sins are washed away.

(c) There is a difference between atonement and regeneration. Putting powder on a spot on a handkerchief will cover the spot, but will not cleanse it. The spot will not stay covered very long. The only way to clean it is to send it to the laundry. After that, it is clean but full of wrinkles. We must be ironed with a hot iron so as to rub out the wrinkles. Ephesians tells us about God's ironing.

(d) In the revised version of the New Testament the word "atonement" is translated "reconciliation"— Rom. 5:11.

15. Sheol.

In the Old Testament when the saints died, they went down to Sheol; but in the New Testament Christ went up, and He washed away their sins and ours.

16. God.

(a) The mystery and character of God given us first from His work.

(b) Then revealed from His Word.

(c) Then from His Son.

(d) And finally from the Spirit in the believer's life.

17. Legislation.

(a) In the Old Testament there is progress. It involves a covenant relationship based on sacrifice. It is expressed in worship. It involves a consecration of time (Sabbath), substance (tithes), and self (burnt offering).

(b) In the New Testament the key is in the fact that it is spiritual—Romans 12:1. It should be translated "spiritual" service instead of reasonable.

CHAPTER TWELVE

The Full Mention Principle

XI. FULL MENTION PRINCIPLE.

a. Definition—that principle by which God declares His full mind upon any subject vital to our spiritual life. Somewhere in the Word, God gathers together the scattered fragments that have to do with a particular truth, and puts them into one exhaustive statement. That is His full mind concerning that truth.

b. Passages that show the full mind of God.
1. Resurrection—I Cor. 15—resurrection of the Saviour and of the believer.
2. The tongue—James 3. A marvel, mystery, malice; destructive, devilish, demonized organ.
3. Restoration of Israel—Romans 11—The Bible is full of reference to this, but Romans 11 summarizes.
4. Trials and triumphs of faith—Hebrews 11.
5. God's discipline of His children—Heb. 12:1-11.
6. The Church—Ephesians 1-3.
7. Principles of the Kingdom of Heaven—chapters 5-7 of Matthew. The Code of the Kingdom and the Laws that will be in effect when the Kingdom of Heaven is established on earth, are presented there.
8. The vicarious sacrifice—Isa. 53.
9. Righteousness by faith—Rom. 3:10-21.
10. Godly repentance—II Cor. 7.
11. Law—Exodus 20.
12. The full panoply (suit of armour)—Eph. 6:10-17.
13. The nature or natures of Jesus Christ—Heb. 1 and 2.
    Chapter 1—Son of God, better than the angels.
    Chapter 2—Son of man, lower than the angels.
14. The final judgment—Rev. 20. This is the Great White Throne Judgment, and is mentioned only once in scripture.
15. Last things—of this day in which we live—Matt. 24.
16. Spiritual gifts—Chapter 12-14 of I Cor.

c. Illustrations of this law. These summaries may not always be complete chapters, but may be found in a verse.
I Cor. 1:30—summarizes all of Christ's work in a sentence and gives us knowledge of God, knowledge of ourselves, and knowledge of Christ.

1. Love—I Cor. 13. I Cor. 12, 13, 14 should always be studied together.

All through the Bible are references to the love of God for man, but in I Cor. 13 we find everything that God has to say about love. Charity is the word used, but the meaning has been changed since the time when the Bible was translated. Moody once said, "This chapter ought to be read in church once a week." But we have to do more than just read the chapter; we have to live it. There is a beautiful tradition of the last days of the Apostle John: As Jesus looked into the faces of His disciples for the last time, He said, "Little children, love one another." They said, "You have told us that before." He said the second time, "Little children, remember what I have told you from the beginning, love one another." They said, "We have heard that before. Give us a new commandment." But He said a third time, "A new commandment give I unto you, that ye love one another." All the commandments are bound together in that statement, that we love not ourselves, but others.

(a) This thirteenth chapter is right in the heart of a discussion of spiritual gifts bestowed by God on the people of the church in Corinth. Chapter 12 has to do with the gifts, but chapter 13 goes on to give us something better than spiritual gifts. Chapter 12 discusses the gifts which are a manifestation of the power of God; in chapter 13 we see that love which is the manifestation of the nature of God.

(1) It is much more important for us to manifest the nature of God than to have some spiritual gift to manifest the power of God. "God is love."
Of all the churches in the New Testament, the church that had the greatest number of gifts was the church at Corinth, and in the beginning of this hymn of love, Paul refers to the highest gift in that miracle-gifted church.

((a)) Verse 1—"Tongues of men and of angels." Though he spoke in a language as pure as heaven itself, words without love would be only words. Jesus Christ spoke in words that were so simple that even the poor and ignorant could understand Him, but, "Never man spake as this man." His heart was full of love. His heart was the heart of God. That is why His simplest words became sublime.

((b)) Verse 2—Prophecy. The supreme gift of this church.
The gift of speaking God's will and God's Word, and of sharing God's super-knowledge.

Knowledge of mysteries. The privilege of understanding the revelations of God. "Knowledge"—knowledge of the nature of scripture. "Faith"—the faith of one who is saved so as to work miracles—faith to accomplish the wonderful and incredible.

(2) But love is greater than faith, and all these things without love are nothing.
   ((a)) Verse 3—Giving of goods and body. This brings no profit in that day when we stand before Christ. Love must be back of it all. Personal sacrifice without love profiteth nothing.
   ((b)) Message of this verse.
      ((1)) Love must be supreme in the human heart.
      ((2)) Love must be supreme in the human mind.
      ((3)) Love must be supreme in the human will and life.

(3) Verses 1-3: Five of life's most valued treasures—the things which men seek; eloquence, learning, power, benevolence, and devotion: God takes all five and throws them away when they are not prompted by love.

(4) Characteristics of love; how it works out in practice:
   ((a)) "Love suffereth long and is kind." If you are going to live a love life you will walk a path of sorrow. God is love, and when He walked on earth He was a Man of Sorrows. God is saying that the path of the Christian must be one of suffering. Yet in this suffering, the Christian is kind. God is love, and God suffered for us—"Love never wears out." William Tyndale said, in the midst of persecution, "Take away my goods, take away my good name, yet so long as Christ dwells in my heart, so long will I love you not a whit the less." When patience is tried, love suffereth long. Love hasn't any nerves, and is never driven crazy. Love's patience is never exhausted. Love bore the spit in the face, the thorns on the brow, the mocking, and then Love said, "Father forgive them." Love is kind to everyone—kind in the home, kind to friends, and kind to enemies.
   ((b)) Love is a seven-fold regulator and restrainer.
      ((1)) "Love envieth not."
            It is not jealous, and is very ignorant in the sense that it knows no envy. Envy and jealousy in the life are like rust on iron; they will wear out the one who is envious. Being jealous is a sin that is abominable and almost universal. Christian workers are not exempt. Jealousy and envy come from the flesh, not from the Spirit, just as truly as drunkenness and adultery come from the flesh. There is no other possible way to obtain victory over this awful sin except having a heart filled with love by the Spirit of God. "For envy they delivered up Christ." Envy will lead to deceit and murder.
      ((2)) "Love vaunteth not itself." It is not boastful, never makes a parade, never tries to show off. Christ was meek and humble, and made Himself of no reputation.
      ((3)) "Love is not puffed up"—is not susceptible to flattery. There is pride of race, pride of face, and pride of grace; and the last is the worst. Christ was meek and lowly. The more we love others, the less we will love ourselves. Be careful in keeping yourself humble that you do not give the appearance of pride in humility.
      ((4)) "Love doth not behave itself unseemly." Not unbecomingly. Love is never loud, vulgar, nor offensive. It is always considerate of others, always courteous. Love will make a man to be a gentleman, and a woman to be a gentlewoman.
            Training and breeding will not always make one to be courteous, but love is courteous by instinct. Love will cause a Christian to walk worthy of his calling.
      ((5)) "Love seeketh not her own." Love and selfishness will never be found in the same heart. Christ pleased not Himself.
      ((6)) "Love is not easily provoked." It isn't touchy, and doesn't dare a person to knock a chip off one's shoulder. One who really loves can not be affronted or misunderstood or irritated.
      ((7)) "Love thinketh no evil." Taketh no account of evil done it. Love, as an accountant, never takes account of the evil done to it. It does not keep books, or, if it does, Love never makes an entry. It never thinks of revenge. "Revenge is sweet" is not true. There is no sweetness in hatred. Strong translates it, "Love taketh no inventory."
   ((c)) "Love rejoiceth not in iniquity, but rejoiceth in truth." Love takes no joy in sin. Love can never smile at the fact of sin, but will be heavy-hearted when a saint falls into sin.
   ((d)) "Love beareth all things." Love will bear slights, neglect or insult. "Beareth" means "covereth." Love throws a mantle over the faults of others and hides their shortcomings. "Love roofeth over." The sins of the Old Testament saints are not mentioned in the New Testament. Love covers. In the Old Testament we read that Lot was a worldly man, but in the New Testament we read that he was a righteous man. God's love has roofed over Lot's past life. Bearing these things does not mean soft sentimentality. Christ did not hes-

itate to tell the Pharisees what He thought of them, but He did not criticize behind their backs. Every time He rebuked a person, He spoke to that person directly. "Love stands in the presence of fault or failure of others with a finger on the lips."

((e)) "Love believeth all things." Love is trustful, not doubting. Some people doubt everybody. They think everybody else is all wrong. Love will believe all good about others. Love will be quick to impute good motives.

((f)) "Love hopeth all things." Love hopes when others have ceased to hope. Love looks on the good side and discovers the good rather than the bad in man.

((g)) Love endureth all things." That means to persevere with patience. Paul endured all things, because of his love. Love will be patient with the wrongs and offenses of a brother. Love believeth all things.

This is the only chapter in the writings of Paul in which he does not mention the Lord Jesus, and yet He is there. Substitute "Christ" in the place of love or charity.

((h)) "Love never faileth." "Falleth" rather than "faileth," in the sense that a petal falls from a faded flower. This flower, however, never fades; it blooms forever and love never falleth.

((i)) But now abideth these three, and the greatest of these is love. Prophecies shall fail, tongues shall cease, knowledge shall vanish away, but when all things pass away, love abideth. This thing that abides is the greatest gift of all. The time will come when faith no longer abides, but faith will be sight. Hope will be swallowed up in realization. The greatest of these is love, which is the oldest. Love can say, "Before faith and hope were, I am." Love was before the world; it is eternal.

2. The tongue—James 3.

Even Moses was shut out of the land because he spoke unadvisedly. In the law it says not to go up and down talebearing. Here James is speaking against idle words. Words manifest sin and ungodliness—"Be swift to hear, but slow to speak."

(a) Verse 1—"Masters"—means teachers. Teachers are held to more strict account. This explains the word and applies it to the hearts and lives of the hearers. If you keep to the truth you are apt to be unpopular.

If there is one place where it is easier to stumble than any other, it is the tongue. "The right use of the tongue is a sign of perfection"—Lk. 11:53, 54. Jesus kept control of His tongue. The tongue is a bucket with which you bring up that which is in your heart.

(b) Verse 2—If you are able to bridle the tongue, you can control the whole body.

(c) Verse 3—It is a small bit by which the whole horse is controlled; if a man can bridle the tongue, he can control the whole body—Ps. 32:9. A horse with the bit on its tongue follows his mouth with the whole body. So the tongue can lead the whole body into sin.

(d) Verse 4—The ship is large, but is controlled by the rudder. A horse is moved by will, a ship is moved by the wind. Watch your tongue and avoid shipwreck. A rudder is small in comparison to the ship, but it controls it. Even so, the tongue is small, but it can influence the whole body.

(e) Verses 5, 6—Behold how great a fire a little word kindleth. You can start a forest fire with a little spark. The tongue is a fire able to destroy. Fire spreads, and the scope of the tongue is so wide it is called a "world of iniquity." There is no divine law that the tongue cannot break.

It defiles the whole body by the soot and smoke of slander. It can lie, defend sin, and lead into sin. It is a hellish flame that kindles the tongue.

(f) Verses 7, 8—The tongue can no man tame. It is a "restless" evil, disorderly and uncontrolled, fickle, unreliable, and full of deadly poison. Words may destroy anything, even the very life of the church, (gossip and slander).

(g) Verses 9-14—Fountain, fig tree, and olive tree—none of these give two things from one, and yet from the same mouth comes good and evil speech. We have double-dealing with the tongue. The tongue can no man tame, but it can be tamed of the Spirit of God. Who can cleanse a man's mouth and tame the tongue?

CHAPTER THIRTEEN

The Context Principle

XII. CONTEXT PRINCIPLE.

a. Definition.

1. That principle by which God gives light upon a subject through either near or remote passages bearing upon the same theme. Every sentence or verse in the Bible has something that precedes it and something that follows it—except Gen. 1:1 and Rev. 22:21.

2. Every verse must be studied in the light of its context. Never take a verse out of its setting and give it a foreign meaning.
Examples.

(a) Ram and He-goat—Dan. 8.
Ridiculous statements will be made unless one studies the context; in this case, the rest of the chapter.

(b) Valley of dry bones—Ezek. 37. This is not the Church. The context says it is the whole house of Israel. There are some passages in Scripture that will be absolutely dark without the context.

(c) The Bible can be made to prove anything, but NOT when studied in the light of the context. You can pick out a verse or part of a verse, and use it to prove a theory, and make it mean something God never intended it to mean. That is not treating Scripture fairly.

    (1) Phil. 2:12.
"Work out your own salvation with fear and trembling." What about the context? God works in you, and then you work it out. Verse 14 gives the method of doing His will.

    (2) Rom. 8:28.
"All things work together for good." This is not what the scripture is saying. "To them that love God," and more than that, "to them that are the called according to His purpose."

    (3) John 6:37.
"Him that cometh to me, I will in no wise cast out." But notice the first of the verse—"All that the Father giveth me shall come to me, and him that cometh to me . . . etc."

(d) Psalm 2:8, 9.
This is quoted as a missionary text perhaps more than any other verse. People talk as though the reign of Christ would begin when they ask for it. They seem to think that we have to work and to go on and on, and when the whole world is saved, then the kingdom will come.

    (1) This is not a missionary text. It does not say that the faithful worker on the field will be given the heathen. The next verse says, "thou shalt break them with a rod of iron." This is not the way a missionary does. Verse 8 hasn't anything to do with missions. It has to do with the Son of God and His kingdom. It does not refer to converting the world by the gospel, but to the rule of Christ.

    (2) God's wish is that the world shall be evangelized before Christ returns. It does not mean that the world is growing better and better, and will some day be perfect. The world is growing worse and worse. When the Kingdom is set up, it will be a kingdom of judgment. This world is going down even as in the days of Noah, and the day will come when God must say, "I can stand it no longer." Christ will rule the Kingdom with a rod of iron.

(e) Acts 16:31.
This verse is often read without the context. The last part of the verse says "And thy house," which was a special commandment. From the context we find that this verse was spoken to a man who was under conviction. That jailer had seen himself in the presence of God. When the earthquake took place, this jailer thought that the prisoners had fled, which would mean death to him, under the Roman law. So he was going to save the government the trouble and was ready to take his own life. Since it was dark, he could not see that the prisoners were there. When Paul cried to him, "We are all here," he did this because he knew what was in the mind of the jailer. Then the jailer called for a light, and coming to Paul and Silas, he said, trembling, "What must I do to be saved?" He was not referring to a physical death, but he was under conviction of sin. To this Paul and Silas said, "Believe on the Lord Jesus Christ, and thou shalt be saved." This then, is a word to be spoken to the man who is under conviction. A man who is not under conviction needs something else. This is not a command to those who are not under conviction of sin. If a man is not under conviction he must be shown that he needs a Saviour. He must be brought under conviction. "Believe" is not all he must do; he must have something to believe on. You must tell him about Christ before he can believe. They spoke unto him the Word of the Lord, and to all that were in his house, with the result that the jailer rejoiced, believing in God *with all his house*. Of course, each person had to believe for himself.

(f) Titus 1:2—A sermon was preached over the radio recently in which the preacher said that there was more than one God, taking from that verse Tit. 1:2 the words, "which God." This is an extreme case, but shows what is going on today.

3. Statements of Bible teachers.
   (a) Torrey—"Too much importance cannot be laid upon a close study of the context."
   (b) Todd—"Consideration of the context in examining any verse or passage is of the utmost importance. Failure to do this is one of the causes of misinterpretation of scripture."
   (c) Moyer—"Too many preachers prepare a message and then hunt a text to fit it. That is not a text, it is a pretext."
   (d) Lockhart—"The context is the key to the meaning."

4. Near contexts. The near context will throw light on scripture and explain passages that are dark and difficult to understand.
   (a) Gen. 35:2.
       (1) The passage.
           Jacob says, "Put away the strange gods from among you." At first reading it looks as though Jacob and his family had become idolators, and that they must put away these idols before going back to Bethel. These idols, however, were not for the purpose of worship, but rather were old family heirlooms, probably valued because they were silver and gold. Rachel brought some of them from her father's house, but we never read of any of the family worshipping them.
       (2) The context.
           The explanation may be found in the context. Where did they get these idols? In Gen. 34:26-29, the sons of Jacob despoiled Shechem, the Hivite, and took everything of value out of that house. These idols were valuable, and so were taken. That is where they secured the idols of strangers.
   (b) I John 4:17—Perfect love. Verse 16 explains that that is God's love for us.

5. Remote contexts.
   Sometimes the context is very near the verse, as in the case of the ram and the he-goat. Everything, however, should be studied in the light of the whole Bible.
   (a) Gen. 18:20, 21.
       God told Abraham that he was going to destroy the cities of the plains, which included Sodom, Gomorrah, Gaza, and two others. Abraham prayed, but he prayed for only one city. No reason is given here as to why Abraham was influenced by feelings of humanity, but if that were true, why should he pray for only one? Why not for all?
       The context gives the explanation—Gen. 14:12. We read of Lot, Abraham's nephew, who dwelt in Sodom, which is the reason why Abraham was so concerned for this city. Someone was there who was bound to him by ties of blood.
       Another lesson: God has more than one way of answering man's prayers. The reason Abraham prayed was for Lot's deliverance. God did answer Abraham's prayer—and He didn't answer it. He spared the nephew, but did not spare the city.
   (b) Gen. 24:15.
       Here we read that Rebekah was the daughter of Bethuel, son of Milcah, the wife of Nahor, Abraham's brother. This doesn't look right—the granddaughter of Abraham's brother married to Abraham's son. How could the daughter of the third generation be old enough to marry a son of the second generation?
       Context—Gen. 18:11, 12. Isaac practically was born in the same generation as his wife. A similar case—the parents of Moses.
   (c) Gen. 37:25, 28, 36; 39:1.
       Some of the "higher critics" charge that this is an outstanding example of discrepancies in the Bible. The Midianites and the Ishmaelites are all mixed up—Judges 8:24. Here again we have the Ishmaelites among the Midianites.
       Context—Gen. 16:11, 12; 25:2. Ishmael and Midian were half-brothers, and they settled in the same country and led the same kind of life. The Ishmaelites and Midianites refer to the same people. From Judges 8:24, it seems that all the Ishmaelites were Midianites, but not all the Midianites were Ishmaelites. A modern example is this: All Canadians are British, but all British are not Canadians.
   (d) Judges 5:8.
       There was not a shield or a spear seen among the army of Israel. It was an unarmed army. Judges 3:16—Ehud had to make his own dagger.
       Judges 3:31.
       Shamgar slew the Philistines with an ox-goad, because he had no other weapon. Judges 14:5, 6—Samson, the mighty man was unarmed. Why were these men unarmed?
       Context—I Sam. 13:19-22. There was no smith found through all the land, for the Philistines had taken them all away so that the Israelites could not arm themselves against their enemies. In the

days of Israel's liberty, men drew the sword, but in the days of the oppression, Israel used other weapons.

(e) II Chron. 22:11, 12.

Athaliah, the wicked queen, mother of the king, slew, as she thought all the seed royal. There was in the palace a princess who had married a priest, Jehoiada. God was preparing for what was to come. When the queen started out on her murders, the princess Jehosheba took the baby prince, Joash, and his nurse and hid them in the temple for six years. Now, how could you hide a baby? You could hide the body, but how would you hide his cry?

Context—II Chron. 24:27. In the previous reign, the house of God had fallen, had been broken up, and needed repairing. The reason was, because king Ahab's wife, Jezebel, introduced the worship of Baal into the land of Israel and the rest of the people followed their king, so in the course of time they took all the vessels of the House of God and carried them to the temple of Baal, where they worshipped.

The temple of God was deserted and no one ever went there. They worshipped Baal instead of Jehovah to such an extent that Elijah thought that he was the only man left who did worship God. It is easy to see, therefore, why the temple of God was the best place in which to hide the baby king, because no one ever worshipped there.

(f) Hezekiah's prosperity—II Kings 18:13-36.

Hezekiah was forced to pay a large tribute to the Assyrians, and was without wealth. In Isaiah 39:2 we find a direct contradiction. What are we going to do?

Context—II Chron. 32:22, 23, gives the explanation. The Lord saved Hezekiah from Sennacherib and the people brought presents.

(g) John 21:15.

These are words of the Lord Jesus, "Lovest thou me more than these?" One preacher, when explaining this verse, said that by "these," Jesus meant the fish they had just caught, and that we should not love temporal things more than the Lord. It is true that we should love the Lord first, but that is not the correct interpretation of this verse.

Context—Matt. 26:31-33; 14:27-29. Peter had said that though the others were offended in Jesus, he would not be, and that he would love the Lord a little better than the others. Yet, he got up and cursed, stating that he did not know the Lord. In the picture given in John 21, Peter comes to the shore with the others, and they gather round the fire. That fire must have reminded Peter of that other fire where he had warmed himself on the day of the denial. Now the Lord says to him, "Lovest thou me more than these?"—other disciples. Peter is proud no more. He says to the Lord, "Thou knowest."

(h) Jer. 32:4; 34:3. Cf. Ezek. 12:13.

How is a man going to go into Babylon and see and talk with the king and die in the land, and yet not see it?

Context—II Kings 25:6, 7. He was taken to the king outside of Babylon at Riblah where he talked with the king and saw him. Then, after his eyes had been put out, he was taken into Babylon where he stayed until he died. He saw the king, but never saw the land.

(i) When you come against modernistic teaching you can disprove it by the context principle. Example: God is the Father of all men. This is one of the favorite teachings, and they say that the sinner is a prodigal son, and needs to come back to the Father. But the sinner is not the prodigal son; he is of his father, the devil, the wicked one. A sinner is a *creature* of God, not a son of God; but the modernist says, "God is the Father of all men."

They use Eph. 4:6—One God and Father of all. They make a universal application of this Scripture. "You can prove anything by the Scripture." This application is an error that is Satanic, and its refutation comes through the Scripture.

Context—The book of Ephesians is not addressed to all people, but to all saints. Weymouth says, "This book is addressed to God's people in Ephesus; to those who believe on the Lord Jesus Christ." This passage teaches that God is the Father of all believers. There are many passages in the remote context which will refute this "ism"—John 1:12, 13. Gal. 3:26: etc. To shed Bible light on Bible problems, let the context speak. If a man covets a sane, logical, balanced, sound knowledge of Scripture, he must study the passages in the light of the context.

6. How chapter divisions may cause error in the truth.

(a) Matt. 16:27, 28: 17:1. The post-millennialist will say, "You say the kingdom is not here. How about this verse? Those men have been dead a long time, and this verse says they should not taste of death till they see the kingdom."

Context—Chapter 17. It does not say they shall not taste of death till He comes, but until they see. Then chapter 17 goes on, and after six days Jesus taketh Peter, James and John who had been standing with Him (vs. 28 in the sixteenth chapter). They saw the glory of Christ's coming and kingdom, and they saw the promise fulfilled, which Christ had made concerning His coming.

II. Pet. 1:16-18—Peter himself says, "WE saw." Peter was there. They saw His majesty, which pertains always to a king. They were eye-witnesses of the power of the Lord Jesus Christ.

(b) I Cor. 12:31 and 13:1—Chapter division sometimes breaks into the middle of a sentence. The proper punctuation at the end of 12:31 should be a colon, rather than a period.

(c) I Cor. 10:33 and 11:1—Chapter 10 tells of Paul's own self-renunciation. The thought is not just that alone, but is continued in 11:1, "Be ye followers of me." Chapter division cuts off the application.

(d) Mark 2:23-28—This passage should be linked up with verses 1-5 in chapter 3. Jesus said that the Son of Man is the Lord of the Sabbath, and in the next verses goes on to prove that He is the Lord of the Sabbath.

(e) II Cor. 6:18 and 7:1. 7:1 sums up the previous argument.

(f) Matt. 19:30 and 20:1. These two should go together.

(g) Isa. 53. This should begin back in chapter 52, with verse 13.

7. Use of context principle in comparing spiritual things with spiritual. This shows the value of the context principle as declared by God Himself in I Cor. 2:12, 13. We find spiritual things only in the Book of God and it would be useless to compare the books of man. This is a command to compare scripture with scripture.

(a) Other translations of these verses.
"Unfolding spiritual things spiritually."
"Unfolding Biblical things in Biblical words."
"By spiritual words are spiritual things explained."
"Explaining spiritual things in spiritual words."
"The correct way to explain inspired things is in inspired words."
"Comparing, unfolding, explaining."
It is the revelation of a God-given method of understanding scripture. There is only one way to explain the Bible, and that is with the Bible. Since the Bible is divine, it is folly to try to explain it by the things of man. The Bible will throw light on any problem it brings up. It is self-explanatory. Never depend upon man for any explanation of any Bible problem; go to God and you will find the solution in His Book. Bible illumination comes through the Bible itself. That is the value of the context principle.

(b) Rom. 3:10-19—How Paul used the context principle. Shows what the Spirit thinks of the principle.
    (1) In chapter 1 Paul deals with the Gentile and his sin. In chapter 2 he deals with the Jew and his sin, showing that the Jew has missed the righteousness of the law.
    (2) In chapter 3, then, Paul is rounding out his argument. After declaring that all men are sinners, he proves it by the use of scriptures. Using the context principle, Paul goes back into the Old Testament to prove the universality of sin.
        ((a)) This is making use of the "proof-text method" called grasshopper exegesis. This does not mean bolstering up your ideas with scripture, but getting your ideas from scripture. Starts, "As it is written." This is the method of teaching used fifty and seventy-five years ago, and many modern teachers ridicule this method, saying that it is out of date. There is no reason why preaching should be changed. The Bible has not changed, the message is not changed, nor is the need of man changed. We would be better off if men preached the way their fathers did.
            ((1)) Compare a book of sermons written fifty years ago with a book of sermons written in this day. Fifty years ago, you will find they preached doctrine, but today they are preaching froth and foam. The world is full of men who are called preachers, but they are merely peddlers of stories. When we call them wonderful preachers it is a sad commentary on our intellect. God calls on us to preach the Word. You can get plenty of people to respond to stories, but will the results be lasting? Use the proof-text method and declare the truth. You may use illustrations. They are legitimate, because the Lord Jesus Christ used them, but He did not tell stories.
    (3) Contexts used by Paul.
        ((a)) Rom. 3:10-12. Paul, in proving that all men are guilty sinners goes back to Psalm 14:1-3 as the context.
        ((b)) Rom. 3:13—Context Psalms 5:9; 140:3.
        ((c)) Rom. 3:14—Context Psalm 10:7.
        ((d)) Rom. 3:15-17—Context Isa. 59:7, 8.
        ((e)) Rom. 3:18—Context Psalm 36:1.

(c) Rom. 15:9-12. Another sample of Paul's use of the context.
    (1) He is seeking to prove that the Gentiles are really included in God's mercy. It was very difficult for the Jew to believe this, because he thought God was the God of the Jew only.
    (2) Paul proves his point by referring to Isa. 11:1, 10; Ps. 18:49; Isa. 42:6, 7; Deut. 32:43.

8. How to use this principle. Dr. Pierson calls it the principle of comparative mention. Passages of scripture may be compared or contrasted.

(a) Law and Grace. When you declare the truth concerning law and grace, it will:
  (1) Do you good.
  (2) Help your people.
(b) The new man and the old man—Col. 3:5-14 and Eph. 4:22-24. Line up the new and old man before the people and contrast them as to walk, members, standing, state, attire, etc.
(c) The Adversary and the Advocate. Contrast Christ and Satan—Gen. 3:15. There is a wonderful contrast all through scripture.
  (1) The adversary is continually accusing the believer, while the Advocate is defending him.
  (2) The adversary tries to entangle the believer, while the Advocate is always at the right hand of God, standing righteous before God when the believer proves to be unrighteous.
  (3) The adversary sends evil spirits to possess, while the Advocate sends the Holy Spirit.
(d) The Paracletes.
  John 14:16—translated Comforter.
  Means "One called alongside to help." Both the Holy Spirit and Christ are called by this name, Paraclete, and they are the only Ones in Scripture who have this name.
  (1) Christ is the paraclete (advocate) in heaven, and the Holy Spirit is the paraclete (comforter) on earth.
  (2) The Holy Spirit comes from God to represent God to the believer, and the Lord goes before God to represent the believer to God.
  (3) The Holy Spirit becomes our representative of Christ on earth. Christ becomes our representative in heaven.
  (4) The Holy Spirit makes intercession with the believer, and Christ makes intercession for the believer.
(e) Contrast between the Son of God and the son of perdition. There is a marvelous parallel between the two.

Christ	*Anti-Christ*
The Truth	The lie.
The Way	The deceiver
Public ministry 3½ years	Public ministry 3½ years.
Coming One	Coming One.
Morning Star	Star of the morning.
Prince of Princes	A prince.
Will have many diadems	Will have ten crowns.
All power from heaven	All power from Satan.

CHAPTER FOURTEEN

The Agreement Principle

XIII. THE AGREEMENT PRINCIPLE.

a. Definition.

That principle under which the truthfulness and faithfulness of God become the guarantee that He will not set forth any passage in His Word which contradicts any other passage.

1. There are no contradictions in scripture; there is organic unity. Though there are 66 books, yet it is perfect unity as shown in structure, history, purpose, doctrine, and theme, which is Jesus Christ. There are always critics who declare that the Bible is full of discrepancies, inaccuracies, contradictions, and errors, but the Bible is not a Bible of mistakes, and this is guaranteed by the God of truth and faithfulness— Psa. 119:90; John 17:17.

2. If the Bible is a book of errors, then we must reach one of two conclusions.

   (a) The Bible is not God's book; for God is faithful.

   (b) If it is God's book, then God is not faithful. Both these conclusions may be rejected—Num. 23: 19; Rom. 3:4; Deut. 32:4; Tit. 1:2. There are a lot of books written by man which do not contain the truth, and many commentaries on scripture do not contain it. God is the Author of the Bible, through the Holy Spirit, and the Bible is a perfect unity, though ridiculed by many modernists.

b. Examples of this principle.

This agreement principle is illustrated by Bible testimony on topics of human disagreement. There are some things in scripture upon which the scriptures agree, but on which human beings are disagreed.

1. Gathering of the Jews. Many say God is through with the Jew. If you talk of the time when Israel will be the head instead of the tail there will be disagreement among men; but not so in scripture. God is agreed all through the Bible concerning the dispersion and regathering of Israel—Deut. 30:1-3; Isa. 11:12; Ezek. 36; Ezek. 37; Jer. 23:3; Matt. 24:31; Rom. 11:25,26; Amos. 9:14-15. The Old Testament and the New Testament are perfectly agreed on this subject.

2. Is the world growing better or worse? People say that it is getting better in spite of the evidences of decay and corruption. Others say it is getting worse—no agreement at all. The Bible is agreed upon this subject as well—"As it was in the days of Noah." "As it was in the days of Lot." "When the Son of Man cometh will he find faith in the earth?" "In the last days perilous times shall come." Some people seem to think that the Lord will come back because the world is getting so good, but the truth is that the world is so *corrupt* that He must come.

3. Contrast between the writing of Paul and James—James 2:24; Rom. 4:2-4. Paul says you are justified by faith; James says you are justified by works. But Paul is showing how the sinner is justified before God by faith, and James shows justification before men by works. God sees our faith, but when we say we have faith, men look for works as a proof. Paul is talking about the fact of justification; James about the fruits of justification. Paul is talking about the doctrine of justification; James about the experience of justification. Paul is rebuking the Pharisees for their lack of faith; James is rebuking the people for their license and lawlessness.

c. Need for accuracy in the study of the Word of God.

Never preach on a text until you have studied it in the light of your concordance; know every word in your text.

There are many so-called errors which would never be set forth by man if every man were accurate.

1. Some of man's errors.

   (a) A man near Chesapeake Bay was a fisher of oysters, and a Christian. He was a member of the M.E. Church, and wanted the church to grant him the license to preach. Since he was very unlearned, the preacher kept putting him off. At last the preacher said that the next time the presiding elder came, he might preach, and get the opinion of the presiding elder. In due time his opportunity came, and he preached on the text, "Thou art an oysterman." He had the Lord Jesus out in the bay fishing for oysters. When he gave the invitation four people responded. Afterwards the preacher said to him, "You made a terrible mistake." The would-be preacher could not understand why, and then the preacher explained that the text should have read, "Thou art an austere man."—Lk. 19:21,22. To which the man replied, "What's the difference? Didn't we get four fish?"

   (b) A preacher of very little education once preached on the text, "He took him and held him and let him go," and was trying to explain how this was done when a man in the audience called out, "He took him and healed him and let him go"—Lk. 14:4. We need to be careful in reading the Bible.

2. How these errors are made.

    (a) Some prophecies were spoken; some were written and not spoken; some were both written and spoken.

        (1) Matt. 27:9—"Which was spoken by Jeremy the prophet." Somebody hunts through the book of Jeremiah for this prophecy and cannot find it, and then will locate it in Zechariah. This is proclaimed as another mistake in the Bible, and many explanations are offered:

            ((a)) Matthew wrote from memory and got the names of the men mixed up, so wrote down Jeremiah instead of Zechariah.

            ((b)) It is a slip of the pen.

            ((c)) The reason why "Jeremiah" was written instead of Zechariah was because Jeremiah's name was used to indicate any one of the prophets just as Ephraim was put in to indicate one of the tribes.

            ((d)) The thirty pieces of silver were in another prophecy written by Jeremiah, which is now lost.

            ((e)) Wordsworth says, "Matthew knew who it was, but wrote Jeremiah instead of Zechariah to show us that it doesn't make any difference." The fact of the matter is that Matthew does not say that Jeremiah wrote it, but says that Jeremiah spoke it. The Holy Spirit is not limited to a written statement. He could tell just as well what Jeremiah said, as He could tell Moses what the Devil said. Zechariah wrote what Jeremiah spoke.

        (2) I Thess. 1:10.

            ((a)) The people at Thessalonica were waiting for the Son, so the verse says. Some say they were not waiting for the Son, but for the Spirit; that the coming of the Son and the coming of the Spirit were the same thing. Those poor people at Thessalonica, then, were waiting for something that had already happened, for the Spirit came at Pentecost. In this they take issue with the Lord Jesus, because He said He was sending another.

            ((b)) Some say that they were waiting for death.

            ((c)) Others, that the coming of the Lord took place when Jerusalem was overthrown. Any view will be taken except the truth of the Lord's return.

d. Let marks of time be noted.

    1. Ezek. 36:25—The word, "Then" is the important word; it indicates the time. This verse does not apply to the church at all. Verses 16-24 explain it; as having to do with the restoration.

    2. Matt. 24:29—The words, "immediately after the tribulation" give the key to this verse.

e. Let marks of place be noted.

    1. Wilkins, concerning the ascension of the Lord, compares Luke 24:51 with Acts 1:9-12, saying that Luke, in the Gospel of Luke, says that Christ ascended from Bethany, and in Acts says He ascended from the Mt. of Olives. He points this out as a mistake in the Bible, and says that since these records differ there is a question as to whether He ascended at all. There is no question about this at all, since Bethany is on the slope of the Mt. of Olives, and Christ could not ascend from Bethany without ascending from the Mt. of Olives.

    2. Sinai and Horeb are the same.

    3. Antioch—be sure to differentiate between them.

    4. Ramah—there are five of them.

f. Dean Stanley, in Smith's Dictionary of the Bible, criticizes Stephen's discourse in Acts 7. We must be convinced first of all, and once for all, that the Bible is the Book of God.

Mark 7:13—The Jews put their traditions before the Word of God. The Catholics put their church before the Word of God; the Mormons put their book of the Mormons before the Bible; Christian Science puts "Science and Health" before the Bible. But the words of the Lord are pure words, and these are the words which the Holy Ghost teaches.

Dean Stanley says that in Stephen's address in Acts 7 there are twelve discrepancies at least, either by variation or addition. Does the Holy Spirit not have the right to make an addition if He wants to do so? Who are we to question Him? An addition is not a contradiction. In His criticism, Stanley says it shows that Stephen handled the scriptures carelessly; and his idea in criticizing is to blast away the foundation truth of the inspiration of the scripture. Here are a few of the so-called mistakes.

    1. Acts 7:14 speaks of Jacob and his kindred, which were seventy-five in all. This Dean Stanley compares with Gen. 46:26, which sets the souls that came with Jacob, besides his son's wives, as sixty-six. There is a difference between the family of Jacob and the descendants of Jacob.

Souls that came besides wives, Gen. 46:26	66
Jacob himself	1
Joseph	1
Joseph's sons	2
Wives of Jacob's sons	5 ⎧ not included
	— ⎨ in
Jacob's family	75 ⎩ Gen. 46:26

2. Acts 7:20 is compared with Ex. 2:2. Stephen says Moses was exceeding fair, while Exodus says he was a goodly child. Dean Stanley says this is an example of the careless way in which the Bible is written. However, in translating the Septuagint into the Greek, the word which was translated "goodly" in Exodus, is the same word which is translated "exceeding fair" in Acts.

3. Acts 7:22 is compared with Ex. 4:10—Acts refers to Moses' education and Exodus to his eloquence. What kind of comparison is this?
    Why not compare Acts 7:22 with Heb. 11:24? It is only common sense to believe that teachers would be provided for the child adopted by Pharoah's daughter. Stanley puts learning and eloquence as synonyms. Does education always make a man eloquent? No.

4. Acts 7:32 is compared with Ex. 3:3. There is no comparison here. There is a comparison between verses 7:32 and 3:6,7, but there is no comparison between verses that do not have the same subject.

5. In Acts 7:22 the statement is made that Moses was mighty in words, and in Ex. 4:10 Moses said, "I am not eloquent." You would not expect a man who was trying to get out of a job to say that he was eloquent. In Deuteronomy, however, Moses made one of the most eloquent speeches made by man. God says Moses was mighty in words, but does not say that he was eloquent.

6. Acts 7:53 and Ex. 19:16. Acts—law received by mediatorship of angels. In Exodus no mention of angels. What of it? Deut. 33:2; Gal. 3:19; Heb. 2:2—the word "saints" means "holy ones" or "angels."

g. Further examples of the use of this principle.

1. Psa. 58:4—One man says that an adder is not deaf, and so the Bible is not true. One Bible student has said, "When a man makes a statement concerning a contradiction in the Bible, I always go to the Word of God to see what it really says." In this instance, God is comparing a man who will not hear the Word with a serpent which will not listen to the music of the snake-charmer, but stops its ears. God is talking of His people; He speaks and they will not hear. They are not deaf, but rebellious.

2. I Sam. 16:17 with I Sam. 17:58. David was Saul's harpist, and when David slew the giant, Saul asked him who he was. This is called a discrepancy. The fact is that Saul asked him who his father was, because Saul had made a promise concerning the father of the man who slew the giant.

3. Luke 9:50 and Luke 11:23. These are not contradictory; they are complementary. Both statements are true under different circumstances. The context will solve the difficulty. Neutrality is sometimes as deadly as opposition, and again sometimes neutrality is effectual. Suppose there is a charge against you, and I know you are innocent. I keep silent. My neutrality is against you. Again, there is a charge against you. I know you are guilty and I keep silent. My neutrality is for you. In Luke 9:50 the question is concerning service. While this man was not banded with the disciples, he was not working against them. But in Luke 11:23 it is a question of warfare between Christ and Satan, and in that case there can be no neutrality. Everyone not *for* Christ is against Him.

4. Gal. 6:2 and Gal. 6:5. Gal. 6:2 says, "Bear ye one another's burdens," and then in 6:5 "Every man is to bear his own burdens." These refer to two kinds of burdens. There are some burdens which you can help another to bear such as sorrow, grief, and poverty. There are other burdens, such as duty and responsibility, which are not transferable. 6:2 refers to burdens of sympathy. 6:5 to burdens of responsibility.

5. Prov. 26:4,5.
    Vs. 4—answer not approvingly. If you answer in folly then you are lowering yourself to the level of the fool. Do not answer him as if he were wise. Jesus was asked many foolish questions, but He never answered them on the same level.
    Vs. 5—Answer him according to his folly, in such a way as to expose his folly, and in such a way that he will not have an opportunity to feel wise, or that he has superior knowledge.

6. John 8:59—Where did the people get the stones when they took stones to throw at Jesus? How did they pick up stones in the temple? The Bible does not say they picked up stones in the temple. They no doubt picked them up and carried them in. A stone was their ordinary weapon and was carried as the modern man would carry a revolver. And if the Bible had said they picked up stones in the temple, Edersheim says they could have found them in the court of the Gentiles, which was unpaved.

7. I Kings 15:14 with II Chron. 14:1,2,3. How could he take away the high places, and then not take them away? There were different kinds of high places in Palestine. Asa took away the high places where the idols were worshipped—I Kings 3:2,4; I Kings 22:43; II Kings 12:2,3; II Kings 15:3,4; I Chron. 16:39-40.

8. II Sam. 24:24; with I Chron. 21:22-25.
    (a) The amount paid by David was 50 shekels of silver, as recorded in II Sam., but in I Chron., it was 600 shekels of gold. Why the difference?
    (b) Professor Smith says that when the Chronicler came to write Chronicles he thought that 50 shekels were not enough, so he lied in a kindly way and said 600, in order to preserve the honor of David. The writer of the book then, was a kindly liar; and if he wrote one lie, then he probably wrote others.

(c) By reading the context we find that the threshing floor became the site of the temple and you could not build a temple 1000 ft. square on a threshing floor. In the first reference, David bought the threshing floor for 50 shekels of silver, and in the second, he bought the place of threshing-floor (whole field), and paid 600 shekels of gold.

9. Acts 9:7 with 22:9. In Acts 9:7 they heard the voice and then in Acts 22:9 they did not hear the voice. The fact is that they heard the voice, but not the words. The word translated "voice" comes from the Greek, "phone," which contains the idea of disclosure. In the Revised Version it reads, "they heard the sound," which is correct. Another reference is John 12:28,29. The people heard the voice, but not the words.

10. Deut. 31:2 with 34:7. Deut. 31:2—"I can no more go out and come in." In Deut. 34:7—"eye not dimmed, and natural forces not abated." The first reference doesn't mean feebleness, but that his days are at an end. Num. 27:17 shows what the phrase means.

11. Ex. 20:14 with Num. 31:18. Exodus says "thou shalt not commit adultery." Numbers says to keep alive the women that have not known men, for themselves. Man says they were to keep the women for their own immoral desires. It was not that, but the women were to be kept as slaves, and as judgment for leading the children of Israel astray.

12. Luke 9:35 with II Pet. 1:17. Luke says, "This is my beloved son, hear ye him." II Pet. 1:17—"This is my beloved son in whom I am well pleased." Turn to Matt. 17:5. The Father said, "This is my beloved Son in whom I am well pleased, hear ye Him."

13. Ex. 20:17 with I Cor. 12:31. Exodus says "Thou shalt not covet." I Corinthians says, "Covet earnestly the best things." In Corinthians the word "covet" means desire.

14. Ex. 9:3 with Ex. 14:9. In 9:3 we read about the cattle in the fields of the Egyptians dying. In 14:9 they used horses to pursue the children of Israel. If the cattle died, how could the horses be alive to pursue? In 9:3 it says that only the cattle in the field would be affected, so those kept in the stables for the army would not be touched. The horses of the Israelites were not smitten, and so Pharaoh could take them, as the Israelites were slaves. "All" may be used to mean all varieties, as well as, without exception. You have to decide its use from the context.

15. Numbers 4:3 with Numbers 8:24,25. In 4:3 it gives the age of the Levites as from 30 years old to 50. In 8:24,25 they were numbered from 25 years up. In 4:3, we have the numbering of the Levites; in 8:24,25, the service of the Levites.

h. Names in Scripture.

1. More than one man may have the same name.
   (a) Saul of Tarsus was not the king of Israel: This might be said in a moment of carelessness.
   (b) How could Jehoram be king in Israel, and king in Judah? He was not. There were two kings of the same name.
   (c) There are three men named James in the New Testament: James the son of Zebedee, James the son of Alphaeus, and James the brother of Jesus.
   (d) There are four Johns: John the Baptist, John the Apostle, John Mark, and just John—Acts 4:6.
   (e) There are ten Simons in Scripture.
   (f) There are many Herods in the New Testament.
   (g) There are six Marys.
   (h) We are inclined to speak of titles as names. Abimelech was the title of the king of Philistia, just as the titles king, czar, president, or kaiser. Agag, Caesar and Pharoah were all titles.

2. Not only do different people have the same name, but one man may have more than one name.
   (a) Jacob—Israel.
   (b) Silvanus—Silas.
   (c) Timotheus—Timothy.
   (d) Levi—Matthew.
   (e) Peter (Gr.)—Cephas (Aramaic)—Simon (Heb.).
   (f) Jehoiachin—Coniah—Jechoniah.
   (g) Saul—Paul.
   (h) Abram—Abraham.
   (i) Sarai—Sarah.
   (j) Joseph—Zaphnath-paaneah (Egyptian).
   (k) Daniel and his friends—Dan. 1.

3. Places may have more than one name.
   (a) Antioch—one in Syria, and one in Pisidia in Asia Minor.

(b) There are three Bethsaidas and five Ramoths.

(c) Bethel is also Luz.

(d) Jerusalem is also Ariel (lion of God).

(e) Egypt is called Ham, and there was a small town on the east shore of the Dead Sea called Ham.

(f) Sinai is also called Horeb.

(g) Sea of Galilee also has other names: Chinnereth, Genessaret, Tiberias.

(h) Dead Sea also called Sea of Plain, and Salt Sea.

(i) Dan—Gen. 14 Abraham pursued the four kings unto Dan. Man says Dan was not established until 400 years after, at the establishment of the tribe of Daniel. There were two places by that name.

(j) Mt. Hor and Moserah—the same place. Num. 33:38 says Aaron died at Mt. Hor and Deut. 10:6 at Moserah.

(k) Bethany—on side of Mt. of Olives.

(l) Hai—Ai.

i. Inaccuracies in Translation.

We must recognize that this may occur; for the translations are not inspired. Many times so-called translations are not translations, but interpretations. Don't make a god of the 1611 version, or any other. However, the answer to many apparent contradictions is found in the translations of men.

1. II Chron. 16:1 with I Kings 15:32,33.

(a) Chronicles says Baasha came in the 36th year of the reign of Asa, while Kings say that in the third year of the reign of Asa, Baasha began to reign and reigned for twenty-four years, dying in the twenty-seventh year of the reign of Asa. This makes the king appear to be fighting against Asa nine years after he was dead.

(b) Look up the word "reign" and you will find that it was the thirty-sixth year of the kingdom of Asa. Reign means dominion, empire, kingdom, realm, and royalty. So what this really says is, "the thirty-sixth year of the founding of the kingdom over which Asa reigned"—II Chron. 14:1; 15:19; 16:1.

2. Rev. 5:8-10.

(a) Here is a picture of the heavenly beings praising God for salvation. There is no scripture which states that Christ died for anyone but the world. There is no hope given for the fallen angels nor for the Devil. The angelic beings are not included in the redemption provided by Christ—Heb. 2:9 —"Christ tasted death for every man."

(b) The revised version gives the correct translation. "He hath redeemed men," not *us*. This translation is indorsed by many great Bible teachers. These creature beings are not redeemed.

3. Jude 14 with II Pet. 2:5.

Enoch is the seventh from Adam, and in Gen. 5 this is confirmed. But in II Pet. 2:5 God spared Noah the eighth person. In the mind of the person who found this apparent discrepancy this is a contradiction, because Noah would be the tenth person from Adam, according to the generations in Genesis. The revised version is correct—"preserved Noah with seven others."

4. Gen. 1:31 with 2:4. A day may be 24 hours in one place, and in another place may mean a period of time.

Gen. 6:19 with 7:2. This is a repetition with additions. The two animals were for propagation, and the seven for sacrifice.

5. Accounts of creation. There are not two accounts of creation. Gen. 1:1 to 2:4 is the introduction to this book of beginnings, of which there are 12 divisions. The over-all account is given in chapter 1 and the details in chapter 2.

6. Gen. 16:4-14 with Gen. 21: A preacher once said that there were two accounts of the expulsion of Hagar. The first record is of the fact that she was mistreated by Sarah and ran away, but the Lord sent her back. Thirteen years later she and her son were cast out.

7. I Sam. 6:19 says 50,070 were slain. That is a great number. The Hebrew says he smote 70 men, two 50's and a thousand, or 1170 men.

8. Judges 12:6, "fell forty and two thousand." We say 42,000 and here there were only 32,000 of them all together. It should be 2040.

9. Luke 24:39.

(1) Jesus in resurrection body is standing in the midst of the disciples. They think He is a spirit. He says "a spirit hath not flesh and *bones* as ye see me have."

(2) Mrs. Montgomery's translation reads: "Spirit hath not flesh and *Blood* as ye see me have." He didn't have *blood* after the resurrection.

CHAPTER FIFTEEN

The Direct Statement Principle

XIV. THE DIRECT STATEMENT PRINCIPLE.

a. Definition. That principle under which God says what He means, and means what He says.

   1. This is an important principle, and we enunciate this because of the attempts of many people to spiritualize the Word of God and to make it a mystical book. To many people, God's Word is not to be taken literally at all. A tooth, an eye, or an ear, must mean something else, to a person of this type.

   2. There are certain things to be considered, however.

      (a) A word that meant one thing 300 years ago (when the Bible was translated into English) may have a changed meaning today.
      Luke 1:63—A writing table does not mean a rolltop desk, but rather a writing tablet.
      Luke 3:23—"Began to be about thirty years of age." This means, He began His ministry at the age of about thirty years.
      Acts 21:15; I Sam. 17:22—Took up their carriage. This means that which was carried, or baggage. "Wist," "wit," "I do you to wit," are not used today.
      Rom. 1:13; II Thess. 2:7—"Let" did not mean to permit, but rather to hinder, hold back, or restrain.
      I Thess. 4:15—"Prevent" meant come before, precede (See R.V.).
      Phil. 3:20—Conversation refers to life and action. In the revised version it has been changed to citizenship.

      (b) Mistakes are also made by the translators and printers.
         (1) A publishing company had the public aid them in proof-reading the Bible they were putting out, and which they wanted to be perfect. After all their efforts, the Bible came out with, "Holy Rible" on the inside front page.
         (2) The "Place makers" Bible instead of "peacemakers"—Matt. 5:9.
         (3) The "Adulterous" Bible. The word NOT was left out in the commandment, "Thou shalt not commit adultery"—Ex. 20.
         (4) The idle Bible—in Zech. 11:17 "idle" is printed instead of "idol."
         (5) The "murderers" Bible—the murmurers in Jude 16 were called murderers.
         (6) The "Printers" Bible—Psa. 119:161, the word "princes," changed to "printers."
         (7) The "Wife-haters" Bible—Luke 14:26—word "life," changed to "wife."
         (8) The "Vinegar Bible"—Luke 20, the word "vinegar" instead of "vineyard."
         These mistakes are made by man, not by God; and we must recognize that only the first parchments were inspired by God.

   3. How people spiritualize the Scriptures.

      (a) God made man in His own image. A white man declared that God, then, must be white. Others say that the first man was red. Adam means red man of the earth. Therefore He must have been red.

      (b) The four rivers in Eden are supposed to mean prudence, self-control, courage, and justice.

      (c) The parable of the sowing of the wheat. Jerome says that the thirty-fold pertains to marriage, sixty-fold to widows, and one hundred-fold to virginity.

      (d) When you study the Bible don't try to make it a kind of wonder book, or spiritual museum.
         (1) Shakespeare. In 1611 when the Bible was translated, Shakespeare was forty-six years old. Some wise person turned to the forty-sixth Psalm, and found that the forty-sixth word from the beginning was shake, and the forty-sixth word from the end was spear. This was supposed to mean something or other.
         (2) Armistice. Signed on the eleventh hour of the eleventh day of the eleventh month. A wise person turned to the eleventh book, the eleventh chapter, the eleventh verse, which was I Kings 11:11. The kingdom was rent from Solomon, so it must be rent from Wilhelm. But the next verse says it will be rent from Solomon's son. Supposed to be a prophecy to that effect.

      (e) Zion is not heaven, and Jerusalem is not heaven. And the New Jerusalem is not to be in heaven, but a literal city. All these are mixed up. Zion is a hill on which Jerusalem is built.

      (f) People say that the throne of David is in your heart. How many thrones did David have? The throne of David is the literal throne to be set up in a literal city, Jerusalem.

      (g) Augustine says that the disciples were fishing and caught 153 fish. The sum of all the numbers to 17 is 153, so 153 means 17. 10 is the number of the commandments and 7 is the spiritual number. Together they make 17. Therefore the 153 fish stand for the commandments and the Holy Spirit.

b. Figures of Speech.

You will find figurative speech in any book, and it is found in the Bible as well. Since the Bible is oriental in origin, the figures will show the highest of oriental hyperbole. A figure of speech is speech out of form. It is sometimes thrown into a peculiar form and expressed in an unusual manner, in a way that is not just natural, or fashioned according to grammar. This is not from accident or ignorance but from design and for the purpose of emphasis.

1. Common figures of speech.

The thermometer is going up. Crank the car. The furnace has gone out. Take a street car. A hard heart. There are over two hundred figures of speech in the Bible.

2. Rule for studying figures of speech in the Bible.

Words should be understood in their literal meaning, unless such literal interpretation involves a manifest contradiction or absurdity.

3. Examples from Scripture.

   (a) Isa. 1:18—Sins as scarlet.

   (b) Jer. 1:18—"I have made thee an iron pillar, a walled city."

   (c) Matt. 8:22—"Let the dead bury their dead."

   (d) John 2:19—"Destroy this temple." The context explains this figure.

4. Some of the better known figures of speech.

   (a) Metaphor—represents.

   Words are taken from their literal meaning and given a new and striking use. The figure is a distinct affirmation that one thing is another which it resembles. The two nouns must always be mentioned. The figure lies in the verb. "IS" is equivalent to "REPRESENTS."
   Examples: Isa. 40:6; Ps. 18:2; Matt. 26:26-28; John 6:32-65.

   (b) Simile—resembles. Likening one thing to another in terms of comparison.

Examples:—*Metaphor.*	*Simile*
Isa. 40:6—"flesh is grass."	I Pet. 1:24—"flesh is as grass."
Ps. 100:3b—"sheep of his pasture."	Isa. 53:6—"We like sheep."
	Isa. 55:10,11; Jer. 23:29; Matt. 7:24-27; Rom. 112:4,5; I Cor. 12:12; Matt. 13—Parables.

   (c) Metonymy. A figure of speech consisting of a change of nouns. The name of an object is substituted for another which it clearly suggests.

   (1) Container for what is contained.
   "This is the cup of my blood."
   Ps. 23—"preparest a table before me."
   I Cor. 10:21—"drink the cup."

   (2) Cause for effect—Eph. 4:20—"learned Christ," means the teaching of Christ.

   (3) Parents for children—
   Gen. 9:25-27; 49:7; Rom. 9:13.
   Mal. 1:2,3—three hundred years after, children were born; means the descendants, rather than Esau and Jacob.

   (4) Author for works. We speak of reading Shakespeare, Thackery, Hugo, Moses, etc. Lk. 24:27—"Jesus began at Moses," meaning the writings of Moses. Lk. 16:29—"they have Moses and the prophets," meaning their writings—II Cor. 3:15.

   (5) Instrument for effect. Deut. 17:6—"at the mouth of two or three witnesses," meaning their testimony. "The earth was corrupt," means the people—Gen. 6:11. "God so loved the world," means He loved the people—John 3:16. "Why persecutest thou me?" means rather, "Why do you persecute those who are mine?" "I was hungry and ye fed me"—those who are mine.

   (6) Land "mourns"—means untilled etc.
   Rom. 14:15—"destroy not by thy meat"—example leads into idolatry.
   Luke 2:27—"came by the Spirit"—by the direction of the Spirit.
   Matt. 10:34—"came to send a sword"—stands for disturbance.

   (d) Synecdoche. Similar to metonymy, with this difference.

   (1) A part is used for the whole; and the whole for a part.
   Gen. 3:19—"Sweat of the face" stands for the body; "bread," for food.
   Matt. 27:4—"innocent blood," stands for the whole man.
   Acts 27:37—not only *souls*, but men.
   Luke 16:23—the spiritual part of the man.
   John 19:24; Ecc. 12:3; Jer. 8:7—first used as representatives of the whole class to which they belong.

John 20:2—"then laid they Jesus"—the body of Jesus. "They have taken away my Lord"—the body of my Lord.

   (2) Plural sometimes used for singular, and singular for plural.
      Judges 12:7—Did not bury him in pieces, one in each city. Translators have added "one of the" to make it clear.
      Gen. 14:—Lot did not dwell in all the cities of the plain, but in one—Gen. 19:29.
      Isa. 1:3—Ox knows and ass knows—means all oxen and asses.
      Josh. 24:12—sent the hornet—meaning hornets.
      I Cor. 14:19—(speak five with and ten thousand without) means few and many.
      Eccl. 6:3—One hundred children means a great many.
      Ex. 20:6—"thousand" means the whole number.

(e) Personification. Figure of speech whereby an inanimate object, an object of nature, an abstract idea are given attributes of life—Num. 16:32—"earth opened her mouth."

(f) Ps. 114:3,4; Job 3:10.
    Anti-Personification. Living things are sometimes represented as dead. Mephibosheth said to David, "I am a dead dog." (Humility). A dead dog is not good for anything, but a dead horse is good for glue.—II Sam. 16:9—Shimei called a dead dog.

(g) Apostrophe. From the Greek, "To turn"—means to turn away from the readers or hearers, addressing that which is absent as present, or addressing the inanimate or dead thing as living.
    Psa. 114:5-8—the sea is addressed.
    Isa. 51:9—the arm of the Lord.
    Isa. 54:1-5—Israel, the wife of Jehovah.
    I Cor. 15:55—death and the grave.

(h) Hyperbole. A rhetorical figure that might be set forth under the word "Exaggeration," or magnifying an object beyond reality. An overstatement used for the purpose of deep emphasis. No thought of deception.

Ps. 8:6	II Sam. 1:23	Judges 7:12
Jer. 9:1	Amos 9:14,15	Deut. 1:28
John 21:25	Gen. 41:49	Psa. 22:6

(i) Other figures. Sarcasm and irony. (See Job) God said, "Where were you when I laid the foundations of the earth?" Irony—Elijah said to the prophets of Baal, "Call louder, maybe your god is asleep."

(j) Parable. Means to throw alongside. Taking a story and using it to throw light on a subject. Two-fold reason for using the parable.
      (a) To make truth known to the one who wants to know.
      (b) To hide the truth from those who do not want to know. It is an earthly story with a heavenly meaning. An extended simile. Do not make a parable out of something that is not a parable.

(k) The Fable. A brief story or tale introducing individuals or brute creation and endowing them with reason and speech. The oldest fable is the fable of Jotham, in Judges 9:7-20. It had to do with Jotham's own day, but there may also be a lesson for the present. Israel is often called a tree—fig, olive, or a vine. The bramble, no doubt, represents the false Messiah—II Kings 14:8-10.

(l) The Riddle. Designed to puzzle and perplex the hearer. The most celebrated riddle is that of Samson in Judges 14:14.

(m) Contrast—Prov. 11:1.

(n) Comparison—Psa. 84:10.

CHAPTER SIXTEEN

The Gap Principle

XV. THE GAP PRINCIPLE.

a. Definition. That principle of divine revelation whereby God in the Jewish Scriptures ignores certain periods of time, leaping over centuries without comment. This is a principle that is not recognized by all Bible teachers and students.

b. Illustrations.

1. Isa. 61:1,2, with Luke 4:16-21. Why, in Luke's record, did the Lord Jesus stop at the comma in Isa. 61:1,2? In the first coming of the Lord, He came to preach the acceptable year of the Lord. When He comes the second time He will preach of the day of vengeance. This has not yet come. There is already a gap of 1900 years between the clauses of that sentence—Isa. 61:2.

2. I Pet. 1:10,11.
The prophets themselves could not understand what they prophesied concerning the suffering and glory of Christ (His humiliation and exaltation). They did not understand the gap principle. They tried to put these two mountain peaks together, but there was a valley of 1900 years which they did not see.

3. Dan. 9.
The seventy weeks were not weeks of days, but weeks of years, or four hundred and ninety years. Sixty-nine of these weeks have passed.
69 weeks—(Gap)—*One week which has to do with Israel, the restoration,* the day of the "little horn."

4. Hosea 1:4.
Jezreel—(Gap) forty years. *Close of the kingdom of the house of Israel.*

5. Rev. 12:5,6—Birth and ascension (vs. 5) (gap). *Three-and-a-half years of tribulation period—Vs. 5,6.*

6. Isa. 9:6,7—Incarnation Vs. 6a—(Gap)—*Throne of David (not taken yet).*

CHAPTER SEVENTEEN

The Three-fold Principle

XVI. THE THREE-FOLD PRINCIPLE.

a. Definition.

The principle of Bible study in which God sets forth the truths of salvation in a three-fold way; past-justification; present-transformation; future-consummation.

1. This principle expresses the grace of God and shows the fullness, completeness, and richness of our eternal salvation. It is found all the way through the Word of God.

2. This three-fold principle meets the three pre-eminent needs of man:
   (a) Salvation from the wrath of God—Rom. 1:18; 3:23; John 3:36.
   (b) Salvation from the bondage of sin—Rom. 7:15.
   (c) Salvation from physical distress, disease, death, and decay—Rom. 6:23.

3. Every misery and woe of the human race springs from these three conditions of man:
   (a) Separation of the soul from God.
   (b) Slavery in the bondage of sin.
   (c) The mortal and infirm condition of the body.

4. Sin has brought on us:
   (a) Damned souls.
   (b) Sin-blighted lives.
   (c) Death and decay-doomed bodies.

5. God provides for three pre-eminent needs of man in his three-fold plan of salvation. Salvation is something past, something present, and something future. Every Bible student will agree that this is found in the Word of God. The Christian's only foundation is in the finished work of Christ.
   (a) Past—Justification, which gives man a ground for the hope that is within him.
   (b) Present—This aspect is manifested in the daily walk of the Christian who should so live and walk as to honor God. This is possible, not because of what we are in ourselves, but because of the indwelling Holy Spirit.
   (c) Future—The consummation of our salvation will be in eternal glory when the believer is made in the visible and eternal likeness of the Lord Jesus Christ.

6. Man is saved from the:
   (a) *Penalty of sin.*
   This is past, and has to do with the wrath of God. "He was wounded for our transgressions" that we might not be wounded. God laid our sin on Him.
   (b) *Power of sin.*
   Salvation from the habit of sin and the bondage of sin, in this present day. Whenever a Christian is given over to fleshly desires and appetites he does not have fellowship with God, and does not have victory. His life is powerless and barren. No life that is filled with fleshly desires and worldly activities is ever fruitful.
   (c) *The Presence of sin.*
   When this salvation has reached its consummation, we will be given not only a redeemed soul and spirit, but also a redeemed body. Some people think that if you have enough faith you will not have any bodily ills; but immortality will not come until Christ returns.

7. Man could not meet these needs in his own strength.
   (a) God knows that man could not get right with God, so God laid the foundation for this remedy in the cross.
   (b) God knows that man is too sinful and weak to live aright, so He bestowed upon us the Holy Spirit, and has given Jesus Christ a place in heaven as our intercessor and advocate.
   (c) God knows that man cannot get out of the grave, nor give himself a new body, so God provided the resurrection; or rejuvenation, as the case may be.

b. Illustrations from Scripture.

1. Tit. 2:11-13—Gives us the three-fold work of Jesus Christ.
   Cross—past.
   Throne—present.
   Coming—future.

2. II Cor. 1:10—
   He hath, He doth, He will deliver.

3. I Thess. 1:3—
   Faith, labor of love, patience and hope.

CHAPTER EIGHTEEN

The Election Principle

XVII. THE ELECTION PRINCIPLE.

a. Definition.

That principle of divine revelation whereby God in working out His purposes set aside all firsts and established all seconds.

1. God has a purpose, and this is worked out all through Scripture.

2. For example: Rom. 9:10-12. The purpose of God declared that the elder should serve the younger; and nothing can set this aside. It is clear and candid. The seconds that the Lord establishes are established on the basis of the cross.

3. The reason why God sets aside the firsts, is because the firsts are of the flesh and of Satan; and the seconds are associated with the spiritual and with the Lord Jesus Christ.

b. Illustrations:

1. Heb. 10:7-9—Sacrifices under the law are compared to the sacrifice of the Lord Jesus Christ. The sacrifices of the Jewish altars are set aside for the sacrifice of the Lord Jesus Christ.

2. Examples in families of Scripture:

    (1) Cain set aside for Abel.

    (2) Japheth set aside for Shem.

    (3) Ishmael set aside for Isaac.

    (4) Esau set aside for Jacob.

    (5) Reuben set aside for Judah.

    (6) God set aside the first and chose the second, or a second. "Except a man be born again"—the first birth is not enough; only the twice-born man is accepted.

3. Adam had two possible grounds of access to God. Before the fall, he had access to God and fellowship with God on the ground of his own continuance in righteousness. But, because of one evil deed, fellowship with God was lost, and communion was cut off. As soon as sin entered in, what did God do? He made provision for clothing Adam and Eve by slaying animals. No man can enter in the presence of God by good works, but only by the shedding of blood.

4. Cain and Abel. The above truth is brought out in this incident also. God set aside the offering of the first, and established the second.

5. Gen. 48:8-19—Jacob crossed his hands, and by this act, the second son of Joseph received the blessing that the first should have received. In the crossing of Jacob's hands we have a figure of the fact that all things are based on the cross.

6. II Pet. 3:13—Sin has access to both earth and heaven at the present time, but God will establish a second heaven and earth where righteousness shall reign.

7. According to God's Word, we were lost in our first condition; but by His grace, those who believe are saved by the second condition. God has set aside our first condition on the grounds of the cross of Calvary.

In our first condition, we were without hope; in the second condition we are saved in hope. In the first condition we wandered in darkness and sin; in the second we are walking in the light. In the first condition we were rebels against God, but now we are ambassadors for Him. In the first condition we were hell-doomed sinners, but now we have the hope and assurance of heaven.

The Repetition Principle

XVIII. THE REPETITION PRINCIPLE OR RECURRENCE PRINCIPLE.

a. Definition.
That principle under which God repeats some truth or subject already given, generally with the addition of details not before given.
This principle is closely allied to the progressive mention principle. "Repetitions with additions." Repetitions are made for the sake of additional information.

b. Examples.

1. Gen. 1:2—The creation of man recorded in Genesis 1 is a mere statement of fact, but in the second chapter there are added details. A moral aspect is also added. In the first chapter the name of God used is Elohim, the *creative* title. In the second chapter we have the name LORD or Jehovah, God's *redemptive* title. This is the name of God when He enters into covenant relationship with man.

2. "Verily."
   (a) The repetition may be of a single word, phrase, or sentence, and that is always significant and of importance—just as if God were saying, "Take note here."
   Note how many times the Lord Jesus said, "Verily, verily."

   John 5:24   John 6:47
   John 5:25   John 6:53
   John 6:26   John 8:34
   John 6:32

   (b) Truth concerning hell.
   The mind of natural man has always rebelled against the thought of hell. This is treated by the Lord in a three-fold repetition—Mark 9:44-46-48. A simple statement, but one that men need to face.

   (c) Judgment of the stubborn nation—Isaiah 6:10.
   This passage is found in the Bible seven times—six times besides Isa. 6:10. This concerns the judgment of judicial blindness on Israel.

   (1) It was first given in Isaiah.
   (2) When the Lord Jesus came and the nation treated Him as they treated God the Father in the Old Testament, and rejected Him, then Jesus pronounced judgment on them and quoted Isaiah 6.
   (3) In the Old Testament God the Father dealt with them; in the Gospels, God the Son worked with them; in the Book of Acts the Holy Spirit tried to reach the hearts of the people of Israel. But this could not be done, and in the Book of Acts through the pen of Luke, and the mouth of Paul, the Spirit pronounced the judgment of blindness upon Israel, and quoted Isaiah 6.
   (4) Paul in the Epistle to the Romans quotes Isaiah 6, concerning judgment on the nation of Israel. It brings out the amazing fairness of God's dealings with man. Judgments that men fully deserve are not meted out until sufficient warning has been given.
   (5) References: Isa. 6:10; Matt. 13:14; Mark 4:12; Luke 8:10; Jn. 12:40; Acts 28:25-27; Rom. 11:8.

3. The Book of Revelation.
   You can never understand this book aside from the Repetition Principle. It is a series of visions with the coming of Christ as the climax. This is repeated three times in the book, each time with added information.

4. The ministry of Paul.
   In the Book of Acts, which begins with the ministry of Peter, we have a record of Paul's ministry, and in all of the record he seems to be preaching only to the Jews. Only toward the end of the book Paul says to the Jews that he is now going to preach to the Gentiles. In the Epistles, however, we have the repetition of the record of Paul's ministry, and in this we find the record of another marvelous activity, the establishing of churches among the Gentiles. It is a repetition with added details. We have the same period, the same preacher, but two lines of ministry.

5. History of Israel.
   It is given in the Old Testament, and is repeated in the Book of Acts in the sermon of Stephen, with added details, not contradictions. In Romans we find a record of Israel's wanderings, which is a repetition of the record in Deuteronomy.

c. You will often find that in the repetition, the divine viewpoint is given, while in the first account, man's viewpoint alone is given.

1. Books of Chronicles and Kings.

In the books of I and II Chronicles, and I and II Kings (with I and II Samuel really part of Kings) the same period of history is recorded. Chronicles, however, is a repetition with a spiritual application, spiritual thought, and spiritual information. In Kings, history is recorded from man's viewpoint. In Kings we have the facts of history; in Chronicles we have God's thoughts and words about these facts. In Kings God reveals the course of events; in Chronicles God reveals the reason for or meaning of these events. In Kings we see how man ruled; in Chronicles we see how God over-ruled. Kings is governmental; Chronicles is ecclesiastical. Kings is kingly; Chronicles is priestly. Kings is written from the viewpoint of the natural; Chronicles from the supernatural. Kings, of things earthly; Chronicles, of things heavenly. God's purpose in Kings is to give the whole history of Israel's kingdoms in a complete way.

2. Differences between Kings and Chronicles.

The priestly aspect of Chronicles compared with kingly and natural aspects of Kings.

(a) Wars vs. revival. In Kings, there are three chapters (88 verses) given over to the wars of Hezekiah —II Kings 18:19:20:. And there are three verses given to the great revival in Israel during his reign—II Kings 18:4-6. Here the emphasis is upon his wars. In Chronicles, there are three chapters given to the great revival under Hezekiah—II Chron. 29:30:31:. Only one chapter is given to the wars—II Chron. 32:.

(b) Ark of the Covenant. In II Samuel one chapter is devoted to the removal of the ark to Jerusalem, II Sam. 6. In Chronicles three chapters are given to this event—II Chronicles 13, 14, 16. Emphasizes Levites, temple, and religious life.

(c) David's great sin. In Samuel, two chapters are devoted to it—II Sam. 11:12:. In Chronicles, it is not mentioned. When God forgives He forgets.

(d) Reign of Saul. It takes twenty chapters in I Sam. to tell of the long and disastrous reign of the first king, Saul, who was not a man chosen after God's own heart, but after the eyes of the people. In Chronicles his reign is disposed of in one chapter. He is a type of the flesh and man after the flesh is not important to God.

3. The word "because" in Chronicles. In Chronicles we oftentimes find the word "Because" or a similar word. In King's the record says, "This happened." In Chronicles, "This happened because." God is behind the scenes and showing something not revealed before—the cause of the event.

(a) II Chron. 12:14.

(b) II Chron. 13:18—Israel prevailed because they relied on the Lord.

(c) II Chron. 14:11, 12—In Kings we read of Asa and his wars, but in Chronicles we find the word "so." There is no "so" in Kings. Asa won his battles because he came to God and prayed to Him.

(d) II Chron. 16:9—therefore.

4. The temple.

You will find more about the temple in Chronicles than in Kings, because the religious side is being emphasized. Solomon, Ahab, Hezekiah, etc., are not made much of in Chronicles. The cause of their failures is given only to show the result and the working of God.

d. The Four Gospels.

1. Reason for having four gospels which are repititions of the life of Christ. Not, as some think, for a complete biography. The reason above all others is given in John 20:30, 31. The New Testament is the outgrowth of the Old. The Old Testament is the root and the New is the shoot. "The New is in the Old contained, and the Old is in the New explained." The Old Testament is filled with prophecies concerning Christ which are fulfilled and explained in the New. The very first verse of the New Testament links up with the Old Testament.

(a) The prophecies concerning Jesus Christ which are recorded in the Old Testament may be classed under four heads:
    (1) King—Psa. 2:6; Isa. 32:1; Dan. 9:25.
    (2) Servant—Isa. 42:1; Isa. 52:13.
    (3) Son of Man—Isa. 7:14; 9:6, 7; Dan. 7:13, 14.
    (4) Son of God—Isa. 9:6, 7; 40:3-9.

(b) Christ is set forth in the Old Testament as the Branch, and Old Testament name:
    (1) Jer. 23:5—The Branch—the king—Lion.
    (2) Zech. 3:8—The Branch—my servant—Ox.
    (3) Zech. 6:12—The Branch—the man—man.
    (4) Isa. 4:2—The Branch—of the Lord—Eagle.

(c) Christ is introduced four times in the Old Testament by the word "behold."
    (1) Zech. 9:9—Behold the king.
    (2) Isa. 42:1—Behold, my servant.
    (3) Zech. 6:12—Behold, the man.
    (4) Isa. 40:9—Behold your God.

(d) The New Testament
    (1) Matthew — presents Christ as King   — Sovereign — appeals to Jews.
    (2) Mark   — presents Christ as Servant — Servant   — appeals to Romans.
    (3) Luke   — presents Christ as Man   — Seed   — appeals to Greeks.
    (4) John   — presents Christ as God   — Son   — appeals to Church.

These are not really four pictures of Christ, but there is one picture presented in four different ways.

2. Another possible reason for writing these four Gospels.

Each would appeal to a different class of people. When Christ was crucified there was an inscription placed over His head, and it was written in three languages: Greek, Hebrew and Latin, the languages of the three principal peoples.

(a) Matthew is the book that would appeal to the Jews. Some say John should be used in dealing with Jews, but this is not true. The Jew does not need proof that the Messiah was to be Deity; what he needs is proof that Jesus was the Messiah. This proof is found in Matthew from the first verse, "The Son of David, the son of Abraham." The only Jew who could prove that He was the son of David and of Abraham was Jesus. The Jews kept their records in the temple, and when the temple was destroyed, the record was destroyed also. The only records of His genealogy are those which God gave in the two gospels.

(b) Rome was not interested in a Jewish King. The keyword of their government was service. Rome worshipped military service in her government. They were not interested in the same things the Greeks were interested in, which were poetry and literature. The gospel of Mark would appeal to the Romans. It is a short Gospel, full of action.

(c) The Greeks were interested in poetry, song, and literature. They also had one high ambition, and that was to produce a perfect man and a perfect race. At one time Greece slew all defective children in order to destroy all defects from the race. Their gods were not made in the form of beasts but in the forms of men. They were interested in the perfect man, and they would find that in Luke. This book has been called, by an agnostic, the most beautiful book ever written.

(d) The fourth group is for the Christian. If you are a Christian your favorite gospel is John.

Paul knew how to preach to these different groups. To the Jews he preached Jesus the Messiah, and to the Gentiles he preached Jesus the Son of God.

3. Now these aspects are presented in the four gospels. This does not mean that Matthew, for instance, wrote *only* of Christ as King, but it was this aspect which is in the foreground.

(a) Matthew. Key verse 1:1.
    (1) The expression "kingdom of heaven" is found thirty-two times in Matthew and nowhere else in the New Testament.
    (2) John the Baptist's preaching concerning repentance, "for the kingdom of heaven is at hand," is found only in Matthew.
    (3) The wise men came saying, "Where is he that is born king of the Jews?" This is recorded only in Matthew.
    (4) When Jesus was tried they charged Him with claiming to be King. When they nailed Him to the cross, the inscription, "This is the King of the Jews," was nailed over His head.
    (5) He was an absolute King, placing His word above the law of Moses. He asserted His authority by the words, "I say unto you," fifty-four times. He demonstrated His authority by pronouncing woes upon them.
    (6) The record of His birth in Matthew says He was born King of the Jews. In Luke 2:11—"Unto you is born a Saviour."
    (7) In Matthew, He was crucified because He claimed to be King of the Jews: in John, because He said He was the Son of God. Both are true, for both charges were brought against Him. In the Sanhedrin they charged Him with claiming to be the Son of God, but before Pilate they charged Him with being a seditious king.
    (8) Matthew begins with the genealogy of the King—His birth, baptism, and testing. It includes the calling of His cabinet together, the constitution of the Kingdom (set forth in Matt. 5, 6, 7), the credentials of the King (set forth in Matt. 8, 9,—not found in the other Gospels), the messengers sent out, the reception, and rejection of the message. In chapter 11 Christ begins to tell of the change which has come to the kingdom, "It is like." This is followed by the ministry of the rejected King, His trial, and crucifixion, because He said He was King of the Jews.
    (9) Ascension. There is no record of the ascension in Matthew because He is to be a King on earth.

(b) Mark. Key verse 10:45.
    (1) Christ is set forth as the Servant of Jehovah, not the servant of man. Servant of man—mere humanitarianism.
    (2) No genealogy is given. He is only the messenger or servant. No servant holds his position on the basis of ancestry. When one applies for a position, one's ancestry does not make any difference; it is the recommendations that are required.

(3) Matthew gave the genealogy because it was necessary for a king.

(4) Christ's recommendation is given at the beginning of the book of Mark, "This is my Son." It is God's recommendation.

(5) There is no record of His origin, birth, boyhood; no reference to Bethlehem and no account of His youth.

(6) All through the book we find a word which is a servant's word. It is translated into English in three ways: "straightway," "forthwith," and "immediately." This word is found eighty times in the New Testament, and forty of these in the book of Mark alone.

(7) Jesus is never called "Lord" in Mark until after His ascension, with one exception in 9:24. This should be omitted as in the Revised Version.

(8) There is no "our Father" in Mark.

(9) Jesus is never called King, except in derision, and is called the Son of David only once.

(c) Luke. Key verse 19:10. Opens with wail of bereaved mothers and ends, "woe, woe."

(1) Christ is presented as the Son of Man—"The Son of Man is come to seek and to save that which was lost."

(2) It is filled with songs and parables. It is the book from which we get some of the old church hymns.

(3) It is the book the artists love. The great majority of the Bible pictures are based on Luke.

(4) Christ's humanity is emphasized in Luke. His genealogy in the third chapter traces his ancestry back to Adam. Matthew's genealogy traces Him back to Abraham through David. This is to prove His right to the throne of Israel. In Luke He is the Son of Man, whose ancestry is traced back to Adam. Every man came from Adam. If we have descended from something else, then we are something else, not a man.

(5) The gospel of Luke is the gospel of prayer, and you will find verses here that are not found in the other books. The other gospels tell of His deeds, but Luke says that He prayed before He did them.

(6) As a man, He was dependent upon God. We too often think that we do not need to pray, but if Jesus Christ needed to pray, how much more we?

(7) In Matthew 10: when Jesus sent out the disciples, He sent them to the lost sheep of the house of Israel, but in Luke 9: He sent them to all men. His humanity is brought to the front.

(8) There is a difference between the parables. In Matthew they begin with, "The kingdom of heaven is like." In Luke they begin—"A certain man."

(9) It is in Luke you find Him as a man in the garden of Gethsemane. Only here we are told of the drops of blood and of the awful agony in the garden.

(d) John. Key verse 20:30, 31.

(1) John emphasizes the Deity of Christ, the Son of God. Luke says, "Unto you a child is born," but John says "Unto us a Son is given."

(2) No human genealogy is given. Christ was God Incarnate. In Matthew He was born a king, in Luke He was born into the family circle, but in John He is God Incarnate. A genealogy would be out of place. Who can write the genealogy of God?

(3) You will find no record of the temptation, the transfiguration, the baptism (this is mentioned only by John the Baptist), or of His birth. Very little is said about Nazareth—His home is in the bosom of the Father.

(4) The miracles in the first three gospels are mighty works, but in John they are signs of His deity.

(5) Four times He claimed to be God, and He also claimed omnipresence—John 3:13. He claimed to be one with the Father—John 5:18. He was crucified because He claimed to be the Son of God. They were going to stone Him because He said He was the Son of God, but they did not because He was the Son of God.

(6) No record of ascension because God is omnipresent.

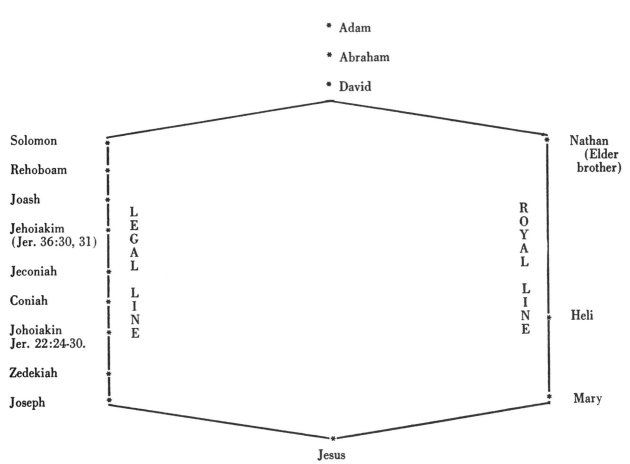

MATTHEW'S GENEALOGY
(42 names)

LUKE'S GENEALOGY
(77 names)

* Adam

* Abraham

* David

Solomon

Rehoboam

Joash

Jehoiakim
(Jer. 36:30, 31)

Jeconiah

Coniah

Johoiakin
Jer. 22:24-30.

Zedekiah

Joseph

L E G A L   L I N E

R O Y A L   L I N E

Nathan
(Elder
brother)

Heli

Mary

Jesus

MATTHEW'S GENEALOGY (Matt. 1)

This genealogy starts with Abraham, and it is most interesting. There are some names omitted from this by God, because of sin in that line. Beginning with Abraham, we follow the line to David, Solomon, and Rehoboam. Under Rehoboam the nation was divided into the northern and southern kingdom. Farther down the line we come to Jehoiakim, and Jehoiakin was his son—Jer. 22:24-30; Jer. 36:30. How could Jehoiakin be childless? This did not mean that he would have no children, but that his sons were cursed as far as this line was concerned. Not a single son would sit on the throne, although they had the right to the throne.

Joseph was a son of David. That is what the angel called him. He had the title to the throne of David, because Joseph was a descendant of Jeconiah. All of Jeconiah's sons had a title to the throne, but none of them could sit on it. Joseph was of the line of David. Apparently God's promise must come to naught. This must have given the devil great joy, for he must have thought he had succeeded in breaking this line. For even if Joseph did have a son, that son could not use his title because he too would be a son of Jeconiah.

Concerning Zedekiah, the judgment said that Coniah's sons would not reign. When Nebuchadnezzar beseiged Jerusalem, he appointed Zedekiah king. (Zedekiah was Coniah's uncle . . . brother of Jehoikim, the father.)

LUKE'S GENEALOGY (Luke III)

Goes back to Adam, but corresponds to Matthew's genealogy from Abraham to David. Nathan was an elder brother of Solomon and had the same mother and should have been on the throne instead of Solomon—I Chron. 3:5, II Sam. 5:14. Solomon had the throne and apparently Nathan did not make any objections. Absalom tried to take the throne but Nathan's mouth was closed. No doubt his mouth was closed for that same reason that the Lion's mouths were closed when Daniel was in the den. God closed it. Heli and Joseph were both sons of David, but Joseph had the title to the throne. However, the title did not do him much good because he could not use it. Heli had a daughter named Mary, a distant cousin to Joseph. These two became engaged. This working out of the two genealogies is one of the most wonderful things in Scripture. God's curse on Jeconiah is nullified by the other line. An engagement in the Orient is sacred. It is usually about a year in length and cannot be broken without a divorce. Those engaged were considered man and wife.

Two thousand years have made a difference. Mary is now honored, but in that day she was not. Joseph was a just man, and he wanted to do what was right. When Mary was found with child before their marriage, there were three paths open to Him: He could make her a public example and by the law of Moses she would be stoned; he could give her a private bill of divorcement; he could marry the girl and legitimize the child. Joseph, being a just man, must choose between the first two and he decided to divorce her. But God could not allow this to happen, and an angel was sent to Joseph. So when the time came for the marriage, they were married.

When Joseph married Mary and her child was born in wedlock, it meant that in the eyes of the law, Jesus Christ was a son of Joseph, and that was what He was. It does not say that Joseph begat Jesus. Jesus was not the child of Joseph, but He was the son of Joseph in the eyes of the law. Joseph was the legal father of Jesus. Jesus was the literal son of Nathan and the legal son of Solomon, so he received the title to the throne of David. Jesus, the legal son of Joseph, was heir to the title from Jeconiah, but He was not the son of Jeconiah. Suppose that another son of Joseph wanted to claim the throne—Jesus had the title. Joseph had the title, but had no child. If Jesus did not rise from the dead, then the Bible would be untrue, for all this proof would be worthless. He had a Father in heaven Who begat Him and a legal father on earth. He had all rights of the first-born. He had the right to the throne through Joseph legally and through Mary He had the right and could rule because not of the seed of Jeconiah. No other Son of Joseph could sit on the throne. There was only one person in the whole universe of God to whom the throne could rightfully come, and that was Jesus. He had the blood of David through Mary. Suppose someone should dispute Solomon's right to the throne and demand the throne through Nathan's name — Jesus meets that claim. How the devil fought the line of Solomon and tried to destroy it! He did not know that Jesus was not coming through that line at all. At one time his whole line depended upon one small baby, Joash.

Jehoshophat was in the regular line. Jehoram slew all his brethren so that he and his sons were all that were left—II Chron. 21:4. The Arabians came and slew all of the sons except Ahaziah—II Chron. 21:16, 17; 22:8-14. Then when Ahaziah was slain, Athaliah slew, as she thought, all of the sons. Joash, however, escaped. There was a period of time when he was the only one in that line. When the time came, that little king who had been hidden in the house of God came forth to take the throne, just as a king will someday come from the house of God—II Chron. 23:11. There is a deeper meaning than the proof of the humanity of Jesus in the genealogy of Luke.

CHAPTER TWENTY

The Synthetic Principle

XIX. THE SYNTHETIC PRINCIPLE, OR PRINCIPLE OF LITERARY STRUCTURE.

a. Definition.

That principle under which God superintends the literary structure of the Bible so that it is constructed in introversion, alternations, or combination of both.

b. Explanation.

Everything that God does is perfect: Everything in nature and the Book; everything in the world and the Word. God is not the Creator of that which is imperfect. A blade of grass is perfect and so is a drop of dew. Man's most perfect creation is a razor-blade—smooth, sharp. But put it under a microscope and the edge would look like this: W But a blade of grass under the same microscope is perfect.

Snowflakes are perfect. If 10,000 snowflakes were photographed, you would find no two alike, yet they are all alike in structure. They are all six-pointed.

The same perfection that you find in nature, you find in Scripture. When you find the same perfection in Scripture that you find in nature, then you have proof that the God Who created is the God Who wrote.

c. Alternation.

1. Meaning. Alternate members to an outline or alternation.

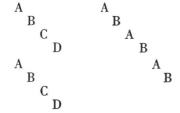

2. Examples:—showing the beauty of the structure of the Word of God.

(a) Book of Jonah.

A. Commission 1:1, 2
　B. Disobedience 1:3
　　C. Consequence 1:4-17
　　　D. Prayer 2:1-9
　　　　E. Deliverance 2:10
A. Commission 3:1, 2
　B. Obedience 3:3, 4
　　C. Consequences 3:5-10
　　　D. Prayer 4:1-3
　　　　E. Correction 4:4-11

(b) John 3:20, 21.

A. Everyone that doeth evil hateth the light.
　B. Neither cometh to the light.
　　C. Lest his deeds be reproved.
A. Everyone that doeth truth.
　B. Cometh to the light.
　　C. That his deeds may be made manifest.

(c) Prov. 31:10-31.

A. Her husband—10-12.
　B. Her occupation—13-19.
　　C. Her character—20.
　　　D. Her household—21.
　　　　E. Herself—22 (What she is on the outside).
A. Her husband—23.
　B. Her occupation—24.
　　C. Her character—26.
　　　D. Her household—27, 28.
　　　　E. Herself—29, 30 (what she is on the inside).

(d) Matt. 23:16,17.
   A. Woe unto you blind scribes.
      B. The temple and the gold.
   A. Ye fools and blind.
      B. The gold and the temple.

(e) Acts 2:14-36.
   A. Appeal—men of Judea—14,15.
      B. Reference to Joel—16-21.
   A. Appeal—men of Israel—22-24.
      B. Reference to Psalm 16: 25-28.
   A. Appeal—men and brethren—29-33.
      B. Reference to Psalm 110: 34-36.

(f) Joshua 4:1-9—Memorial.
   A. Twelve men—1,2.
      B. Twelve stones—3.
         C. The place—3.
   A. Twelve men—4.
      B. Twelve stones—5.
         C. The memorial—6,7.
   A. Twelve men (figure of speech, tribes figuratively) 8.
      B. Twelve stones—8.
         C. The place—8,9.

(g) II Thessalonians.
   A. Introduction. Grace and peace—1:1,2.
      B. Thanksgiving—1:3.
         C. Reason—1:3,5.
            D. Obtaining of rest and glory—1:6-10.
               E. Prayer for them—1:11.
                  F. Name of the Lord be glorified—1:12.
                     G. They gloried in Him—1:12
                        H. Admonition—2:1-12.
      B. Thanksgiving—2:13.
         C. Reason—2:13.
            D. Obtaining of glory—2:14,15.
               E. Prayer for Paul—2:16-3:1.
                  F. Word may be glorified—3:1.
                     G. Hearts directed to God's love—3:5.
                        H. Admonition—3:6-15.
   A. Conclusion—Peace and Grace—3:16-18.

d. Introversion.

1. Example
   A.   A.
      B.   B.
         C.   C.
      B.   C.
                              B.

2. Examples from Scripture.
   (a) Isa. 6:10.
      A. Make the heart of the people fat.
         B. Ears.
            C. Eyes.
            C. Eyes.
         B. Ears.
      A. Heart.

   (b) Luke 1:68-79.
      A. Visitation—68.
         B. Salvation—69.
            C. Prophets—70.
               D. Enemies—71.
                  E. Covenant—72.

E. Oath—73.
D. Enemies—74,75.
C. Prophet—76.
B. Salvation—77.
A. Visitation—78,79.

(c) Psalm 117.

A. Praise—1.
B. Reason—2a.
B. Reason—2b.
A. Praise—2c.

(d) Psalm 23.

A. Supply, pasture and water. Spoken of "He"—1-3.
B. Danger—death, rod and staff—spoken to "thou"—Vs. 4.
B. Danger—enemies, table and cup, spoken to "thou"—Vs. 5.
A. Supply, goodness, and mercy—spoken of "Lord"—Vs. 6.

e. Other examples.

1. Ezek. 36:26,27. Alternation.
   A. New heart.
   B. New Spirit.
   A. New Heart.
   B. New Spirit.

2. Jer. 17:5-8. Alternation.
   A. Cursed is the man who trusts man—5.
   B. Shall be like the heath (a shrub in the desert)—6.
   A. Blessed is the man that trusts God—7.
   B. Shall be like the tree—8.

3. I Cor. 3:6,7. Alternation.
   A. I have planted.
   B. Apollos has watered.
   C. God giveth the increase.
   A. Neither is he that planteth.
   B. Nor he that watereth.
   C. But God that giveth the increase.

4. Psalm 1: Alternation.
   A. Blessed is the godly man—vs. 1.
   B. Shall be like a tree—vs. 3.
   A. Ungodly are not so—vs. 4.
   B. Are like the chaff—vs. 4.

5. Psalms 8 and 150 begin and end the same—Introversion.

CHAPTER TWENTY-ONE

The Principle of Illustrative Mention

XX. PRINCIPLE OF ILLUSTRATIVE MENTION.

a. Definition.

It is that principle by which God exhibits by illustrations of judgment, His displeasure at various forms of sin and disobedience.

(1) He speaks by way of judgment for violation of His command. He gives a decisive sign of hatred of sin and then is silent for a long time.

(2) If God visited every sin with deserved punishment as soon as a law was broken, the human race would soon become extinct.

b. Examples.

1. Lying to the Holy Ghost—Acts 5:1-11 Ananias and Sapphira. This illustrates what God thinks of this sin, yet if all who commit it were punished in this manner there wouldn't be any Church.

2. Idolatry—Judgment of Babel is an example of judgment of idolatry—Gen. 11:

3. Graven images—Story of the golden calf and its judgment—Ex. 32:

4. Profanity of Holy things—Death of Korah—Num. 16—Nadab and Abihu—Lev. 10:1, 2.

5. "Thou shalt not kill." Cain had a mark because "Vengeance is mine saith the Lord" Gen. 4:15.

6. Family impurity—Judgment on Sodom—Gen. 19:

7. Theft—Judgment on Achan—Josh. 7:

c. This principle should encourage Scriptural illustrations in preaching.

CHAPTER TWENTY-TWO

The Double Reference Principle

XXI. DOUBLE REFERENCE PRINCIPLE.

a. Definition.

It is that peculiarity of the writings of the Holy Spirit, by which a passage applying primarily to a person or event near at hand, is used by Him at a later time as applying to the Person of Christ, or the affairs of His kingdom. Human writers may not have had this in mind, but the Spirit knew.

b. Examples.

1. Hosea 11:1—"Out of Egypt have I called my son."
The Holy Spirit applies it to the experience of Christ when taken into Egypt and brought out—Matt. 2:14, 15. It also refers to Israel. Israel nationally, was a son, but Christ was a greater "Son."

2. II Sam. 7:12-16—Davidic covenant. It has to do with Solomon in one sentence, and the very next verse goes beyond to Christ.

3. Deut. 18:15—Statement concerning a prophet to follow him. The reference here is to Joshua and yet it looks forward to Christ also—Acts 3:22, 23.

4. Jer. 50: and 51:
Predicted judgment on Babylon. It has not yet been minutely fulfilled. There is reference here to a future Babylon that will be destroyed—Rev. 18:9-21.

CHAPTER TWENTY-THREE

The Christo-Centric Principle

XXII. CHRISTO-CENTRIC PRINCIPLE.

a. Definition.

It is that principle by which God shows:
1. The mind of Deity is eternally centered in Christ.
2. All angelic thought and ministry are centered in Christ.
3. All Satanic hatred and subtlety are centered at Christ.
4. All human hopes are, and human occupations should be, centered in Christ.
5. The whole material universe in creation is centered in Christ.
6. The entire written Word is centered in Christ.

b. Explanation.

1. The mind of Deity is eternally centered in Christ.

   (a) This is seen, first of all, in the fact that Christ was in the form of God; the mind of God was in Him —Phil. 2:5; Heb. 1:3.
   We do not see the sun, but the rays of the sun, and yet the rays are of the sun. It is the same with God and the Son of God—Heb. 1:8. He has all the perfections of God. He is the visible image of the Invisible.

   (b) God was unseen by men before the Incarnation except in the Theophanies of the Old Testament. "He that hath seen me hath seen the Father" expressed the power of God in His mighty works.
   He is the image of the invisible God. Jesus was, or is God. He had a mind big enough to hold the thoughts of God and a heart big enough to hold the love of God.

   (c) He is the Creator of all things.
   He is the sum and aim and end of all creation—John 1:3; 1:10; Col. 1:16, 17; Heb. 1:3; 3:4; Rom. 11:36; Col. 1:17; II Cor. 8:9.
   He is the heir of all things—Heb. 1:2. Why heir? He gave up all the riches and rights He had as God, and became man to die and be raised and ascend to heaven, and be heir of all things.

   (d) Eph. 1:4—before the foundations of the earth, all was centered in Him. Rom. 5:14—Adam was the figure of Him that was to come.

2. All Angelic thought and ministry are centered in Him.

   (a) Isaiah 6: with John 12:41.
   The vision of the figure on the throne being worshipped by the Seraphim shows Jesus. In Revelation there is a throne surrounded by angelic beings worshipping the Lamb.

   (b) Luke 1:—angels announced His birth.

   (c) After temptation—angels came and ministered to Him.

   (d) Matt. 25:31—He will return surrounded by angels—II Thess. 1:7.

   (e) I Peter 3:22—angels are subject to Him.

   (f) Heb. 1:6—all the angels of God worship Him.

3. All Satanic hatred and subtlety are centered at Christ.

   (a) Rev. 12:
   Here we have the sun-clad, and star-crowned woman. The red dragon is ready to devour the child. The woman is Israel, the child is Christ, and the dragon is Satan. The child is caught up to God. Here is a picture of Satan trying to prevent the coming of the Seed.

   (b) "Conflict of the ages."
   This is the war Satan carried on all through the ages, trying to prevent the coming of the Seed.

   (c) From Gen. 3:15 to Revelation.
   (1) Before flood—attempt to corrupt mankind—Gen. 6.
   (2) Abraham called and warfare again.
   (3) In Egypt—
   ((a)) Tried to wear out the life of the people by hard labor.
   ((b)) Command to kill men. God intervened and allowed Moses to be reared in the very home which he would later be turning against.
   ((c)) Command to cast all boy babies in the river.

(4) War against royal line.
    ((a)) Athaliah tried to wipe out the royal line. One baby saved by the marriage of a priest and a princess.
    ((b)) In Esther—planned complete destruction of Jews.
    ((c)) When seed was born (edict of Herod) male children to be slain.
    ((d)) Satan entered into Judas. (This is said of no other man).

4. All human hopes are, and all human occupations should be, centered in Him.

(a) We can get eternal life from no other. In hope we have desire and expectation—John 1:29; Acts 4:12; Heb. 1:3.

(b) All human hopes are in Him from Adam on. No one could help Jesus when He was on the cross. God the Father couldn't help Him for He was a substitute for sinners, and Mary (His mother) couldn't help Him because she was a sinner. There was nothing else for God to do but smite. If the only blood that was shed had been that of bulls and goats, no one would go to heaven. Blood of goats covers but does not *wash away* sin. Jesus Christ does not merely atone for us or for anyone; He washes our sins away.

(c) All occupations should be centered on Him—Col. 3:17; I Cor. 10:31.

(d) If we put Christ where He belongs in our lives many saved souls will be the result.

5. The material universe in creation and preservation centers about Him—Col. 1:16; Heb. 1:3.

6. The entire written Word is centered in Christ.

(a) This is the only Book that gives the past, present, and future of man; but man isn't the theme of the Book.

(b) It is the only Book to give the past, present, and future of Satan, the nations, and the Church.

(c) The living embodiment of the Bible is Christ. He is the perfect example of the perfect Man. What is said of the living Word is said of the Written Word—Rev. 19:13; Luke 5:1.
The life of the Bible is Christ. Wherever the Word of God is preached and where it is received Christ acts on the heart and the life.

(d) Its viewpoint is Christ.
    (1) It is the history of Adam (first man) and Christ (last Adam, and second man).
    (2) The first man put the second man to death. He couldn't stand the holiness of the second.

(e) Every page of the Book speaks of Christ, as indicated in the following article:

Christ in Every Book of the Book of Books

By R. T. Ketcham, D.D.

In *Genesis* He is the Creator and Seed of the woman. 1:1; 3:15.

In *Exodus* He is the Lamb of God for sinners slain. Chapter 12.

In *Leviticus* He is our High Priest. Entire Book.

In *Numbers* He is the Star out of Jacob. 24:17.

In *Deuteronomy* He is the Prophet like unto Moses. 18:15.

In *Joshua* He is the Captain of the Lord's Hosts. 5:13-15.

In *Judges* He is the Messenger of Jehovah. 3:15-30.

In *Ruth* He is our Kinsman Redeemer. Chapter 3.

In *Samuel* He is the Despised and Rejected King. I Sam. 16 to 19.

In *Kings* and *Chronicles* He is the Lord of Heaven and Earth. Entire Books.

In *Esther* He is our Mordecai. Chapter 10.

In *Job* He is our Risen and Returning Redeemer. 19:25.

In *Psalms* He is the Blessed Man of 1.
He is the Son of God of 2.
He is the Son of Man of 8.
He is the Crucified One of 22.
He is the Risen One of 23.
He is the Coming One of 24.
He is the Reigning One of 72.

He is the Leader of Praise of 150.

In *Proverbs* He is our Wisdom. Chapter 4.

In *Ecclesiastes* He is the Forgotten Wise Man. 9:14-15.

In *Song of Solomon* He is "my Beloved." 2:16.

In *Micah* He is the Everlasting God. 5:2.

In *Nahum* He is our Stronghold in the Day of Wrath. 1:7.

In *Habakkuk* He is the Anchor of our Faith. 2:4.

In *Zephaniah* He is in the Midst for Judgment and Cleansing. 3:5 and 15.

In *Haggai* He is the Smitten Shepherd. 13:7.

In *Zechariah* He is the Branch. 3:8.

In *Malachi* He is the Sun of Righteousness.

In *Matthew* He is the King of the Jews. 2:1.

In *Mark* He is the Servant of Jehovah. Entire Book.

In *Luke* He is the Perfect Son of Man. 3:38; 4:1-13.

In *John* He is the Son of God. 1:1.

In *Acts* He is the Ascended Lord. 1:8, 9.

In *Romans* He is our Righteousness. 3:22.

In *I Corinthians* He is the First-Fruits from among the dead. 15:20.

In *II Corinthians* He is made Sin for us. 5:21.

In *Galatians* He is the End of the Law. 3:10 and 3:13.

In *Ephesians* He is our Armor. 6:11-18.

In *Philippians* He is the Supplier of Every Need. 4:19.

In *Colossians* He is the Preeminent One. 1:18.

In *I Thessalonians* He is our Returning Lord. 4:15-18.

In *II Thessalonians* He is the World's Returning Judge. 1:7-9.

In *I Timothy* He is the Mediator. 2:5.

In *II Timothy* He is the Bestower of Crowns. 4:8.

In *Isaiah* He is Our Suffering Substitute. Chapter 53.

In *Jeremiah* He is the Lord our Righteousness. 23:6.

In *Lamentations* He is the Man of Sorrows. 1:12-18.

In *Ezekiel* He is the Throne Sitter. 1:26.

In *Daniel* He is the Smiting Stone. 2:34.

In *Hosea* He is David's Greater King. 3:5.

In *Joel* He is the Lord of Bounty. 2:18-19.

In *Amos* He is the Rescuer of Israel. 3:12.

In *Obadiah* He is the Deliverer upon Mount Zion. Verse 17.

In *Jonah* He is the Buried and Risen Saviour. Entire Book.

In *Titus* He is our Great God and Saviour. 2:13.

In *Philemon* He is the Father's Partner. Verses 17-19.

In *Hebrews* He is the Rest of Faith and Fulfiller of Types. 9; 11; 12:1, 2.

In *James* He is the Lord of Sabaoth. 5:4.

In *I Peter* He is the Theme of Old Testament Prophecy. 1:10-11.

In *II Peter* He is the Long Suffering Saviour. 3:9.

In *I John* He is the Word of Life. 1:1.

In *II John* He is the Target of the Anti-Christ. Verse 7.

In *III John* He is the Personification of Truth. Verses 3, 4.

In *Jude* He is the Believer's Security. Verses 24, 25.

In *Revelation* He is the King of Kings and Lord of Lords. 19:11-16.

CHAPTER TWENTY-FOUR

The Numerical Principle

XXIII. THE NUMERICAL PRINCIPLE.

The Number One in Scripture

Someone has truly said, "Strengthening to the believer's heart is the subject of Spiritual arithmetic, as revealed in God's Word." Such a subject that One Supreme Mind must have been the author of all the books of the Bible.

The number ONE is a primary number. All other numbers depend upon ONE. It precedes and produces all other numbers; that is, every digit is dependent upon number ONE.

This is God's number; without Him nothing could exist. "In the beginning, God . . ." No creator—no creation. No designer—no design. Without a former, there can be no formation. No Saviour can mean only one thing—no salvation.

There cannot be two firsts. The number two confirms that there is a difference. We are admonished to "seek first the Kingdom of God and His righteousness." Our own will excludes God's will. Many Christians have heard the still, small voice whisper, "This is the way, walk ye in it." But because the way of self is accepted, God's way is rejected. His way promises comfort. Man's way produces confusion. He is the One in Whom all blessing flow.

The first number EXCLUDES all other numbers. In this, we make a distinction as far as God is concerned. He did not have to create a world; He was not compelled to form the first man; He could have excluded the human race. But His condescending grace was brought down to sinful man through His Son, Jesus Christ.

God formed Adam for the purpose of fellowship. That fellowship was broken because Eve listened to Satan and added, omitted, and altered the Word of God. In Genesis 3 we find that she added "neither shall ye touch it"; she omitted the word "freely"; she altered "thou shalt surely die." She knew God's will, but heeded Satan's will. God could have exterminated Adam and Eve because of His displeasure at sin, but He came down to them in the garden to clothe them in animal skins. They recognized their sinful deed, became conscious of their sin, and made themselves aprons of fig leaves. But there is no blood in a fig leaf. There must be a life sacrificed. This prompted the slaying of animals in order that they might be clothed in coats of skins. This is the first mention of a life for a life to atone for sin, and points forward to Calvary where the Lamb of God, through His shed blood, expiates sin. He gave His life a ransom for us. He came to this earth with a nature capable of death, to die for the sinner. He became partaker of our nature, that we might become partakers of His nature. He became friendless that we might have a friend. Because God did not desire to see us excluded, He gave His Son to die that all who might believe in His finished work, might be *included*. The sinner who stands at the Great White Throne Judgment will be forced to utter, "God excluded me because I did not acknowledge the finished work of His Son for me."

The number ONE stands alone, independent of all others. God is independent; we are dependent. If we come to the realization that Jesus Christ was clothed in His earthly nature and needed to pray to His Father, then it will not be difficult to impress the state of our dependence upon Him. How often we limit His power by turning to man to lift burdens and share financial difficulties. How often He must be grieved to witness our independence of Him. God is ONE Who has a solution for every sorrow. When shall we learn to get back to the kindergarten of faith and once again study the BOOK, the ONLY BOOK, the ONE BOOK which dissolves doubts and promises a performance of the supernatural?

Number TWO affirms a difference. And because all men have not believed in number ONE, the human race is divided into two classes—those in Christ and those outside of Christ. Number two proves that there is a distinction between those in the first Adam and those in the last Adam. Number two explains why God had to call in the Garden of Eden, "Adam, where art thou?" Sin produced conviction and prompted Adam to hide from God. Because of the totality and universality of sins today, the same question rings out from Heaven into your very presence, "Where art thou?" As to where you are, there are two possibilities, but there can be only one answer—in Adam or in Christ; you are either saved or unsaved. That's why we read in the Word of God, "The wages of sin is death, BUT the gift of God is eternal life through Jesus Christ our Lord" (Romans 6:23). "He that hath the Son hath life, BUT he that hath not the Son shall not see life, but the wrath of God abideth on him" (John 3:36). "For God so loved the world (sinners) that He gave His only begotten Son (salvation) that whosoever (sinners) believeth in Him should not perish BUT have everlasting life" (salvation) (John 3:16).

If you have thwarted every opportunity to hear the simplicity of the Gospel message and the truth that Jesus Christ died and arose from the dead for your sins, then abolish such rejection and in humility ask, with the Philippian jailer, the question pointed to Paul, "What must I do to be saved?" You will receive the only answer that has come down through the ages, "Believe on the Lord Jesus Christ and thou shalt be saved" (Acts 16:31).

In the study of number ONE, we are brought to that principle of Bible study called the "First Mention Principle." The first recorded words of Jesus given by the Spirit of God were, "Wist ye not that I must be about My Father's business?" How this throws light on His last words spoken upon the cross, "It is finished!" What is finished? His Father's business. "He came to be obedient unto death, even the death of the cross."

The first ministerial words of the Lord Jesus Christ were repeated three times: "It is written." This gives us light concerning the ministry of the Lord Jesus, all in accordance with the Word of God.

The first book of the Bible gives the supremacy of God in creation, in the giving of life, and the sustaining of life. In the first book we have the beginning of righteousness and justification by faith. It contains the suffering of Christ and His glory as predicted in Joseph. It contains the death and resurrection of Christ in the offering of Isaac. The way of man and the way of God are seen in Cain's firstfruits and Abel's lamb.

Remember this then, there could not have been two firsts, and there have never been the first two. The word of God never speaks of two firsts, because there is only one first and that is God. There is no real beginning apart from Him. He is first in time and rank. Everything begins with God—creation, redemption, and salvation.

The Number Two in Scripture

The second number, TWO, is the number of division and separation. Number TWO affirms there is a difference. In Exodus 8:23 we read that God said, "I will put a division between My people and thy people."

In the first chapter of Genesis we discover that the earthly waters are divided from the heavenly waters. Then too, we read that God divided the night from the day. Here is a hint of the separation of saved and unsaved. Light and darkness will not mix. God makes a distinction. As far as God is concerned, only TWO men ever lived. The human race is divided into TWO classes. Because the first Adam failed—the last Adam, Christ, became a substitute for us. The first man, Adam, brought sin. The second man, Christ, brought salvation.

Now there are a great many TWO'S in Scripture. Sometimes the SECOND is evil. Eve was the second human being created. She had known only ONE supernatural Being, God. But a SECOND personality came into the garden, and that personality brought about the fall. The ONE supernatural Being was God; the SECOND supernatural being was Satan.

It is interesting to note that in the New Testament, wherever there is a second Epistle you will find that the second is the one which has some special reference to the enemy. II Corinthians emphasizes the power of the enemy. II Thessalonians concerns the working of iniquity, the son of perdition. II Timothy discusses the ruin of the Church, while I Timothy gives us the rule of the Church. II Peter shows the great apostasy at work. In II John —the Anti-Christ is mentioned by name.

Thus, the number TWO suggests separation and division. There are two birds, one slain and one set free. There are two goats, one slain and one set free. There are two masters; two covenants—old and new. We have Cain and Abel; Ishmael and Isaac; Jacob and Esau; Vashti and Esther. In Genesis 3:15, we have the woman and her seed and Satan and his seed. In Leviticus 10:10 we read of the difference to be made between the clean and unclean. In II Corinthians 6:14 we discover a distinction between righteousness and unrighteousness; between light and darkness. Scriptural illustrations seem endless. Think of law and grace; Christ and the anti-Christ; good and evil; leavened and unleavened. Paul speaks, in I Corinthians 15 of the natural body and the spiritual body. First it is sown in dishonour—second, it is raised in glory; sown in corruption, raised in incorruption; sown in weakness, it is raised in power.

May we call your attention to the great separation chapter, Genesis 19, where Lot and his daughters are separated from those who are destroyed in their sins. The chapter is full of the figure TWO. Take your Bible and read carefully this chapter and note the "two angels" in verse 1: the two classes of age, "old and young," in verse 4; the "two daughters" in verse 8: two classes of standing, "great and small," in verse 11; the two places, the "plain and the mountain," in verse 17; the two cities, "Sodom and Gomorrah," in verse 24; the two agents of destruction, "fire and brimstone," in verse 24; the two dwelling places, "house" and "cave," in verses 3 and 30; the two children, "Moab and Ben-ammi," in verses 37 and 38.

Another great separation chapter for study is Matthew Ch. 7. We call attention to the man with the mote and the man with the beam; the strait gate and the wide gate; the narrow way and the broad way; the way which leadeth unto life and the way which leadeth unto destruction; the good tree and the corrupt tree; the wise man and the foolish man; the house built on the rock and the house built on the sand; the house which stood and the house which fell.

Our number in this study calls our attention to witnessing — "that in the mouth of two or three witnesses every word may be established." Our Lord said, "It is also written in your law that the testimony of two men is true. I am ONE that bears witness of Myself, and the Father that sent Me beareth witness of me."

Our Lord sent forth the "seventy" by "two and two." Other illustrations of two witnesses are Caleb and Joshua, Moses and Aaron, Elijah and Elisha, Paul and Barnabas, Peter and John, Moses and Elijah at the Transfiguration, two angels at Christ's Resurrection and the two men in white apparel who testified at His ascension that He would return again.

The following phrases, which witness to the fact of future punishment and eternal separation occur only TWICE in Scripture. "The fire that never shall be quenched," Mark 9:43-45. "Cast into the fire," Matt. 7:19 and John 15:6. "The furnace of fire," Matt. 13:42, 50. "Everlasting fire," Matt. 18:8; 25:41.

The following word has reference to witnessing and occurs only TWICE in Scripture. The Greek word "alethuo," found in Galatians 4:16 — and Ephesians 4:15, is translated first "tell the truth" and then, "speaking the truth."

May the Word, with its TWO witnesses—the Old and the New Testament, become more precious to us as we study the writings of the Holy Spirit.

The Number Three in Scripture

With "THREE" we come to the number of union, approval, approbation, co-ordination, completeness, and perfection. It is the number of the Trinity. THREE persons in One God — THREE Members of Divine perfection.

In Isaiah 6, the Seraphims in praising God said, "Holy, Holy, Holy." It is significant that they stopped at THREE. Four "Holy's" might have made it more majestic, but these Beings were declaring the tri-unity of God. We speak often of distinction in the Godhead, but perhaps we should say that there is a threefold personality. A little girl (and should we not go more to children for the simple definition) once said, "THREE in One and One in THREE, and the One in the middle stands for me."

Truly there are only THREE definitions of God. God is Love! His love surpasses illustration, defies comparison, and beggars description. God is Light! What light is in the material world, God, the source of material light, is in the spiritual. God is Spirit! The Father of love gave His Son to light a world dark in sin; and the Holy Spirit glorifieth the light of the world along with His work of reproving the world of sin, righteousness, and judgment.

The resurrection of our Lord on the THIRD day speaks of divine power. Human power could not accomplish it. Jonah was THREE days and THREE nights in the great fish as a sign of Christ's burial and resurrection.

Christ was crucified at the "THIRD hour." He hung on the cross six hours — THREE in darkness and THREE in light. At noon God threw a funeral pall over the cross; it was the darkest moment of all history. The Father turned His face from the Son. Christ's tormentors could no longer see the agony on His face. The inscription over His head was written in THREE languages suggesting the completeness of man's rejection of Christ, but on the THIRD day, after the burial, He arose victorious; thus the divine completeness of number in study.

THREE persons were raised from the dead by Christ; Jairus' daughter, the widow's son, and Lazarus.

Here is completeness of divine power in every human stage of existence, for the daughter of Jairus was twelve years old, just a girl; the widow's son at Nain was of adult age, a young man; Lazarus was full grown, an elderly man.

There are THREE offices of Christ, showing His perfection. He was Prophet, Priest, and King. The completeness of His Shepherd care is seen in His THREE titles—the Good, the Chief, and the Great Shepherd.

The perfection of Christ in His temptation is shown in His THREE-fold use of, "It is written."

Now the completeness of sin is seen in this manner. There is the THREE-fold testing of man, which was also the complete testing of Christ—lust of the flesh, lust of the eye, and the pride of life. These temptations led to the fall of Eve. She saw that the fruit was good for food, pleasant to the eye, and desirable to make one wise. In the wilderness Satan tempted Christ: "change the stones to bread" — lust of the flesh; "view the kingdom" — lust of the eye; "cast thyself down" — pride of life.

There are THREE enemies of man; world, flesh, and the devil. There were THREE great apostates: Cain, Balaam, and Korah. Consummation of sin is reached in Revelation when we come to the, "THREE unclean spirits" — the unholy trinity of evil. Thus we discover that Satan is the great "ape" of God. He delights in mocking the Holy One. But God's grace puts the "Prince of darkness" in the shadows, even as we glance through the Old Testament. There was the tabernacle with its THREE divisions—the Outer Court, the Holy Place, and the Holy of Holies. In its construction, THREE metals are used—gold, silver, and brass. Here is Deity clothed in humanity to free us from judgment. THREE colors are mentioned—blue, purple, and scarlet. The Heavenly One, rejected as King, gives His life a ransom for many. Theres were THREE entrances — the gate, the door, and the vail. THREE feasts in particular — the Passover, the Feast of Weeks, and the Feast of Tabernacles, give us the atoning sacrifice of the Saviour at His first coming, the Holy Spirit's coming, and the Millennial reign of Christ.

THREE times the Father spoke from Heaven to His Son, showing His pleasure in the Son's obedience and the completeness in carrying out the mission for which He came—Matthew 3:17; 17:5; John 12:28.

Have you ever had your attention called to the trinity of persons linked together in Scripture? There is divine perfection here in God's over-ruling of the world's history. We suggest a few: Shem, Ham, and Japheth; Gershom, Kohath, and Merari; Saul, David and Solomon; Hananiah, Mishael, and Azariah; Peter, James and John.

The perfect nature of the Promised Land might be suggested if one notices that the returning spies carried THREE things; grapes, pomegranates, and figs.

A beautiful picture of complete consecration is given us as we study the healing of the leper or the consecration of a priest. Blood and then oil were used in the anointing. The blood was placed on the tip of the right ear, on the thumb of the right hand, and on the toe of the right foot. Thus, a THREE-fold consecration: to hear God, to serve God, and to walk with God.

The little book of Jude is filled with the number THREE: three-fold salutation; three-fold meditation; three-fold example of Divine retribution; three-fold expression of sin; three types of apostates; three classes of evil workers, and a three-fold doxology.

For your meditation we give God's THREE great gifts of grace; faith, hope and love. Faith speaks of our own dependence; hope speaks of our own lack; love speaks to us of God. Faith is an imitation of God; hope is the aspiration to God; love is the manifestation of God. Faith and hope acquire blessing, but love bestows blessing. Before hope and faith, love said, "I am." Love was before the world. Love is eternal. Love is the nature and whole of God.

The Number Four in Scripture

In our previous studies, we have examined the first three numbers. Number one is that of primacy and unity. It is God's number, for there can be no other first. Separation and division are associated with number two. The first number excludes difference while the second affirms there is a difference. Three speaks of Divine completeness and perfection.

In this brief study we examine number FOUR, the creation number. FOUR has special reference to the earth. On the fourth day, material creation was finished. There are four regions of the earth: North, East, South, and West. The day has four divisions: morning, noon, evening, and midnight. There are four seasons in the year — spring, summer, autumn, and winter. There are four lunar divisions: first, half, full, and last. In Scripture, there are four corners or quarters of the earth. Family, tongue, nation, and country, designate the fourfold division of mankind—See Genesis 10:20, 31; Revelation 5:9; 7:9; 11:9; 14:6.

The fourth commandment refers to the earth. The fourth clause in the Lord's Prayer refers to the earth. The four Gospels present the earth-life of our Lord. Four women are mentioned in our Lord's earthly geneology: Thamar, Rahab, Ruth, and "her that had been the wife of Urias." There are four kinds of flesh mentioned in I Cor. 15:39. We have the four Hebrew children in the book of Daniel; four in the fiery furnace; four world empires; four winds of heaven — Daniel 7:2, 3. We have four kings mentioned in Daniel: Nebuchadnezzar and Belshazzar, kings of the Babylonian Empire; along with Darius the Median and Cyrus the Persian. Ezek. 21 gives the four judgments upon the earth. Created beings are to be found in heaven, on the earth, under the earth, and in the sea. In this connection we note that the cherubim of Ezekiel 1:5, 6; 10:9, 11, 14, 20, 21, had four faces, four wings, four sides, and four wheels. And even more interesting becomes this passage when we realize that the Cherubim execute God's will in connection with His creative works.

It is not surprising to discover that the story of the children of Israel wandering about in the wilderness is found in the fourth book of the Bible, Numbers. It is truly an earthly book and suggests a picture of our walk on earth.

Many messages have been given on the four kinds of soil mentioned in our Lord's parable in the thirteenth chapter of Matthew — the wayside, the stony, the thorny, and the good.

We believe that never before, as in the present age, have the power and subtlety of Satan been so manifested. We are premillennial in our doctrine. We believe that the millennium is still future, and that Christ will come to set up His kingdom. In Revelation 20:2 when Satan's present power on earth is put to an end in the Millennium, he is given a fourfold description: "The dragon, that old serpent, which is the Devil, and Satan." He is imprisoned in the bottomless pit during the one thousand year's reign of Christ; and the mention of his four names in this passage seems to emphasize the fact that his earthly power is somewhat taken away from him.

Examine the fifth chapter of Revelation and notice the parallelism between verses twelve and thirteen. Those are heavenly creatures giving a sevenfold ascription of praise to the Lamb in verse twelve. But the earthly creatures of verse thirteen ascribe only a fourfold message of praise.

We are not alone in looking forward to that day when the King of kings shall return to set up the Davidic Kingdom. There is a King in heaven without a throne, but He awaits that day when He shall return to a people pleading for His coming. How different from His first coming, which was one of rejection. When our Lord gave His discourse on the Mount of Olives, about events which should transpire and precede His return, He spoke to only four. "Peter, James, John, and Andrew asked Him privately, 'tell us, when shall these things be?'" Thus there is a spiritual meaning and significance hidden behind this number four. There must be a Supreme Mind back of the inspired writings and that One Supreme Mind is God Himself.

Striking illustrations are discovered upon examining the numeric value of names. These numeric values of the Hebrew and Greek alphabets, that is, the number which each letter of the respective alphabet stands for, give us 888 as Christ's number. In contrast with this triplet of numbers we find that the man of sin in Revelation is 666 (Six is man's number). How amazing! A trinity of evil in opposition with a trinity of good. But back to our number in study. Damascus, the oldest city in the world, has a numeric value of 444.

The Number Five in Scripture

The number FIVE is significant of God's wonderful grace. In Genesis 1:20, 21 we read of the manifestation of His grace in bringing living beings into existence on the fifth day. In this first chapter the Hebrew words, translated "life," "living," and "living thing," occur five times. How wonderful, the thought that God, Who brought life into the natural world, can bring spiritual life through His Son, Who is the Light of the World. On the first day of creation, the Hebrew word for light appears five times—God's grace in bestowing light upon a dark world.

I am fearful in the writing of this number, since it speaks of grace. Who can attempt to explain or define it? It defies comprehension. Man-made definitions are so inadequate. The simplest, I suppose, is this, "Grace means pure unrecompensed kindness and favor." The easiest to remember—GRACE, God's Riches At Christ's Expense.

But let us now examine further this divine usage of our number in study. Truly there is nothing in us to call forth the divine favor of God. This was true in the case of Abraham. But God called him and made a covenant with his seed forever. When God made that covenant it was stamped by number five.

Five animals were slain—Gen. 15:9. When God called unworthy Abram, He manifested His grace by changing the fifth letter and substituting the fifth letter of the Hebrew alphabet — Abraham. The numerical value of this letter is five. The same thing was done in the changing of Sarai to Sara*h*.

The Tabernacle in the wilderness is marked with number five. God's grace to helpless sinners is seen throughout the structure. The pillars of the outer court, supporting the fine twined linen, were five cubits apart and five cubits high. The brazen altar, where the sacrifice was offered, was five cubits by five cubits in construction; again manifesting the grace of God where the substitute was offered, and pointing forward to Calvary to the vicarious suffering of the Sinless One. This altar was, however, three cubits high speaking of Divine approach, for our Saviour is the Way, the Truth, and the Life.

There were five pillars at the Eastern end of the Holy Place. This was called the Tabernacle door, and reminds one of the five great names given our Lord is Isa. 9:6 — Wonderful, Counsellor, The Mighty God, The Everlasting Father, The Prince of Peace.

Israel knew something of the grace of God. How could Moses bring two million people out of Egypt? He didn't! God did. God brought them out in great grace, and when they were lined up they were five in ranks. They were in perfect weakness, but the invincible power of Jehovah was with them. God said, "Five of you shall chase one hundred." He did not say, "Five shall chase a hundred," but "Five of YOU . . ." If God be for us who can be against us? What difference how many there are? "They that wait upon the Lord shall renew their strength . . ."

Jesus looked out upon the hungry multitude and said, "What shall we do?" The disciples said, "Send them away." The Lord said, "What have you?" The answer was "Five loaves." The Lord Jesus took the five loaves and fed five thousand. Out of that five came abundance, enough for the whole crowd.

In Eph. 4:11 we are told of five ministries—apostles, prophets, evangelists, pastors, and teachers. Through these five outlets went forth the Gospel of the grace of God.

When God wanted to picture the earth-life of Christ, He did in the four Gospels; but when He wanted to picture His grace, He did so in the five offerings of Leviticus, chapters 1-7. Offerings for sins of omission, sins of commission, our sinful nature, and our sinful deeds that we might have peace.

Perhaps the most difficult verse in the Bible to be understood by Christians under trial is Romans 8:28, "And we know that all things work together for good to them that love God, to them who are the called according to His purpose." But did you ever notice God's goodness and grace in the five-mentioned truths following this verse? Did *foreknow*, did *predestinate*, has *called*, has *justified*, will *glorify*. And these, all of grace, not because we deserve them.

Paul says (I Cor. 14:19) : "Yet in the Church I had rather speak five words with my understanding, that by my voice I might teach others also, than ten thousand words in an unknown tongue." If one expects power and fruit-bearing in his preaching, God's grace and power must be manifested. Many there be today who sound forth with ten thousand words but say little. With an educational background and power in delivery, they have forgotten the text: "Not by might nor by power, but by My Spirit, saith the Lord of Host."

In our studies of numbers in Scripture we have been giving instances of certain words used. We suggest here the Greek word "Parakletos," which means, "one called alongside to help." It is used five times, occurring in John 14:16, 26; 15:26; 16:7. It is translated "Advocate" in I John 2:1.

"Agalliasis" meaning "exceeding joy or gladness," occurs in Luke 1:14, 44; Hebrews 1:9; Acts 2:46; Jude 24. In Luke, Zacharias is told by the Angel that many shall rejoice at John's birth. The name "John" means "Grace of Jehovah." How glorious then that "Agalliasis" (used FIVE times) should first be used here, in showing the joy and gladness to be expressed at the birth of one whose name means GRACE of Jehovah.

We suggest one five-fold phrase used. "Bless the Lord, O my soul," is found in Psalm 103:1, 2, 22; 104:1, 35.

The Number Six in Scripture

Number SIX is man's number and brings to light the sad state of human incompleteness. Man was created on the sixth day. God said that six days would mark the number of man's labor. Six is significant of man as trusting in his own powers and believing that he can get along without God's help. Man is evil, corrupt, and Satanic in his rebellion against the Almighty.

There are six generations recorded of Cain of whom Scripture says, "who was of that wicked one, and slew his brother."

God's love is intimated but not manifested until we reach the book of Deuteronomy. He was compelled to bring the waters of judgment upon the earth because of His displeasure with sin. This was "in the SIX hundredth year of Noah's life."

In our study of the previous number we saw how the number five was predominate in Abraham's life, even to the changing of his name Abram, and his wife's name, Sarai. We repeat this to show the parallelism between Abraham and Lot, for in the history of Lot, we read of SIX downward steps as he feasted his eyes upon Sodom. (1) He lifted up his eyes, (2) he chose, (3) he journeyed east, (4) he dwelt, (5) he pitched his tent toward Sodom, (6) he dwelt in Sodom.

Twice in the Old Testament there steps out a wicked man, and these are both marked with six. Goliath was six cubits tall. He wore six pieces of armour. His spear's head weighed 600 shekels of iron.

Nebuchadnezzar set up an image of gold. It was 60 cubits high, and six cubits in breadth. Six kinds of musical instruments were played to denote the time of worship. These instruments were the cornet, flute, harp, sackbut, psaltery, and dulcimer.

In passing, we mention the "man of great stature" in II Sam. 21, who had six fingers on each hand and six toes on each foot.

There are six words used for man in the Bible. Adam, Ish, Geber, and Enosh in the Old Testament; Anthropos and Aner in the New Testament.

The book of Hosea is a remarkable book, and full of symbolical teaching. It has to do with the wife of Hosea. God used the relationship of these two to illustrate truth. Hosea was told to marry an unchaste woman, that is, a woman not worthy of him. God said to Israel, "I took you when you were not worthy of me and after I had taken you, you left me." Hosea's wife also left him. Wicked Israel sought good things from idolatrous nations instead of from God. In Hosea 2:5 we have a list of SIX things sought. "I will go after my lovers, that give me my bread, and my water, my wool and my flax, mine oil and my drink." In verses eight and nine of the same chapter, seven things are enumerated which God gives: corn, wine, oil, silver, gold, wool, and flax. Seven is one of God's perfect numbers and we shall present its significance later.

When the children of Israel in Egypt thought of foods, they were six in number. In Numbers 11:5 they are listed as fish, cucumbers, melons, leeks, onions, and garlic. Egypt is a type of the world and these foods are typical — perhaps tasty and flavored, but unsatisfying. What a contrast to the list of seven foods in Canaan as found in Deuteronomy 8:8, which are wheat, barley, vines, fig trees, pomegranates, olive oil, and honey. Study these foods and you will discover that here are strengthening, satisfying, and sustaining qualities.

Reginald T. Naish gives us an interesting word in regard to this number. We quote: "Here is an interesting instance of six, showing its spiritual significance, as given in Psalms 9 and 10, which, in the original, are connected by an acrostic, each verse of these two Psalms commencing with a letter of the Hebrew alphabet, the acrostic running consecutively through both Psalms. But in the middle the acrostic, SIX letters of the Hebrew alphabet, mem, nun, samech, ain, pe, and tsaddi, are omitted! When we come to study the reason, we find that both these Psalms have as their subject, "the man of the earth" (Psalm 10:18), or Antichrist — "That wicked one," "who opposeth and exalteth himself above all that is called God, or that is worshipped." And the cry of the godly goes forth in that evil time, "Arise, Lord; let not man prevail; let the heathen be judged in Thy sight. Put them in fear, O Lord; that the nations may know themselves to be but men" (Psa. 9:19, 20).

Perhaps it may seem out of place to continue a word in regard to acrostics when it will be observed that the following has no bearing upon our number in study. We well realized that Bible writers were inspired and yet are amazed at their literary ability. For example, there are twenty-two letters in the Hebrew alphabet. Perhaps you have noticed in some Bibles a Hebrew letter at intervals of every eight verses in Psalm 119. Each of the first eight verses began with the first letter of the alphabet. In verses 9 through 16, each verse begins with the second letter, etc.

The book of Lamentations is made up of five chapters. Chapters 1, 2, 4 and 5 have twenty-two verses, each verse beginning with a letter of the Hebrew alphabet, all being used in their proper order. Chapter three contains sixty-six verses. The first three verses begin with the first Hebrew letter; the next three verses begin with the second letter. This continues until each Hebrew letter is used three times to complete the sixty-six verses. Of course, this cannot be discerned in the English Bible.

There is a man in the New Testament who is marked 666. It is the number of a man because the Word says so—Rev. 13:18. This looks to the great super-man, the man of sin, yet to come.

In Genesis 22 we find the words, "burnt offering" mentioned six times in referring to man's offering. The seventh (the ram) is the offering which God provided. Man's offering comes short of perfection. A lamb is provided by God, which is a seventh offering.

At Christ's trial and crucifixion, there were six persons who bore testimony to His innocency. (1) Pilate, Luke 23:14; (2) Herod, 23:15; (3) Judas, Matt. 27:3; (4) Pilate's wife, Matt. 27:19; (5) The dying thief, Luke 23:41; (6) The Centurion, Luke 23:47.

Notice the six main divisions of the Book of Jude:
1. Introduction—"Sanctified and preserved."
2. Exhortation—"Contend earnestly."
3. "Certain men"—False teachers exemplified—"These."
4. "Certain men"—False teachers prophesied—"These."
5. Exhortation—"Keep yourselves in love."
6. Conclusion—"Preserved and sanctified."

Notice how the divisions answer to one another. That is, 1 to 6, 2 to 5, and 3 to 4. It is natural to expect such a book, describing the rebellion of man, to be marked by number six.

Six times the men of His generation said that Jesus had a demon. This is man's blasphemous accusation. The accusation continues today, perhaps in a different form. And yet we read in Scripture that these were those who found no fault in Him. He has been taken into the laboratory and torn apart but if men would carefully analyze Him, they would fall at His feet and worship. Stubborn man, however, is today exercising his own will. God has permitted man to run things; and what a mess our old world is in today!

The Number Seven in Scripture

This is the number of divine fulness, perfection, and completeness. It is one of the perfect numbers, and comes from a Hebrew word meaning "to be complete," "to be full," "to be satisfied," "to have enough."

We first wish to show the use of this number outside of scripture. Botany is divided into seven branches. There are seven stages in the life of a fruit-bearing plant: fruit, stem, leaves, flower stalk, flower, root, seed. The plants that are beneficial to man as cereal food, are seven in number. They are found in all parts of the world. The cereals that God made for the food of man are wheat, oats, barley, maize, rice, rye, and millet. The human voice has seven ranges: bass, baritone, tenor, counter alto, alto, mezzo soprano, and soprano. There are seven terms for volume in music: ff, f, mf, m, mp, p, pp.

It is interesting to note the number seven in the body. The human body is composed of seven tissues: brain, nerve, blood, et cetera. There are seven parts to the body: four limbs, head, neck, and trunk. There are seven holes in the head: two ears, two eyes, two in the nose, and one mouth. There are seven ribs connected to the breastbone on each side. There are seven bones in each wrist, seven muscles between the bones in the hands and feet, seven classes of colors of the eyes, seven openings in the throat, seven more bones in the backbone of a child than in an adult. When we were seven months old we began to cut our teeth. When we were seven years old we began to lose them. There are seven types of connecting tissues, seven layers of ventricles in the heart, seven bones in the neck. There are seven stages of man: infancy, childhood, adolescence, et cetera. There is a marked change in the body every seven years. There are seven classes of relationship of first degree: father, mother, sister, brother, wife, son, and daughter. Seven circumstances govern the action of man: who, what, where, with what assistance, why, how, and when. There is a seven day regulation of the pulse-beat: for six days out of seven the pulse beats faster in the morning than in the evening. On the seventh day it beats slower in the morning than in the evening. We need to rest. Man's way always is a poor substitute for God's way.

Now let us turn our attention to the large place which number seven occupies in the Word of God. It is a good number to study in the Book of Revelation, which is a marvelous demonstration of the use of number seven.

The last book of the Bible is the book which fills up and completes the Scriptures. It fills the Word of God full and nothing can be added. In Revelation we find seven churches, seven seals, seven trumpets, seven personages, seven vials, seven dooms, and seven new things. In Revelation 1, there are seven glories of the Son of Man: head, hairs, eyes, feet, hands, mouth, and countenance. There are seven beatitudes of blessing: Rev. 1:3; 14:13; 16:15; 19:9; 20:6; 22:7; 22:14. The word "Jesus" is found seven times in Revelation. The words "Jesus Christ" are found seven times. The vengeance and wrath of God are found seven times. However, the word "dragon" is found thirteen times, and that is the number of evil. The keyword to the book of Hebrews is "better." There are seven better things in Hebrews: covenant, promise, substitute, hope, sacrifice, word, and resurrection.

There are seven walks in Ephesians. There are seven precious things in Peter: I Pet. 1:7,19; 2:4,6,7; II Pet. 1:1,4. In Gen. 12:2,3 we have seven parts of the covenant. Exodus 6:6-8 gives us the seven-fold promise to Israel. There is a seven-fold sprinkling of blood in the book of Leviticus. Naaman was told to dip seven times in the Jordan. Seven miracles are recorded in John's Gospel. In this same gospel we have repeated seven times, "Mine hour." There are seven sayings on the cross and these are made up of forty-nine Greek and Arabic words (seven times seven). The righteous are spoken of seven times in Gen. 18, where Abraham carried on intercession on behalf of Sodom and Gomorrah. In the twenty-second chapter of Genesis the angel of the Lord called out "Abraham, Abraham;" and there are seven people throughout Scripture who received this double call: Abraham, Jacob, Samuel, Moses, Martha, Simon Peter, and Saul (Paul). Seven earthquakes have taken place in Scripture: (1) at Horeb—Ex. 19:18; (2) at the victory of Jonathan and his armour bearer—I Sam. 14:15; (3) when God revealed Himself to Elijah at Horeb—I Kings 19:11; (4) in Uzziah's reign—Amos 1:1; (5) at Christ's death—Matt. 27:54; (6) at Christ's resurrection—Matt. 28:2; (7) when Paul and Silas were in prison—Act 16:26.

You will notice in the eleventh chapter of Isaiah in the second verse, that there is a seven-fold description of the Holy Spirit as resting upon our Lord. Seven gifts are given in Rom. 12:6-8: prophecy, ministry, teaching, exhorting, giving, ruling, and showing mercy.

An instructive study can be made if one examines the number of significant words used only seven times in Scripture. The Greek word "apthartos" means immortal or incorruptible. It is found in Rom. 1:23; I Cor. 9:25; I Cor. 15:52; I Tim. 1:17; I Pet. 1:4,23; I Pet. 3:4.

The Greek word "agape," which means love, occurs seven times in John's Gospel.

The phrase, "a new song," occurs seven times in the Old Testament and is always given in connection with the second coming of our Lord. In Psalm 29 the phrase, "the voice of the Lord," is found seven times.

Truly, our number in study is the number of spiritual perfection, and since the author of the book, the Holy Spirit, is perfect, then we can fully understand the frequent occurrence of the number.

Illustrations of the use of the number are so many that they would fill a book and we have only cited a few of the examples.

In the first chapter of the Bible and in the first verse, we have an example of the beauty of this number. That first verse contains seven Hebrew words, and these seven words have twenty-eight letters, or 4 times 7. The gematria or the merit value of these three nouns in the verse, "God," "heaven," and "earth," is exactly 7 7 7. The first three words have fourteen letters, the last four words have fourteen letters, the fourth and fifth words have seven letters, and the sixth and seventh words have seven letters. We stand amazed when we discover that there are over thirty different combinations of seven in the first verse of the Bible. Here is divine authorship! There is no man who ever lived who could devise such a mathematical problem as arranged in the first verse of the Bible.

In closing, we cite one further illustration. There were seven men who lived to be over 900 years of age. Adam, Seth, Enos, Cainan, Jared, Methuselah—with Noah, the perfect man, as the seventh. Lamech, the father of Noah, is marked by an age of 777 years.

The Number Eight in Scripture

Number EIGHT is the number of resurrection.

The ark, a type of Christ, passed through the water, a picture of death. When it rested on Mt. Ararat there came out eight people—that is resurrection. On the eighth day there is a new beginning. That also makes it a resurrection number. The first day of the week is a resurrection day. The sign of circumcision was placed on a Jewish child on the eighth day, the sign of separation—a new beginning. When a priest was consecrated, the ceremony took seven days, and on the eighth day the priest took up his new work. When Saul was king (a man of the people's choice) there was nothing but trouble. God chose David, a man after God's own heart; and David, instead of being a man of splendid stature, was the eighth son—a youth. He was a new beginning.

There is a beautiful typical picture in the twenty-fourth chapter of Genesis. Abraham's servant goes out to seek a bride for Isaac—typifying the calling out by the Holy Spirit of the heavenly bride of Christ. In this chapter we find Isaac's name mentioned eight times; and he is a type of Him Who is the heavenly Bridegroom, "the resurrection and the life." His wife, too, is mentioned eight times only; six times she is designated as a "wife," then as "my master's son's wife"—which is a type of the first resurrection when the Bride is called to the marriage supper of the Lamb.

In reading through the Word we find eight cases of resurrection mentioned, apart from our Lord's resurrection and those saints that came out of their graves at that time. There are three references in the Old Testament, three in the Gospels, and two in the Acts.

The writers of the New Testament who give us the record of Christ's life, death and resurrection, and the part the Holy Spirit plays in this day, number eight. They are: Matthew, Mark, Luke, John, Paul, James, Peter and Jude.

It is not our purpose to go into addition, subtraction, and multiplication in regard to the numerical principle, but it is interesting to note the numerical values which are all multiples of eight in regard to our Lord's name as mentioned in the New Testament. These names are: Saviour, 1408; Lord, 800; Christ, 1480; Messiah, 656.

There are many beautiful uses of the number eight which any Bible student can discover for himself as he reads God's Word. For example—David was the eighth son of Jesse, while Solomon was the eighth son of David. Both of these are pictures or types of Christ, Who is the Resurrection and the Life. Bethlehem, where Christ was born, is mentioned exactly eight times in the New Testament.

Revelation is the book of the kingdom, and the power, and the glory. It is the book of new beginning—of the One Who rose from the dead. In Rev. 1 there are eight references to the Old Testament. Verse 5—Isa. 55: 4; Verse 7—Dan. 7:13; Verse 7—Zech. 12:10; Verse 8—Isa. 44:6; Verse 11—Isa. 44:6; Verse 12—Zech. 4:2; Verses 13-15—Dan. 7:9,13; 10:5,6; Verse 16—Isa. 49:2.

The Number Nine in Scripture

Number NINE is the number of judgment, finality, and completion.

When Christ hung on the cross He took our place to receive our judgment. He was nailed to the cross at 9:00 in the morning, the third hour of the day. He dismissed His Spirit at 3:00 in the afternoon, the ninth hour of the day. He was nailed to the cross at the time of the morning sacrifice; and His work, suffering, and judgment were completed at the ninth hour. We read that there was darkness over all the earth until the ninth hour. And the sun was darkened, and the veil of the temple was rent in the midst. And when Jesus had cried with a loud voice, He said, "Father, into Thy hands I commend my spirit;" having said thus, He gave up the ghost.

There is a nine-fold "fruit of the Spirit" given in Galatians 5:22, 23: "love, joy, peace, longsuffering, gentleness, goodness, faith, meekness, temperance: against such there is no law." This "fruit" speaks of finality, for there is nothing more needed, as wrought by the Holy Spirit's presence in our hearts. We note here also that there are nine gifts of the Spirit, as shown in I Cor. 12:8-10. They are: the word of wisdom, the word of knowledge, faith, the gifts of healing, the working of miracles, prophecy, discerning of spirits, divers kinds of tongues, and the interpretation of tongues.

There is a fullness of blessing that comes to the Israelites through obedience to God's commands. The Israelites were told not to sow nor reap in the seventh year, and God promised that He would make the sixth year bring forth fruit for three years if they obeyed. He tells them that they should eat yet of the old fruit until the ninth year, so that they would be provided for until what they had planted in the eighth year came to maturity.

The word, "amen," translated "verily," is used by our Lord ninety-nine times according to the Revised Version, and the numerical value of this word is also ninety-nine. Here is finality, for in this word is God's final offer of mercy to hell-deserving sinners. This word is a warning to the sinners to take heed. This is a day when God shows mercy because of another, Jesus Christ, Who died in the sinners' stead. But some day the judgment of God must fall upon all those who have rejected His free pardon. God's wrath and judgment are yet future, and the Christian can be thankful that he will not be there on pay day when wages are paid. If there is one thing that is certain, it is this, "pay day some day."

Other striking instances of the number nine are as follows: The northern kingdom fell in the ninth year of Josiah's rule. In Haggai 1:11 we have a ninefold judgment on Israel. There are nine records of stoning in the Word. There are nine cases of people afflicted with blindness—Gen. 19:11; 27:1; 48:10; Judges 16:21; I Sam. 4:15; I Kings 14:4; II Kings 6:18; 25:7; Acts 13:11. There are nine recorded instances of people afflicted with leprosy.

For further study we give the following words occurring only nine times in Scripture: (Abussos), bottomless pit—Luke 8:31; Rom. 10:7; Rev. 9:1,2,11; 11:7; 17:8; 20:1,3. The word "Raz," meaning a secret, occurs in Dan. 2:18,19,28,29,30,47,47; 4:9.

The word "Ouranos," meaning heaven, has a numerical value of 891, or 99 times 9. Here is completion as far as we are concerned, for we shall have our glorified bodies, and go to dwell forever with Him Who redeemed us. The same Jesus Who walked this earth and gave His life a ransom for many, shall call out His own some day. That will be a day when we can say with Paul, "O death where is thy sting, O grave where is thy victory?" The words "Houtos," "Ho," "Jesous," meaning "this same Jesus," have a numerical value of 1998 or 999 times 2.

The Number Ten in Scripture

Number TEN is the number of perfection or completeness in divine order. It is a perfect number. It is the number of sufficiency according to God's purpose in divine order and human responsibility.

The human body has five fingers on each hand, ten in all. Here is human responsibility in divine work. Ten toes speak of human responsibility in divine walk.

In the ten commandments we see the completeness of God's claim. They give human responsibility Godward and manward. No man ever met that responsibility. Man is guilty before God and in need of redemption.

In the Old Testament (Exodus 30:13) redemption money is ten gerahs. Man's responsibility in giving to God is one-tenth.

The completeness of God's judgment upon Egypt is seen in the ten plagues. The completeness of Israel's rebellion against God is seen in Numbers 14:22 "... and have tempted me now these ten times, and have not hearkened to my voice."

Noah was the tenth of the antediluvian patriarchs. The Word says, "Noah was a just man, and perfect in his generations, and Noah walked with God."

Have you noticed the Gospel story in the meaning of the names of the first ten patriarchs in Genesis 5? Adam—man; Seth—appointed; Enos—subject to death; Cainan—sorrowful, lamenting; Mahalaleel—from the praise of God; Jared—one comes down; Enoch—learning obedience or trained; Methuselah—dying he shall send; Lamech—to the poor brought very low; Noah—rest. Now read those meanings and see that glorious revealed gospel sentence. Man, appointed, subject to death, sorrowful and lamenting. From the praise of God, One comes down, (Christ) learning obedience or trained, dying, He shall send, to the poor brought very low, rest.

In our previous articles, we have studied various numbers in relation to the tabernacle in the wilderness. Coming by the outer court and Holy Place we arrive in the Holy of Holies, God's Holy Presence, manifested in the Shekinah Fire. This division was a cube of ten cubits in length and breadth and height. The inside linen curtains of the tabernacle were ten in number. The laver typifies the Word of God and it is mentioned ten times. In studying Solomon's Temple we discover a ten-fold mention of the laver. There were ten lavers in Solomon's Temple.

I have been told that the word Hallelujah is the same in every language. It is the Hebrew word for "Praise ye the Lord." There is a perfection in such praise seen in the fact that there are ten Psalms that begin with "Hallelujah."

In Psalm 119, there are ten words which are descriptive of God's Word: way, precepts, commandments, testimonies, law, sayings, statutes, judgments, righteousness, and word. Upon examination you will find that one of these occurs in every verse of this Psalm with the exception of just one verse. The name, "our Saviour" as our "Surety," is given in verse 122.

Paul gives witness to a ten-fold security of the saints in Rom. 8:39,39, for he says that neither death, nor life, nor angels, nor principalities, nor powers, nor things present, nor things to come, nor height, nor depth, nor any other creature, shall be able to separate us from the love of God.

In that great covenant made with Abraham, we read of ten nations which are included. The Kenites, Kenizzites, Kadmonites, Hittites, Perizzites, Rephaims, Amorites, Canaanites, Gergashites, and the Jebusites.

We have said that number ten speaks of divine order. The Greek word for order is "Taxis." How strange that the word occurs only ten times—Luke 1:8; I Cor. 14:40; Col. 2:5; Heb. 5:6,10; 6:20; 7:11,11,17,21.

The last form of Gentile World Power is suggested in Revelation 17:12. Here is man again trying to set up a program of peace and perfect order, not realizing that there shall be no peace until the Prince of Peace arrives.

But man, as experience has shown, will fail again. Jesus Christ will return to set up His Kingdom and rule the world from His throne in Jerusalem. This will be the one thousand year period or Millennium. 10 x 10 x 10, or in other words, ten to its third power. This illustrates the perfect order which will some day be upon the earth.

The Number Eleven in Scripture

Number ELEVEN is the number of disorder and imperfection. Note its significance in Genesis 32.22. Jacob has been in Padan-aram and is returning to the Holy Land with his eleven sons. Benjamin is not yet born. His name, meaning, "son of sorrow," speaks of the Lord who came from heaven to earth to suffer, and Who will come again to reign as King upon the earth. As Benjamin came to complete the house of Jacob and alter the total of sons from eleven to twelve, so the coming of Christ will change the present world disorder and disorganization into a rule of perfect peace of which the number twelve speaks. Even after the twelve sons were born, one was sold. Here again we are back to number eleven, showing the disorder in Jacob's household.

It is interesting to notice from this passage and others how number eleven points forward to the Millennial reign of Christ and end-time. To those who believe the Word, God's midnight hour will soon strike. The number eleven foretells the disorder to come, which will usher in our Lord as the King of kings. Another scripture showing the hidden prophetic significance of our number in study, is found in Genesis 37:9. The eleven stars in Joseph's dream seem to point forward to that time when the Jewish people will accept the government and rulership, of the Lord Whom they once refused as their King.

God was forced to send His chosen nation into captivity because of their stubbornness and rebellion. Two of the last kings each reigned eleven years. They were Zedekiah, who refused to listen to God's Word through Jeremiah; and Jehoiakim, who tore up God's Word. When the rule of these two wicked kings ended, the Jewish nation was cast out of the Holy Land and the times of the Gentiles began. So it was in the eleventh year of Jekoiakim, that Nebuchadnezzar began to carry away the inhabitants, and in the eleventh year of Zedekiah, he finished it.

Only one more day would have brought God's people into the Promised Land. But Deuteronomy 1:2 says it was an eleven-day journey to where they turned back in unbelief. Failure to make the complete twelve-day journey resulted in their forty years wandering in the wilderness. Forty is the number of testing and will be studied later.

The second curtain of the tabernacle coverings was made up of eleven curtains (Incompleteness).

In the Book of Acts there were eleven disciples—incompleteness. The vacancy was filled by one who took the place of Judas.

In Matthew 20:6-9 we read of laborers who were hired in the eleventh hour and were paid the same wages as those hired earlier. The eleventh hour workers caused disorder.

Words used eleven times are "KATABOLE" and "PSEUDOPROPHETES." The former means foundation, or literally, "cast down." The latter is translated, "false prophet."

The Number Twelve in Scripture

This number speaks of governmental perfection or rule. Service, power, and deliverance are manifested in a perfect system of government. The sun and moon were made to rule the day and govern the night, and they do it by passing through the twelve signs of the Zodiac which completes 360 degrees—30 x 12.

Our Lord chose twelve apostles. They were leaders or rulers in the affairs of the early church. They are to eat and drink at "My table in My Kingdom and sit on thrones, judging the twelve tribes of Israel." Thus they share in that perfect governmental rule of our Lord during His Millennial reign.

God's city, Jerusalem, is to be perfectly governed in all details. John's vision portrays twelve gates and at the gates twelve angels. The wall of the city has twelve foundations and in them the twelve apostles of the Lamb. The length, breadth, and height of the city were 12,000 furlongs.

Our Lord tells us that He could have prayed to His Father for twelve legions of angels. (Fulness of perfection in Angelic power).

Solomon is a type of Christ and his reign portrays the reign of Christ in the Millennium. Solomon had twelve officers over all Israel. He had 12,000 horsemen. We read in connection with his throne, "Twelve lions stood there on the one side and on the other upon the six steps: there was not the like made in any kingdom."

In the first thirty years of His life, there is only one activity of Jesus mentioned, and that was when He was twelve years of age—"I must be about My Father's business." We could paraphrase His Words, "I must do what My Father rules for me."

In the book of Judges (a judge was a ruler) there were twelve judges. The book of Judges is a book of apostasy because Israel was continually going away from God. There were twelve judges, but thirteen rulers, the thirteenth being Abimilech, a usurper.

Words used twelve times are, "OIKODESPOTES" meaning master or ruler of the house, and "AULE" meaning court, hall, or palace. It signifies a place of government or authority.

The Number Thirteen in Scripture

Number THIRTEEN is the number of ill-omen, rebellion, and apostasy. Its first occurrence is in Genesis 14:4—"Twelve years they served Chedorlaomer, and in the thirteenth year they rebelled." As stated before, number twelve speaks of governmental rule. But in this verse thirteen appears and proves rebellion and government resisted. Beginning at this point, and appearing throughout Scripture, thirteen suggests rebellion, sin, and disobedience.

Gen. 17:25 informs us that Ishmael was thirteen years old when he was circumcised. This rebellion was foreshadowed even before he was born, for we read that he was to be a wild man—his hand against every man, and every man's hand against him. Ishmael was not the promised seed but he was part of the promised multiplication of Abraham.

The descendants of Ishmael through his twelve sons, constitute the Arabian race or nation. They have dwelt in the presence of other nations, and have retained their freedom until this day.

Truly, every man's hand is against them. Egypt tried to conquer them but failed. The Arabs refused to recognize Alexander the Great, and he died before preparation could be made to overthrow them. Pompeii tried and failed. Even Napoleon could not conquer the Arab.

Ishmael was the son of a bondwoman, and Paul tells us in Galatians that he is a type of him who is born after the flesh. Here again is rebellion against one born of the Spirit. The Spirit and the flesh are constant enemies, warring against each other. The flesh can never be improved and Scripture admonishes us to mortify it or put it off.

If one desires to see apostasy centered in one man, he should study the tenth chapter of Genesis. Joktan is the thirteenth in order of the children and descendants of Shem. The names of Joktan's thirteen children are given. Someone has figured out the gematria of Jotkan's name to be 169 or 13 times 13. The gematria of his thirteen sons' names is 2756 or 212 times 13.

Solomon, who built the great temple of God, and became a great rebel against God, entered upon his apostasy in connection with the building of his own house. He was seven (perfection) years in building God's house and thirteen years in building his own house. It is no surprise then to read in I Kings 11:6, "And Solomon did evil in the sight of the Lord, and went not fully after the Lord, as did David, his father."

In the book of Judges, there were twelve judges. There is another, however, who was called a king. This was none other than Abimelech, the usurper who induced the inhabitants to appoint him king. The result—anarchy. Thus, righteous government and rebellion, or apostasy, are seen in the book of Judges.

Twenty kings reigned over the southern kingdom, or Judah. Seven were good rulers, and thirteen led the people away from God.

In the book of Esther lots were cast and the date for the destruction of the Jews, through Haman's wicked devices, fell on the thirteenth day of the month, and in the thirteenh year of Ahasuerus.

The history of Israel is one of rebellion against God. From the beginning to the end they are marked with rebellion. There were thirteen tribes. We often speak of the twelve tribes of Israel, and the land of Canaan was divided into twelve portions. The thirteenth tribe, Levi, did not have a portion, but small portions throughout the other sections. Twelve, as we have previously stated, is the number of governmental perfection, and it was God's design to have perfection; but you can scarcely see a place in the Word of God where they were not in rebellion. They were an apostate nation, but, while there were thirteen tribes, only twelve are ever listed (though not always the same twelve names).

Israel's dietary law as given in Deuteronomy 14:7-19, lists twenty-six unclean articles of food which Israel must never partake (2 x 13).

The twenty-sixth book of the New Testament, Jude, contains a description of an apostate heart (13 x 2).

Mark 7:21,22 gives the thirteen characteristics of an apostate heart.

In the book of Revelation, Satan is called the great rebel thirteen times.

Leaven, which means evil or wickedness, is found thirteen times in the N. T.

The "valley of Hinnom" which means "lamentation" is mention thirteen times.

Paul received thirty-nine stripes (13 x 3).

On the day before the betrayal of Jesus, there were thirteen at the table. Later, Judas went out and betrayed Jesus. There were twelve who were bound together in love, but Judas, the thirteenth, was apart from them all.

Words that may be used for further study and which are mentioned only thirteen times are: "Dianoia," meaning "mind;" "Empaizo," translated "mock;" "Klepto"—"to steal." Words used thirteen times in the Old Testament are: "Chaneph"—"hypocrite;" "Meshuba"—"backsliding."

Most of Satan's names have a gematria or multiple of thirteen. "Dragon"—975 or 75 x 13; "tempter"—1053 or 81 x 13; "Belial"—78 or 6 x 13; "murderer"—1820 or 140 x 13; "serpent"—780 or 60 x 13; "called the devil and Satan" is a phrase with a gematria of 2197 or 13 x 13 x 13.

Someone has called to our attention the name given our Lord in mockery as He was suspended upon the cross, "Jesus of Nazareth." It has a gematria of 2197 or 13 x 13 x 13. Here was rebellion at its height; for our sins were upon the sinless One, and it was Satan's desire to get Him down from the cross. I cannot agree with those who picture Satan wringing his hands in delight and smiling at Christ on the cross. Satan knew Scripture and he knew that Christ was dying on the cross to redeem those of Adam's posterity. In fact, Satan put in the mouths of those at the crucifixion to shout out, "He saved others—He cannot save Himself." If Christ had accepted this challenge, and not died, we would never have known the meaning of redemption.

The Number Seventeen in Scripture

Spiritual perfection or perfection of spiritual order is seen in this number. It is the sum of two perfect numbers, ten and seven. It is not a multiple of any number. It is an indivisible number—a prime number. The seven prime numbers are: 1, 3, 5, 7, 11, 13, and 17.

The eighth chapter of Romans sums up the seventeen blessings of those who are dead and risen in Christ. There is a series of seven and a series of ten. There are seven parts to the question and ten parts to the answer. There is a seven-fold "who shall separate us from the love of Christ?" and a tenfold "I am persuaded that." This is the perfection of God's spiritual order and power—a spiritual and eternal perfection of the believer's standing in Christ.

It appears that when seven and ten are used together, the ten has more weight than the seven. In the second chapter of II Chronicles, Solomon asked for a workman having seven requirements. Hiram sent a workman skilled in ten departments. Solomon asked for a man marked with seven, and received one marked with ten.

In Hebrews 12, there is a contrast between the old dispensation marked with seven and the new dispensation marked with ten.

Verses 6-11 of Psalm 83 name ten enemies combined against Israel. Seven enemies had been destroyed by God. The prayer is that God will remember the seven enemies destroyed, and smite the ten.

There are seventeen angelic appearances recorded in the Gospels and Acts.

Seventeen tongues were spoken on the day which marked the coming of the Holy Spirit from heaven—Acts 2.

There are seventeen prayers of Jeremiah in the first thirty chapters of his book. From there on, a sudden silence.

Words used seventeen times are: Karisma—"gift," always spoken of as God's gifts; Kethab—"Scripture," seventeen times in the Old Testament; Agape—"love," occurs seventeen times in I John; Aphesis—"remission," occurs seventeen times in the New Testament. It is a great word but, one cannot have his sins REMITTED if he REJECTS Christ Jesus. In this dispensation of grace, God is long-suffering and patient, willing that none should perish.

The Number Forty in Scripture

Number FORTY is the number of probation, testing, and trial. The significance of "forty" is seen in the life of Moses who was called to deliver his fellow-countrymen from Egyptian oppression. Forty years Moses was in the land of Egypt, forty years in the desert, and forty years in the service of God. He was forty years finding out that he was "somebody;" then it took him forty years to find out that he was "nobody." Forty more years and he discovered that God was "everybody."

Saul had forty years in which to prove himself worthy of the people's choice. In that forty years, he sinned against the people, Samuel, David, God, and the Word of God.

Perhaps his fruitless life resulted from the fact that there was a great want in Saul. The work of Samuel did not seem to be familiar with him. This in itself would indicate that he was living outside of all religious connections, and dabbling in things secular. One qualification for a king of Israel was loyalty to the Heavenly King. This was the very heart of Samuel's life. But Saul was altogether lacking in the fine characteristics of Samuel.

In Genesis chapter seven, God said unto Noah, "Come into the ark." In our study of the number eight we discussed the resurrection of the eight who stepped out of the ark.

But our number in study is brought out in the fact that it rained for forty days and nights upon the earth.

Forty days Moses was up in the mountain for the transcript of the law.

Forty days the spies were in the land.

Jonah was disobedient and fled from the Lord. But after being chastised he rushed into Nineveh shouting these words, "Forty days and Nineveh shall be overthrown."

Our Lord was tested in the wilderness for forty days. The temptations brought to Him were of the same nature as those presented to Eve—the lust of the flesh, the lust of the eyes, and the pride of life. Satan attacks by the same methods today.

Our Lord was forty days on the earth with His disciples, after the resurrection.

Forty years after the crucifixion came the destruction of Jerusalem.

Forty centuries after Adam, came the fullness of time. When the fullness of time had come, the world had been tested. Man had failed. God sent forth His Son made of a woman, made under the law that we might become adopted sons. God sent forth HIS Son. He was a son from eternity. We are sons in time. He was an Official Delegate from the counsels of eternity. The Omnipotent One came down to the impotent ones.

The Number Fifty in Scripture

This is the number of salvation, and is used approximately three hundred times in the Word.

In Genesis 18 we read of the visit of the Lord to Abraham. It is Abraham's prayer that God will spare wicked Sodom if fifty righteous souls who love God are found within the city limits. Then he asked, "If there shall lack five of the fifty righteous wilt thou destroy all the city for lack of five?" Abraham brought up the number of grace and salvation. Receiving a favorable answer from the Lord at each request, Abraham goes on to the number ten, when he asks if the city will be spared if only this number of righteous is found. This was, as we have stated in a previous article, the number of human responsibility. At this point he stopped praying. He stopped asking and God stopped giving. Perhaps he was afraid of overdrawing his account. Or was he certain God would surely find ten righteous, and that Lot, who dwelt in Sodom, would be saved?

Pentecost was fifty days after the Passover. When it was fully come, 3,000 souls were saved.

The fiftieth year was the year of Jubilee—the year of liberation and restoration. After Joshua led the children of Israel into the land of Canaan, he divided their inheritance among the twelve tribes, "by their families." The portions allotted to the tribes and families were to remain the possession of those tribes and families perpetually—that is, as long as Israel lived in obedience to God. God legislated against the sale of the land. Only in case of extreme necessity or poverty was a man permitted to dispose of his portion, and even then it could not be sold perpetually. It must be returned to the original family in the year of Jubilee. If poverty compelled a man to sell a portion of his inheritance ten years after Jubilee. it could only be sold for the forty remaining years. This was all out of God's goodness. It prevented extreme poverty and also extreme riches. If necessity demanded the sale of a portion of the land, that land could be redeemed by a kinsman, by paying the balance due for the years remaining until Jubilee—Lev. 25:23-28. The same thing was true in the sale of a man himself—Lev. 25:47-55.

In the book of Esther, Haman plotted to wipe out the Jewish race. Of course this is impossible (as Hitler, along with others, found out). Read Jeremiah 31:35-37. Through Haman's evil devices, the day was set when the Jewish race was to come to an end. Haman even went to work and built the gallows on which to hang his enemy, Mordecai. The gallows was fifty cubits high. Now you ask, "Where do you find salvation in the instance?" Salvation is certainly revealed in this story, because wicked Haman, the Jew hater, was placed upon the gallows he had built for Mordecai. Here was salvation again for God's people.

The ark of Noah was fifty cubits wide. The ark is typical of the Saviour. The ark was wide enough to take in all of those who would put their trust in it. The door of access to salvation is wide enough to take in all who put their trust in Christ. How sad that some will turn their eyes from the open door and choose the way which leads to hell!

Robert Ripley, in his book, "Believe it or Not" says,

"Of course you expect to go to heaven when you die. We all do. The hope is in all of us, that when we die, we will go to heaven and rejoin the other members of our family who have passed on.

"Take my advice; make a reservation. Heaven is becoming very crowded and it is extremely doubtful whether you can get in; and should you manage to squeeze yourself past the pearly gates, it is even more doubtful whether you could find your family among all that crowd.

"Now, if we take twenty-five years as a generation, we find that there have been seventy-seven generations since the time of Christ. And if we count only your parents, their parents, and so on backward for that length of time, we find that you will have to meet 302,231,454,903,657,293,676,543 different relatives.

"Our own little world would not hold that stupendous number.

"Mind you, the above figures do not include brothers, sisters, uncles, aunts, nieces, nephews, cousins, and other relatives. Also I am allowing only for 1928 years, although scientists tell us that man has been on earth for countless generations before that time—some estimate it as 100,000 years. And, since science has proved so conclusively that you are related to all animals with four legs or a long tail that have lived on this earth for the last 100,000,000 years, you will have to include them too. They are all your ancestors!

"As a social proposition the celestial outlook appears a bit embarrassing, doesn't it?

"It is apparent that Heaven was filled up several hundred years ago—or about the time Columbus discovered America.

"What to do?

"Obviously there is but one way out. You must die sometime, and since it is so evident that you cannot go to Heaven, where shall you go?"

It is apparent that the one we have just quoted makes light of the eternal abode of the wicked. He seems to believe in heaven, for he quotes from Revelation in another part of his article. But the same Book that describes heaven and all of its glory, is the same Book which gives to us a graphic picture of hell and its inhabitants in the future. Our Lord said more about hell than all of the other Bible characters put together. Mr. Ripley evidently is not sincere in his belief that heaven is a prepared place, for a prepared people; and hell is a prepared place for an unprepared people.

Because of the finished work of Christ on Calvary, the door of salvation is thrown wide open in this day of grace.

Mr. Ripley could have spoken no truer words than those quoted, "Take my advice; make a reservation."

"Believe on the Lord Jesus Christ and thou shalt be saved." "Believe" means trust. "Saving faith" is trusting in someone else to do for us what we cannot do ourselves. The sinner is helpless. He needs a Saviour. Christ is the Saviour Whom he needs.